LIFE OF A YOGI
TEACHERS' MANUAL

SRI DHARMA MITTRA

BE RECEPTIVE

Editor's Note

Namaste, salutations to G-d and Guru. It is a great honor to have been a part of the process by which these sacred teachings have now found their way to you. Yogi Sri Dharma Mittra represents something unique in the varied and booming yoga culture of today. He remains absolutely true to that which he received from his Guru, and yet is also committed to constantly updating that which he disseminates so that this yoga we lovingly call Dharma Yoga is effective and as efficient as possible. This would seem to be a contradiction. How can the teacher transmit something that is both unchanging and constantly improved upon? The answer is to be found in Sri Dharma Mittra himself. Sri Dharma is like a mighty oak tree with a deep and intricate root system. His roots are the decade spent in service to his beloved Guru, absorbing everything his Guru had to share. His mighty trunk is the 50 plus years of constant practice, exploring yoga's every highway, back road and desolate byway, enduring extraordinary tapas to discover the complete nature of the Absolute. The innumerable branches are the many students of Sri Dharma whose lives have been changed forever through contact with this great and humble master over the past half century here in New York City and around the world. Everything is G-d, everything is the tree, but each branch has its own characteristics as a result of deeds from the past and the way of maya here in this material world of name, form and time. To help ensure that each branch has the best possible chance of one day becoming a sturdy tree in its own right, Dharma-ji draws upon his knowledge and experience to give each seeker exactly what he or she needs at exactly the right time and in the right way. This is truly the essence of Dharma Yoga.

This text is the result of many years of labor set into motion by Eva Grubler, Ismrittee Devi Om, and would not have been possbile without the support and help of Yogi Sri Dharma Mittra. I personally want to thank Eva for having entrusted me with seeing this project reach its current state and to the Guru for being ever-willing to answer my endless questions. May this work be a source of inspiration for those of you who discover it, and may it in some way help communicate the great teachings of Yogi Sri Dharma Mittra and the techniques of Dharma Yoga. In Service of G-d and Guru-

—Adam Frei, New York City,
Life of a Yogi Teacher Training Director

Author: Sri Dharma Mittra
Introduction: Adam Frei
All Original Artwork by Sri Dharma Mittra
Graphic Design: Eva Grubler & Michele Gardner
Front Cover Photo: Jeffrey Vock
In Loving Service. Om Shanti.

CONTENTS

Introduction

Living Life as a Dharma Yogi

Introduction

May Lord Shiva protect and guide us;
May He bestow upon us the fruit of knowledge.
May we develop a strong desire for liberation;
May we cherish no ill feelings towards each other.
Om Shanti, Shanti, Shantih.

—Sri Dharma Mittra's
paraphrase of one of the Peace Prayers from *The Upanishads*

Yoga is the path of purification of character and conduct
(the cleansing of one's physical and mental nature) wherein the highest state
of reality and truth may shine undiminished in the hearts and minds of all
beings. The universal principles of spiritual disciplines can elevate the seeker
into eternal God communion. This is the true goal of yoga.

—Sri Dharma Mittra

The Yoga Lived and Taught by Yogi Sri Dharma Mittra

Yoga was born of the rich civilization that flourished in the Indus Valley some 5000 years ago. Ancient stone carvings depicting human figures performing *asana* confirm a direct link between the modern yogic endeavor and its historical roots. The Sanskrit word yoga comes from the root form "*yuj*" which literally means "to yoke". The practitioner seeks to yoke him or herself to God in this lifetime. Yogic philosophy was recorded in the *Vedas* (scriptures), but its techniques were revealed to the Maharishis or great sages across millennia in deep states of meditation.

The nature of human beings is to seek happiness and tranquility, and to gain an understanding of life and our purpose in it. Yoga is a discipline, a technique, and a philosophy that provides insights and guidance to the seeker. Yoga is the art and science of self-care, self-development and Self-realization. It is not a religion, but rather a practical method designed and developed for the purpose of bringing human beings to their highest levels of physical health, mental clarity and spiritual consciousness. Yoga is the science of religion and, in practice, an applied science of the body and mind. The practice and study of yoga helps to bring about a balance of body and mind through which the natural state of health can begin to manifest.

Yoga first influences the mind, which is where the true state of health is formed since mental choices strongly affect the health of the body. The practice creates an internal environment that allows the individual to come to his or her own state of optimum dynamic health. In yoga, a healthy person is a harmoniously integrated unit of mind, body and spirit. Optimum health requires a simple natural diet, adequate exercise, fresh air, a serene and untroubled mind, and the awareness that our deepest and highest Self is identical with the spirit and true nature of God. It follows, logically, that yoga offers instruction and insight into every aspect of life -- the mental, the physical and the spiritual -- and its methods seek to bring about the harmonious unification of all aspects of being.

There are nine main approaches or forms to yoga. Mastery of their essential elements is the path to liberation. The teachings that one will learn and gain exposure to through the "Life of a Yogi" Teacher Training immersions constitute a unique combination of two of these nine forms: Hatha and Raja Yoga. In addition, Hatha-Raja Yoga incorporates many elements of the other seven forms of yoga. This Hatha-Raja Yoga prescribed and lived by Sri Dharma

Mittra represents almost a half-century of life devoted to the direct experience and dissemination of it as a holy science.

The following is a brief summary of the characteristics of the nine main approaches to yoga:

Hatha Yoga (Forceful Yoga) is the path to union through bodily mastery. *Asana* and *pranayama* are the essence of this approach, as is a firm foundation in *yama* and *niyama*. Hatha Yoga is used mainly for physical development, though some mental union (Raja Yoga) is also involved. Hatha Yoga is really a preparation for meditation and is a natural fit for those predisposed to physical action, as it represents the outward quest.

Raja Yoga (Royal Union) is the yoga of mental mastery. This form of yoga relies on the intellect and use of discrimination (*viveka*). When Raja Yoga is mastered, the *yogi* can distinguish between the Real Self and anything other than the Self. Meditation and concentration practices are at the core of this form of yoga, but its foundations are *yama* and *niyama*. Raja Yoga represents the inward quest.

Kriya Yoga is the yoga of purification. This form of yoga can also be considered a sub-category of Hatha-Raja Yoga, since three of the *niyamas* (*tapas, svadhyaya* and *Isvara pranidhana* -- discussed in detail in the First Chapter) are what primarily inform this approach.

Jnana Yoga is the yoga of knowledge. One uses discrimination to find things out and distinguish between that which is real and that which is not real. Through Jnana Yoga, one will be able to go beyond the *koshas* (the five subtle bodies) to discover the Real Self.

Mantra or Japa Yoga involves complete absorption in the repetition of a mantra. Union is achieved through focus on sound and voice. Here, the intersection among the different forms of yoga can be readily appreciated. Mantra can be practiced in any form of yoga.

Yantra Yoga is a Tantric practice that employs the use of *yantras* -- traditional, *mandala*-like shapes used for focusing the mind on one single point. A *yantra* is a pictorial representation of a mantra.

Sri Yantra Diagram

Laya Yoga is another practice of Tantric origin involving deep concentration on inner sounds called *nada* (Divine sounds). The fourth and final pada or chapter of the *Hatha Yoga Pradipika* devotes a number of *sutras* (terse, aphoristic verses) to defining the precise nature of the *nada*.

Kundalini Yoga is another practice derived from the Tantric tradition. *Kundalini* is the dormant power located at the base of the spine. Some of the study of Psychic Development discussed in the chapter devoted to that subject is considered Kundalini Yoga.

Bhakti Yoga emphasizes devotion, for example, to Krishna, but it can be used in combination with any other form of yoga practice. *Kirtan*, the call-and-response chanting of spiritual hymns and mantras, is a popular facet of the Bhakti Yoga tradition.

There are many paths, but the destination is the same -- union with the Highest Self -- union with the Divine. Remember, the great seers and sages of India were no different from us, as we have all been blessed with the greatest boon: a human birth. Let us embrace the lessons they left us, recognizing also that the answer to every question already resides within each of us. It is our hope and prayer that this teacher training will initiate you into a new mode of living where each breath becomes an act of adoration and every right decision brings you closer to the great goal of life. May you be receptive to the grace of God and may you live to realize the Self in this very lifetime. *Om Shanti Om.*

The Life of Yogi Sri Dharma Mittra

Dharma Mittra is the greatest living Hatha yogi in the West.
—Swami Kailashananda

Yogi Sri Dharma Mittra is best known today as a great teacher who is also a true *yogi*. His life's work expresses itself through ethical and humanistic daily rituals that direct aspirants towards the truth that is Self-realization. Sri Dharma's personal practice and direct experience with his beloved Guru on the path of service form the basis for a system that has influenced hundreds of thousands of teachers and students worldwide. Over scores of years teaching in New York City, through his workshops and teacher trainings, his Master Yoga Chart of 908 Postures, his book Asanas: 608 Yoga Poses, his *Maha Sadhana* DVD's and his published articles, Dharma has been a pivotal guide offering committed guidance to his many devoted students. A living manifestation of his initiate name (which translates as universal law; duty; virtue; or righteousness), Sri Dharma continually promotes the *yamas* and *niyamas* -- the ethical precepts of yoga. These guidelines form the firm foundation of his teaching, and one does not have to spend long with Dharma to hear him speak regarding observance of the first *yama, ahimsa* (non-violence). Through practice of this principle in both thought and action, one develops compassion. From this virtue blooms the entire practice of yoga. "If you are involved with violence, your meditation will go nowhere!" "Without the yamas, the ethical rules, there is no yoga!" Sri Dharma tirelessly promotes ahimsa through vegetarianism / veganism and kindness to all living beings.

Sri Dharma Mittra was born on May 14, 1939 into a poor Catholic family of five children in Pirapora in the state of Minas Gerais, Brazil. While still only a teenager, Dharma began to explore esoteric knowledge, and learned of yoga through reading and thoughtful study. He also began to explore the capabilities inherent in the physical body through the practice of *Jiu-Jitsu*, wrestling, weight training and bodybuilding. In 1958, Sri Dharma began seven years of service in the Brazilian National Air Force. While serving his country, Dharma founded and operated a bodybuilding and fitness school called Club Apollo. During this time of his life, Sri Dharma was awarded first place in a bodybuilding contest, second place in weight lifting, and for his achievements was named Mr. Minas Gerais, Brazil. In spite of his many accomplishments, Dharma yearned for more. What he truly desired with every fiber of his being was a living teacher, a Master or Guru, who could help guide him in the discovery of the real nature of why we are here -- to find the True Self on the path of yoga.

In the early 1960's, Sri Dharma's younger brother moved to New York City and met just such a person: Swami Kailashananda or

Yogi Gupta (Gupta was his family name) as he was known in the United States. Yogi Gupta was the only initiated disciple of a cave-dwelling *yogi* and ascetic who was only seen in Rishikesh, India during major Hindu festivals. Most of Yogi Gupta's disciples knew of his Guru only from a single tiny framed photograph that stood in a place of honor on Yogi Gupta's desk in the New York Ashram.

Sri Swami Kailashananda was one of the great sages of modern India and a complete master of all nine forms of yoga. Before renouncing the material world to find God, he had been a practicing lawyer. Known in India as the Psychic Guru, Yogi Gupta was also an accomplished Ayurvedic physician and Vedic Astrologer. He established a hospital and Ashram just up the valley, further into the Himalayas from Rishikesh, known as the Kailashananda Mission.

In 1954, Yogi Gupta was invited to travel from India to speak at a health convention in Chicago. Impressed by the seriousness of the American aspirants, he soon returned to the U.S. and became one of the first illuminated Indian masters to directly transmit the Holy Science of Hatha-Raja Yoga in America.

Dharma's brother was initiated into Swami Kailashananda's lineage as Satya Mittra. Upon receiving news that his brother had met the Guru, Sri Dharma made the difficult decision to leave the Brazilian National Air Force and his family in order to meet with Sri Swami Kailashananda in New York City. Dharma-ji scrambled to gather the monies needed to purchase the one-way plane ticket that would allow him to begin a new life with his intended spiritual father and guide.

Sri Dharma arrived in New York in 1964 and made his way straight to the heart of Greenwich Village where his younger brother was then living. The very day Dharma stepped off the plane, he went directly to have an audience with Yogi Gupta. Sri Dharma recounts that meeting his Guru was like meeting God. For three years, Dharma worked any job he could find in order to have the requisite funds to spend on every class Yogi Gupta taught when visiting from India. Sri Dharma worked as a porter, a busboy, a waiter and a janitor, and devoted any free time to the Guru in Karma Yoga and to practice. When the Yogi Gupta New York Ashram became a reality in mid-town Manhattan, Dharma became a resident and had the great honor of personally serving the Guru whenever he visited the United States. As the blessed disciple, Sri Dharma's duties included preparing Yogi Gupta's meals, shaving his head, cleaning his living quarters and washing and ironing his clothes. This special role gave Dharma-ji the opportunity to often be in close proximity with his Guru so that he could witness and imitate his every action. When Dharma confessed to Yogi Gupta that he was constantly trying to copy him physically, mentally and spiritually, Yogi Gupta shook his index finger at Sri Dharma and declared: "That's it, my son – that's the trick!" After all, true spiritual knowledge can only be imparted psychically.

After three years of Karma Yoga as the Guru's personal assistant, celestial handyman and Ashram juice bar operator, Sri Swami Kailashananda initiated Sri Dharma into the spiritual family in a private ceremony at the Ashram. Dharma received his spiritual name, personal initiate mantra and charged initiate *mala* beads. Upon receiving initiation, Dharma became a *sannyasin* (one who renounces worldly life to focus solely on attaining to God).

In the 1960's and 70's, Yogi Gupta regularly gave free public lectures in rented hotel ballrooms throughout New York City, and Sri Dharma demonstrated *asana* as part of the lectures. Sri Dharma was a beloved teacher of intermediate and advanced students of *asana* and *pranayama* at the Yogi Gupta New York Ashram. Following classes, Dharma would make juice and prepare food for the students and his fellow disciples. Sri Dharma helped to create works of art for the Ashram and its publications, and colorized many photographs of his beloved Guru. Dharma-ji also had the prestigious job of Ashram handyman, installing new plumbing, toilets and air-conditioning systems. Additionally, he was charged with setting up the sound system in hotel ballrooms for the public lectures Yogi Gupta gave after first cleaning the space.

When not engaged in Karma Yoga, Sri Dharma devoted every waking moment to practice. Dharma's traditional path was not easy. On top of being responsible for his daily spiritual and Ashram duties, he had to work an outside job to pay for his classes with the Guru. Sri Dharma worked as a porter in a hotel and as a janitor in a hospital for the $50-a-week required for all programs and consultations with the Guru. Whatever he couldn't cover was put on his tab. At the end of most of those years, Dharma-ji owed some $2000. He would work hard when the Guru was away in order to earn the money to pay off his debt immediately upon Yogi Gupta's return.

In 1975, Sri Dharma asked and received his Guru's blessing to leave the Ashram. He found himself on a New York street corner with no plans, no money, a small shopping bag containing his few possessions and great faith in the path he was on. A couple that were disciple-friends of Dharma saw him on the street, and asked him if he would like to teach in their downtown loft. Since Sri Dharma had nowhere to live or teach at that moment, he readily agreed. Dharma's honest, humble and sincere manner in teaching soon attracted many students, some of whom still study with him today. Sri Dharma soon founded one of the early independent schools of yoga in the eastern United States, called the Yoga Asana Center, and located at 315 Broadway in the City Hall area of New York City. Teachers from the few other schools that existed at that time in New York would attend his classes to learn how to teach and lead classes that included advanced postures and breathing exercises.

Over the succeeding years, the Yoga Asana Center moved to many locations throughout New York City. Throughout this period, Sri Dharma charged only enough money for classes to cover the studio's rent and his food costs. Classes were offered for as little as $1.50 per session and students were often given complimentary sprouts after class. Sri Dharma also offered devotional *kirtans* and vegan pot-luck dinners to the public follow-ing special Deep Relaxation and Healing classes. In 1975, Sri Dharma completed The Sun Salutation Yoga Course Chart, an inspired and helpful yoga program poster. Dharma's daily practice at that time was formidable and consumed most of his waking hours outside of teaching. Hours of *asana* (just a few main poses held for extreme lengths of time), hours of *pranayama* (mostly one single exercise), up to seventy rounds of *japa*, three rounds of Psychic Development per day, various *kriyas* and lots of *dharana* / *dhyana* to uncover and understand the true nature of everything.

Sri Dharma adhered to a mostly live/raw vegetarian diet and observed absolute celibacy and dispassion. In the 1979, the Yoga Asana Center was relocated to 100 West 14th Street at 6th

Avenue. It was an unforgettable haven, hand-built by Dharma-ji. On the street level was a television monitor playing footage of a *yogi* performing an unbelievable, quiet and graceful *asana* practice. Upstairs, students removed their shoes, stepped upon a plush, red carpet and were greeted by the man just viewed on the monitor on the street below. Unique, handmade spiritual items surrounded the students: colorful window shades, meditation pillows and altars. Original drawings covered the walls, including an illustrated tutorial for practicing *pranayama*. Fragrant Indian incense filled the air and mingled with the gentle sounds of birds chirping or Sanskrit chanting from a stereo system. There were special, scriptural tapes Sri Dharma made to help his students realize that they are not the body and not the mind, but God.

In 1984, at the age of 45, Sri Dharma created and published his Master Yoga Chart of 908 Postures as an offering to his beloved Guru. This chart was the result of months of intense work during which Sri Dharma assumed and personally photographed himself in some 1,350 *asanas*. Dharma meticulously cut, pasted and set each individual photo by hand, long before the innovations of the computer age. His students at the time saw the poster as a living, evolving work -- each day when they arrived for class, there were a few more poses posted on its mock-up. Since then, the classic Master Chart has been hung in Ashrams, yoga studios, schools, spas, gyms and homes all over the world. It has been an inspiration and important educational tool for earnest practitioners for almost 30 years.

In order to offer students the opportunity to practice and study outside of New York City, a retreat house in the Catskill region of New York State was established in 1996. For ten years, it served as the preferred location for Sri Dharma's regular students to attend educational immersion retreats and teacher trainings. 1999 saw the genesis of the "Life of a Yogi" Teacher Training Certification program. (Prior to 1999, Teacher Training was achieved through apprenticeship.) The first group offered this official Dharma Yoga Teacher certification was comprised of serious, regular students that were all personally invited by Sri Dharma himself to attend. In the year 2000, Dharma agreed to allow the name Yoga Asana Center to be changed to the Dharma Yoga Center and the practice space was dedicated as the Kailashananda Temple. Since then, there have been several teacher trainings offered each year. The gathering on May 16, 2009 celebrating Sri Dharma's 70th birthday brought 500 students, disciples and friends together from around the world to honor his commitment and perseverance in the service of the dissemination of the holy science of yoga.

At 75 and having just opened a gleaming new temple -- Dharma West at 23rd and 6th, Sri Dharma is still going strong. Dharma-ji's classes are renowned for being both physically and mentally challenging, yet his sense of humor and steady support make attendance a pleasure. New students often find themselves given great personal attention even when the studio, hall or temple is packed. Dharma will often take even the very advanced student beyond where they think they can go. The simple lesson learned from this exchange often leads the student to believe that the seemingly impossible is possible and, with such a teacher, one might realize the Self in this very lifetime. Instruction is clear, concise and to the point. Physical demonstration is always done in a manner that allows the student to recognize the path one may take as they advance in strength and flexibility to achieve the full posture. Having suffered for years and practiced virtually every technique in the yogic arsenal, Sri Dharma wants to prescribe the simplest and most direct course of action regarding any aspect of practice. Yet, for those that are with him often, glimpses of the iron discipline that brought him to the journey's end occasionally peek through. The generosity, humility and humor with which Dharma shares virtually all he knows is perhaps the greatest lesson and gift for those fortunate enough to meet or know him. In the end, it is probably this more than any other quality as a teacher that truly sets him apart.

Dharma Yoga Code of Conduct

Yoga is an integrated way of living defined by strict moral standards. The Ethical Rules serve as a guide for living a moral life. Their observance reflects well on both the individual and the lineage he or she represents. As a teacher trainee ("*sadhaka*") in the Dharma Yoga "Life of a Yogi" Teacher Training programs, one is given the tools, knowledge and a perfect example of how to live every moment as a true *yogi*. Graduates of the DY LOAY TT programs are expected to conduct their lives in consonance with the moral principles of yoga as modeled daily by Yogi Sri Dharma Mittra.

Yoga teachers must adhere to the traditional, yogic code of conduct, as well as the law of the land in which they reside. As practitioners and teachers of Dharma Yoga, one's behavior must reflect the high moral standards espoused in Dharma Yoga. One ought to lead by example and demonstrate always the qualities one would associate with a sincere individual. Actions speak louder than words, and when one takes on the mantle of responsibility (that of one who endeavors to lead others to sacred union with God), one is committed to attempting perfection in every thought, word, action and deed in both the public and private spheres. One must be vigilant regarding how one behaves at all times because even in private, someone is watching.

The Ethical Guidelines: Classical Qualifications of a Sadhaka

One must have at least the desire to possess the following qualities, virtues and attributes. By possessing these, you will surely succeed in yoga.

Sadhakas will cultivate an open mind as regards the Universal Aspect of Being (the Supreme Self or God).

Sadhakas will seek ever to better understand the laws of karma and reincarnation.

Sadhakas will remain committed to following the moral and ethical guidelines espoused by yoga (*yama* and *niyama*) in all areas of their lives and will share this knowledge with their students.

Sadhakas will refrain from consuming the flesh of their brothers and sisters of the animal kingdom and cultivate respect for all living creatures.

Sadhakas will exemplify honesty, truth, kindness, patience and obedience.

Sadhakas will avoid cowardly, dependent or unstable behavior and cultivate strength of character, courageousness and forgiveness.

Sadhakas will take care not to fall under the sway of people.
Sadhakas will remain committed to practicing yoga as a way of life.

Sadhakas are committed to maintaining impeccable standards of professional competence and integrity.

 Sadhakas will avoid teaching or living in a casual manner.

Sadhakas will abstain from giving medical advice or advice that could be interpreted as such unless they possess the necessary qualifications.

Sadhakas will observe moderation in eating, sleeping, recreation, sexual relations and sensual pleasure.

Sadhakas will be kind and non-judgmental in all circumstances, especially when dealing with students and abstain always from acts of arrogance, cruelty, greediness or harshness.

Sadhakas will work constantly toward freedom from "I" and "mine," growing ever less concerned with name, fame, prestige or personal prosperity.

Sadhakas welcome all students irrespective of race, nationality, gender, sexual-orientation, social status, financial circumstance or physical disability.

Sadhakas will accurately and truthfully represent their education, training and experience.

Sadhakas are committed to promoting the physical, mental and spiritual well-being of their students, as well as themselves.

Sadhakas understand the unique student / teacher relationship and will avoid exploiting the trust and potential dependency of certain students.

Sadhakas will always refer students to other teachers if it is in the student's best interest.

Sadhakas will avoid any form of sexual harassment of their students.

Sadhakas will strive to not be critical of anyone or anything, any style of yoga or yoga teacher in particular, practicing non-covetousness and lack of conceit always.

Sadhakas will remain committed to constant study and the practice of meditation.

Sadhakas will strive to offer the fruit of every action to *Isvara*.

A Letter from Sri Swami Kailashananda

Dear Disciples and Devotees,

Devotion is the Lord's highest love; love of one and all, love which never dies. Love which is in you and you are it. Such devotion must crown your spiritual success. As devotion grows, it bears in due course fruit of inner knowledge and Divine perception leading to God-realization. Cultivate devotion through selfless-service, *satsang*, mantra repetition, songs of devotion and meditation. Life without devotion and purity of heart is death and disease. Think of the inspiring devotion of Arunee, Dhroo and Prahlad who achieved the highest goal by devotion and self-surrender. Worldly-life as an end in itself, full of worldly desires and cravings for egotism and attachment to the body for sense pleasure, is the true enemy of devotion. Overcome this enemy by total surrender of self and be free.

May Lord Shiva fill your mind and heart with purity and devotion. May Mother Durga, ocean of compassion and mercy, bless you with radiant health, long life, peace and prosperity. May you all abide in the Lord forever and ever.

*Swami Kailashananda
and Sri Dharma Mittra
1964*

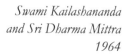

A Letter from Sri Dharma Mittra

Dear Students,

In 1957, my younger brother lent me a yogic book called *Days of Peace*. I still remember the text, which was a detailed description of the state of bliss after one achieves enlightenment or Self-realization (the state of *samadhi* and beyond). That was it! I decided to learn yoga in order to find out: Who am I? What is eternal? Where am I going after this body is discarded? When I was initiated by my Guru, Swami Kailashananda, in 1966, I made up my mind -- this is it! I am going to teach yoga for the rest of my life for a few main reasons:

1. Out of compassion for those who are seeking relief from their pain and suffering due to lack of Self Knowledge.
2. So as to be able to be a full time yogi.
3. Because sharing spiritual knowledge is the greatest type of charity.

I think that teaching yoga techniques for the achievement of Self-realization is one of the highest and holiest positions on this planet, because Self Knowledge is the highest knowledge. This knowledge is real "power" that leads to enlightenment and world peace.

When I teach, I seek always to share the foundation of yoga. That's to say, without it, there will be no Kingdom of the Almighty One, nor will there be even a desire for liberation on the part of the students. I spend lots of time trying to make the students understand and realize *yama* and *niyama*, sometimes passing through lots of difficulties because some students are not receptive. *Yama* is like the ethical rules of every religion -- it purifies the mind and heart. One automatically develops a strong desire for liberation, steadiness in their practice and, eventually, self-control. This leads naturally to success in meditation and the mind becomes fit for a vision of the Almighty One. The *niyamas* include techniques to clean, promote healing, and generate physical and mental powers that all lead one to discover Self-knowledge. The final *niyama (Isvara pranidhana)* invites us to renounce the fruit of all actions to the Lord (the Highest). This is better even than meditation! *Isvara pranidhana* teaches us to surrender the ego. Concentration and meditation methods are indispensable, as well. Finally, the students must learn that their compassion must extend beyond their pets -- it should reach all living beings. Some students immediately understand this and become vegetarians. After all, all living beings love life. They are like us -- they want to be happy and have a family. They fear violence and tremble before death. Students must come to understand that eating animals as food is a great sin and is "out of date". If compassion is fully developed, amazing psychic powers are acquired, such as the ability to know the why and how of everything. So, the best of my best of 53 years of yoga is selected and shared each day with love. This all is a short cut to immortality.

Although I have practiced and taught *yama, niyama, asana, pranayama*, Psychic Development and meditation for many years, the main focus of my practice was and remains Karma Yoga (selfless service) and *svadyaya* (study of scripture). Anyone can practice these two forms of *yoga*, as they require no basic level of physical or mental aptitude, special equipment or intensive preparation, just a great thirst for knowledge of the Real Self and a heartfelt desire to help and love everyone. Karma Yoga is selfless work offered without any strings attached and with no expectation of enjoying the fruits of one's labor. Acting in this way, one gradually loses all selfishness and notions such as: "I am the doer." Thus comes total surrender of the ego. (Egoism is the second cause of pain and suffering.) Why do selfless service? Because without it, there will be no Divine Union, absorption or Self-realization.

The scriptural knowledge and all other knowledge are already contained in the eternal Etheric Records. When the mind is fit to receive them, then, due to *prana's* vibrations and its variations, thoughts are generated and, with the help of *prana*, they materialize in subtle form and are received by the mind. In the case of the scriptures, someone whose psychic channels are totally purified and who is endowed with enlightenment has simply become the vessel for these Divine thoughts to take form through. Surely the knowledge of the scriptures is received and written without any personal touch, because there is no notion of "me" or "I am the doer" involved. The holy person's mind is a perfect channel that does not distort Supreme Knowledge. This Supreme Knowledge that deals with the glories and powers of the Highest One (especially dealing with Self-knowledge) is the holy key that allows the mind to grasp an understanding of: "What is beyond duality and even beyond what the mind can comprehend?" One should approach the scriptures with the highest respect and reverence. While reading or hearing their contents, imagine that you are making direct contact with its point of origin, imagining that one is face to face with "Thee" (the Almighty One – the Supreme Self) receiving instructions.

For all of the above to have an impact, one should start the New Year thinking on Him alone, concerned/absorbed constantly with Self-realization. Also, be ever kind and reverent to all living beings. Share spiritual knowledge with those that are fit to receive it. Start the New Year with love, and it may end up with love. Be ever engaged in *sadhana* and surely success will be the result! Om Shanti, Shanti, Shantih.

With Great Love,

Dharma Mittra

An Interview with Sri Dharma Mittra

Legendary Teachers' Teacher and Yoga Master Sri Dharma Mittra first encountered yoga as a teenager before meeting his Guru in 1964 and beginning his training in earnest. Sri Dharma founded one of the early independent schools of yoga in New York City in 1975 and has taught hundreds of thousands the world over in the years since. Sri Dharma is the model and creator of the "Master Yoga Chart of 908 Postures", the author of *ASANAS: 608 Yoga Poses*, has released two DVD's to date – *Maha Sadhana* Levels I and II, and the Yoga Journal book *Yoga* was based on his famous Master Chart. Sri Dharma continues to disseminate the complete traditional science of Yoga through daily classes, workshops and his "Life of a Yogi" Teacher Trainings, both at his Centers in New York and around the world. For more information on all things Dharma Yoga, please visit: www.dharmayogacenter. com.

You started practicing yoga in the 1960's. At that time, many fewer people were doing yoga than today. How do you think the reasons for yoga practice 50 years ago are different from people's objectives today? If so, what are the differences based on?

Sri Dharma Mittra: A half century ago, yoga was still traditionally taught and received. At that time, the students were mostly interested in enlightenment and Self-realization, and the teachers were few, but were endowed with Divine qualities. Additionally, some were endowed with Self Knowledge and had achieved Self-realization. Most of the students had lots of reverence and obedience towards their teachers. Thus, they were guided to God-realization.

Today, students' needs are different and more complex. Due to technology and countless distractions such as: drugs, junk food, computers and movies, the yoga students are mostly seeking relief from their pain and suffering caused by lots of indulgences. They are seeking yoga for good health, mental powers and, of course, some peace of mind. Very few are after total liberation or Self-realization. The *asanas* multiply greatly in numbers. The teachers are by the hundreds of thousands or so, and there are all kinds of teachers. Some concentrate just on Hatha Yoga, and some teach without *yama* and *niyama* – the ethical rules and observances of yoga. Others are making a business of yoga and, of course, there are still some endowed with liberation or Self-realization, but they are hidden to those who are not yet ready. Yoga is taught in many ways to fit the many needs of today.

Also, today there are many different kinds of students. The feeble student who criticizes the teacher and displays no good conduct; the decent, average student; and the Divine one who is endowed with reverence, obedience and a strong desire for liberation. This is why there are many kinds of teachers -- to fit everyone.

People usually imagine a yogi as a person completely detached from society and concentrated on his or her needs and interests. Is it possible to combine regular human life and deep yoga practice?

SDM: There are many yogis (anyone who studies yoga can be called a *yogi*) who decide to apply most of their time to yoga and renounce most of their worldly desires in order to quickly reach enlightenment. Living alone and dedicated to the welfare of all mankind, they soon enjoy endless bliss, and this is just one small experience of the Almighty One. These are older souls who are born already with Divine qualities such as: discipline in mind, a heart full of love and with one thing only in their mind: to merge in the Almighty One.

For those who are engaged with family, business and the world (householders), surely they too can reach enlightenment in this very lifetime. The difference is that they will have to pass through even more temptations and distractions, but, in the end, this will serve to make the *yogi* strong and powerful.

Be compassionate to all, treat your guest and pets well, and be engaged in constant yoga practice. This is the secret of success. Remember, renounce the fruit of every action to the Supreme One; this then is even better than meditation.

When do the physical exercises on the mat become asana? What does this depend on?

SDM: The physical exercises become *asana* when the body becomes steady and comfortable in the posture and when the *asana* assumes a specific geometric form. (The form is very important, because it will induce in the practitioner a state of consciousness if it is held long enough.) Also, there should be a point for concentration (a drishti) and a specific way to breathe while in each posture.

Due to the pose's physical demands, the physical body is greatly benefited. Glands, organs and muscles may be stimulated or toned, and, in some cases, mental powers are awakened. Thus, the exercise on the mat is turned into *Yoga Asana*.

What does "yoga" mean to you?

SDM: Yoga means: after the settling of the mind into silence through the practice of yogic techniques such as keeping *yama* and *niyama*, being always extremely compassionate to all, through total surrender of the ego, being endowed with Self-knowledge, engaging in lots of reflection and finally resting the mind on Brahman, the Almighty One, for a long time, the individual soul becomes one with the Universal Soul. This Divine Union is yoga. All the techniques are just preparations.

Yoga is usually thought to be a specific teaching from the East. Can a person from the West understand the essence of yoga and practice as part of life there?

SDM: I think that the difficulties that *yogis* in the West face arise mainly during the *asana* practice. In general, the legs of those from India or the Far East can easily find Lotus Pose, because Indians and those from the Far East rarely use chairs and spend much of their time in a squatting pose instead. Also, in India and much of developing world, they are less exposed to junk food and have less attachment to comfort and the distractions that we have in the West due to our technology.

I think that here in the USA is the best place on the planet for the practice of yoga. Without much effort, everything that's needed is right at our fingertips. The best teachers on the planet are here (most of the Gurus are right here in the USA), there is abundant healthy food, there are yoga schools everywhere, through the Internet, most of the scriptures can be delivered overnight to our door and some can even afford to hire a teacher for one-on-one private instruction. All the distractions and temptations in our way are really a challenge for us, and, in conquering them all, we have the chance to put our discipline to the test. Isn't that a blessing?

What about the disciple – what should his or her qualities be? What is the difference between a disciple and a student?

SDM: When the student possesses all the qualities required to become a disciple, the teacher then accepts him or her as a part of his or her spiritual family, and a spiritual name and personal spiritual mantra are given. The teacher will give guidance until the disciple achieves the goal of life: Self-realization. The disciple must be obedient and help the teacher when needed. Thus, disciple and teacher are connected forever.

The regular student is not born spiritually yet, not tested by the teacher and not asked to be initiated, so, one must be qualified to be accepted as a disciple.

What do you teach future yoga teachers?

SDM: Through our "Life of a Yogi" Teacher Training immersions and through our regular courses, future teachers always receive thorough instruction in *yama* and *niyama* – the ethical rules and observances of yoga. They are encouraged to develop supreme compassion and reverence for all beings. Armed with these two, all that is left is to surrender to the Almighty One. Teachers are also taught to give up their ego and to devote lots of time to trying to understand the meaning of *The Yoga Sutras*, *The Hatha Yoga Pradipika*, *The Bhagavad-Gita* and especially *Self-Knowledge* by Shankaracharya. They are taught how to stay clean physically, mentally and spiritually (the *kriyas*). Finally, they are taught to use the yogic techniques for one purpose only: to ready themselves and those they teach for enlightenment.

Now, there are many yoga schools and teachers. How would you describe your way of practice and teaching? What is different at the Dharma Yoga Center from other yoga schools?

SDM: Only knowledge can stop pain and suffering, and this is what I concentrate on with all my heart. Supreme Knowledge as in: "What is the cause of all pain and suffering?"; "What is the greatest impurity?"; "What is eternal?"; "How does one control the mind?"; "What is the nature of the five bodies concealing the Supreme Self?" ; and "How can one reach the state of eternal Bliss?" The foundation of our teaching here is *yama* and *niyama*. Our teachers live according to *yama* and *niyama*; they are vegetarians, and are kind and compassionate to all.

You are famous for creating the "Master Yoga Chart of 908 Postures". Can one achieve Self-realization using just some of them?

SDM: It is conceivable that someone could be physically capable of assuming all 908 *asanas*, but that they still might remain totally ignorant of the True Self. The postures are used to cultivate radiant health, mental powers, mind control and, most important of all, to help one find a comfortable pose to practice meditation in such as: *Padmasana* (Lotus), Egyptian (seated, upright on a chair), *Siddhasana* (Adept's Pose) or any other comfortable sitting pose, so that after one is armed with *yama, niyama*, Self-knowledge, disciplined in mind, self-controlled and full of love, one may stay in it for a long time, eventually becoming one with Him.

Do you consider yoga to be a form of religion? If so, why?

SDM: Yoga is not a religion or a cult, but a set of Divinely-realized techniques which, when practiced correctly, within a short time, help one to achieve radiant health, mental powers and, with the two first steps of yoga (*yama* and *niyama*), spiritual power. With these three powers, one can achieve anything. People of all faiths may practice Astanga, the Eight Steps of Yoga, and enjoy its benefits. Astanga Yoga is really a short cut to immortality. (There are other expressions of yoga that deal with the gods. In these cases, yoga can become very much like religion, in my opinion.)

What is pranayama? Is any breathing exercise pranayama? What is necessary to start pranayama practice?

SDM: Prana = "energy" or "vital force"; *yama* = "control". So, pranayama means: controlling the speed, rhythm, ratio, retention and duration of the breath. By controlling the breath, *prana* is controlled. Combining the above in different ways, each will produce a specific result -- affecting greatly the body and mind.

Some breathing exercises change the state of consciousness, some purify the psychic channels (*nadis*), others, combined with the *bandhas* (locks), join *prana* (descending energy in the body) and *apana* (rising energy in the body) and bring them up to the head, and still others stimulate the chakras (energy centers or vortexes). By performing some *pranayamas*, in combination with a specific *asana*, one may develop psychic powers. Some *pranayamas* are specifically designed for healing purposes. By controlling the breath, *prana* is controlled. To some degree, by controlling the *prana*, the mind is also brought under control.

As long as the breathing exercise is controlled in a specific way, it's *pranayama*. It's necessary to have a qualified teacher to study *pranayama*. Also, the student must be reverent and obedient to him or her. The student must try to be kind to all beings, be moderate in sleeping, eating, should stop eating meat if still doing so, and must be endowed with a desire for enlightenment to achieve any real success in *pranayama*.

One of the yama principles, Brahmacharya, is often translated as "sexual abstinence". To your mind, what is the point of Brahmacharya? Is celibacy required for those who practice yoga?

SDM: *Brahmacharya* means "to be celibate and meet your spouse only when your partner has needs which must be addressed according to the nature of your commitment to them." A householder (one who lives in the world and is involved in its affairs) should be kind to all guests, pets and relatives. Perform your spiritual obligations, be obedient and reverent to your Guru, and avoid entertaining sexual thoughts. Semen is pure Divine concentrated energy, combined with spermatozoa. In one single ejaculation, millions of sperms are wasted. It takes from 70-100 pounds of organic food to produce that single ejaculate, and to replace it. If one is miserable, depressed and lonely, sex may be appropriate if married, rather than taking drugs or drinking. Also, there are yogic techniques to retain the semen during the sexual act itself. If semen is saved, it will turn into spiritual energy, and then boundless energy is available. Also, the body will then give off a sweet fragrance. For those who are looking to accelerate their spiritual progress and reach enlightenment in a very short time, keep celibacy. Remember, *Brahmacharya* also means: "to be free from entertaining sexual thoughts."

One may, of course, practice yoga without celibacy, but progress will be slower due to the distraction of sexual attachment and difficulty in keeping up with the teacher's instructions. Possessing celibacy, tremendous will power is gained.

In old texts on yoga, differences between male and female practice are not mentioned. Asanas are often described from a man's point of view. Do women need special yoga practice? Are some aspects of yoga not available for ladies? What is different between male and female practice?

SDM: Yoga practice is the same for men and women, except for some *asanas* that are not recommended for women. If women are pregnant (over 3 months) or menstruating, there are some poses and *pranayama* that should be avoided. Yoga is truly for all.

In the world of today, yoga has become big business. Doesn't taking money for classes destroy the essence of yoga studies? Where is the balance between the material side of teaching and the spiritual meaning of the practice itself?

SDM: As long as the yoga business' profits are being used to promote, expand and disseminate spiritual knowledge in order to alleviate pain and suffering for the students, the essence of yoga is not affected. There are lots of yoga schools with restaurants, juice bars, yoga shops, massage options, etc., but everything still runs professionally. Rent is extremely high in many cities, and every teacher and employee has to be paid. As a direct consequence, yoga instruction must be offered for a fee.

Even when spiritual instruction is given, there must be some method of exchange. For everything one receives, one should offer up something in return. Asking for free things indicates poverty of spirit. In Ashrams, most students don't pay for the instruction, but they have to do lots of Karma Yoga (selfless work) in exchange. The material side of teaching is really for those who are seeking name, fame, prestige and wealth. The spiritual meaning of practicing is: all yogic practices are intended for Self-realization only.

Yoga instructors are of all kinds: dishonest ones, feeble ones, meat-eating ones, impure ones, unenlightened ones, some who do not possess knowledge of or honor *yama* and *niyama*, others who do know of *The Yoga-Sutras* and about Self Knowledge. All of these are just perfect, with a Divine purpose: to accommodate every manner of student. There are teachers who want to date the students, so they attract students that want to date the teachers. Remember: "Same attracts same." Good students with lots of kindness, obedience, reverence for all beings, who are disciplined in mind and heart, and who possess a strong desire for liberation, without fail, attract the Enlightened Ones (true Gurus) -- teachers that will take the students to the regions of Eternal Bliss or Self-realization. Isn't that wonderful?

Kirtan is an important activity at your yoga centers. Why?

SDM: To wash impure thoughts from the intellect, the waters of devotion are used. Powerful mantras in the form of songs are to be sung with the deepest devotion. It's the easiest way to trigger Divine attention and experience exceeding spiritual bliss. This manner of practice is an esoteric practice in its own right -- Bhakti Yoga. Eventually, everyone passes through it. Of course, there is a time when we have to go beyond the emotions in order to settle the mind into silence. Thus, the mind becomes fit to have a vision of the Almighty One.

Kirtan is indeed a great practice -- it satisfies those who have devotional tendencies. That's why it's important to have it in our Centers, because the students must be encouraged to follow their dharmas (tendencies). My Guru always suggested to us (his students) to practice a little bit of each type of yoga, and then to concentrate more on the one that fits to our dharma. Thus, it will speed and aid spiritual progress.

Could you kindly wish something to our readers?

SDM: The greatest type of charity is sharing or promoting spiritual knowledge to others in need. This supreme knowledge stays until our enlightenment, and it can't be taken from us -- it's really a treasure. This magazine indeed has Divine qualities, because it's doing the highest type of charity -- bringing to thousands of people important knowledge and information that will lead them to the right path, thus relieving their pain and suffering. I thank you for giving me this great opportunity to answer the Divine questions above -- it was really a pleasure for me.

Regarding the aspiring *yogis* who may read these words, I wish you all to be engaged in constant practice -- this is the secret of making progress. Meditate on compassion, stay vegan and seek enlightenment. Be obedient to your teacher and reverent to all. Oh my loved ones, keep *yama* and *niyama*. Then, you have a short cut to Immortality.

Lastly, I love you all. *I am you and you are me.*

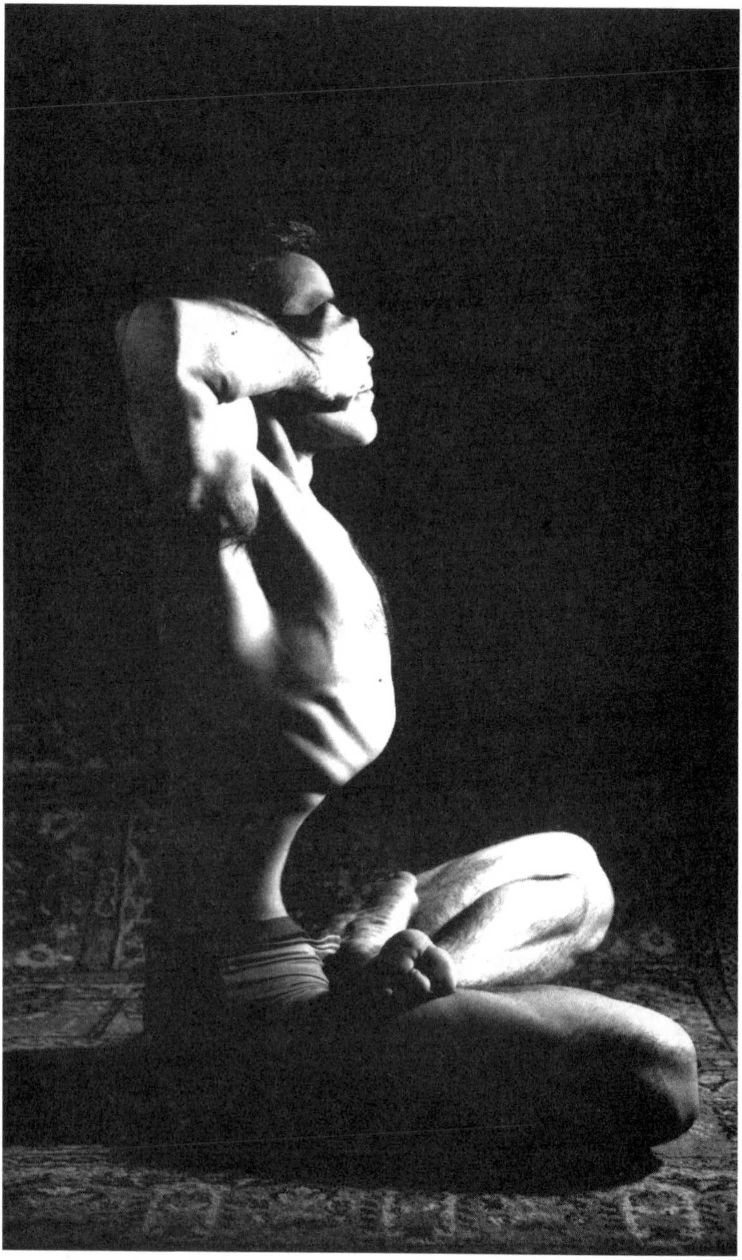

Sun Salutation Yoga Course Chart

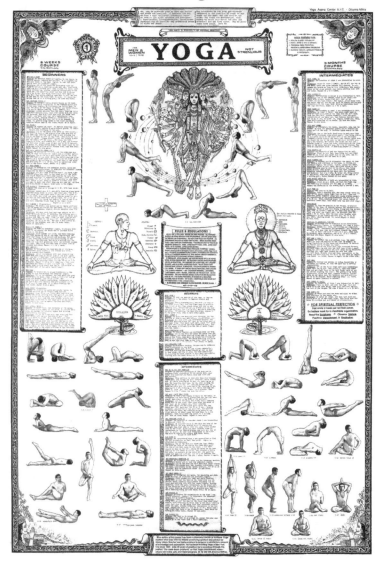

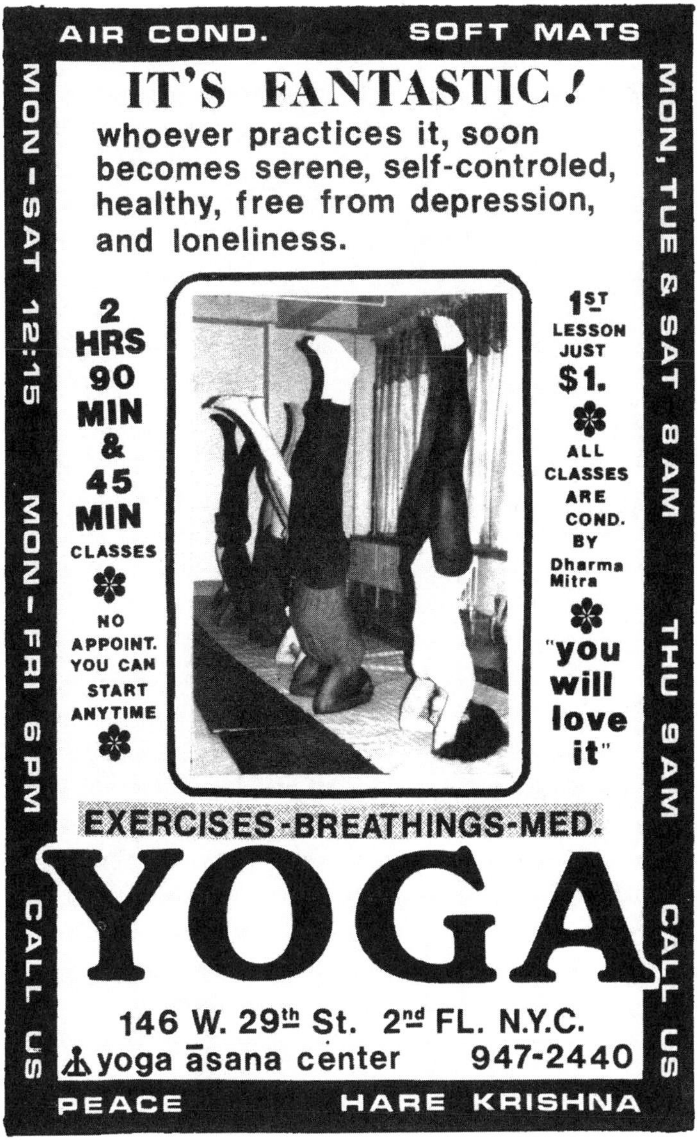
AIR COND.
SOFT MATS
MON - SAT 12:15
MON - FRI 6 PM
CALL US
MON, TUE & SAT 8 AM
THU 9 AM
CALL US
IT'S FANTASTIC!
whoever practices it, soon becomes serene, self-controled, healthy, free from depression, and loneliness.
2 HRS 90 MIN & 45 MIN CLASSES
NO APPOINT. YOU CAN START ANYTIME
1ST LESSON JUST $1.
ALL CLASSES ARE COND. BY Dharma Mitra
"you will love it"
EXERCISES-BREATHINGS-MED.
YOGA
146 W. 29th St. 2nd FL. N.Y.C.
yoga āsana center
947-2440
PEACE
HARE KRISHNA

Master Yoga Chart of 908 Postures

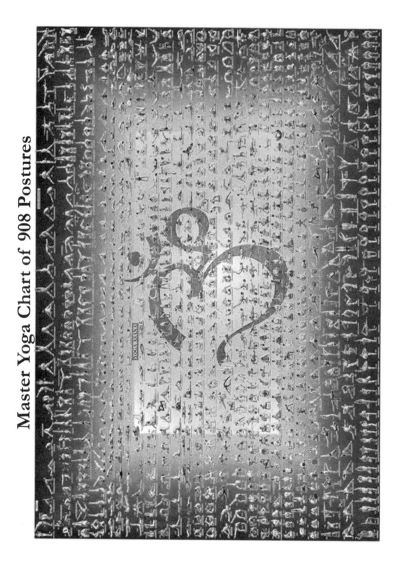

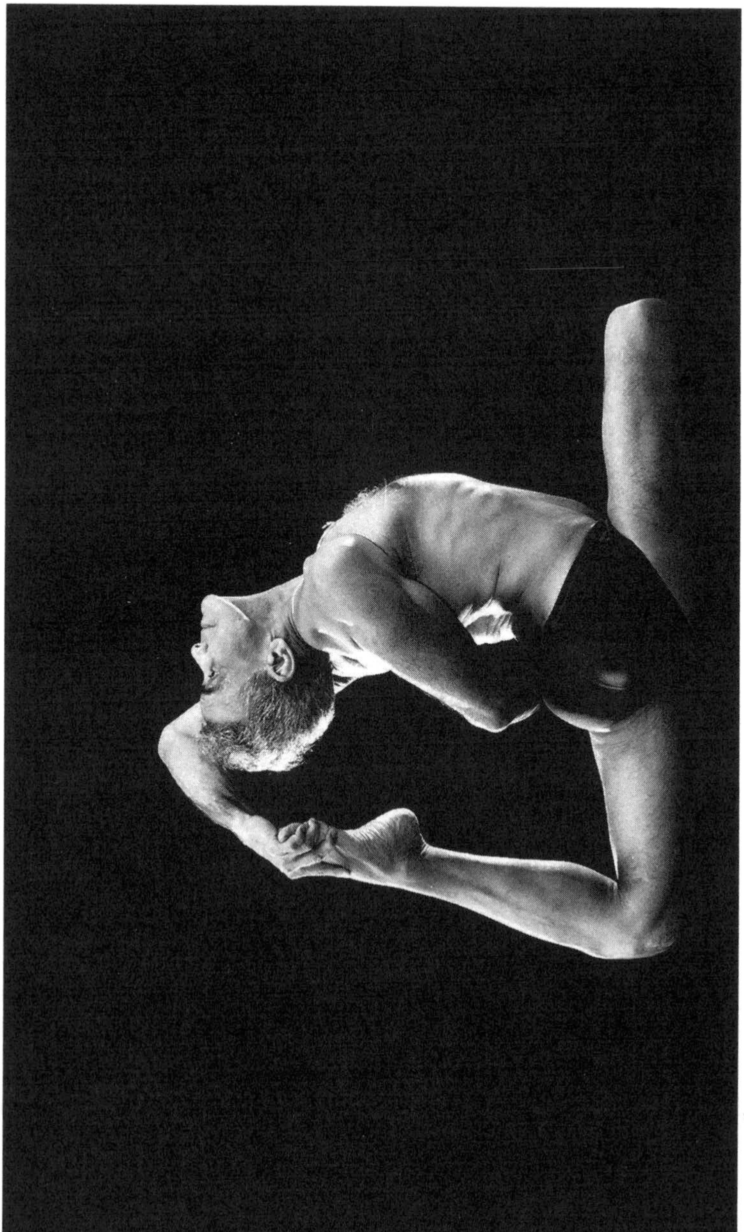

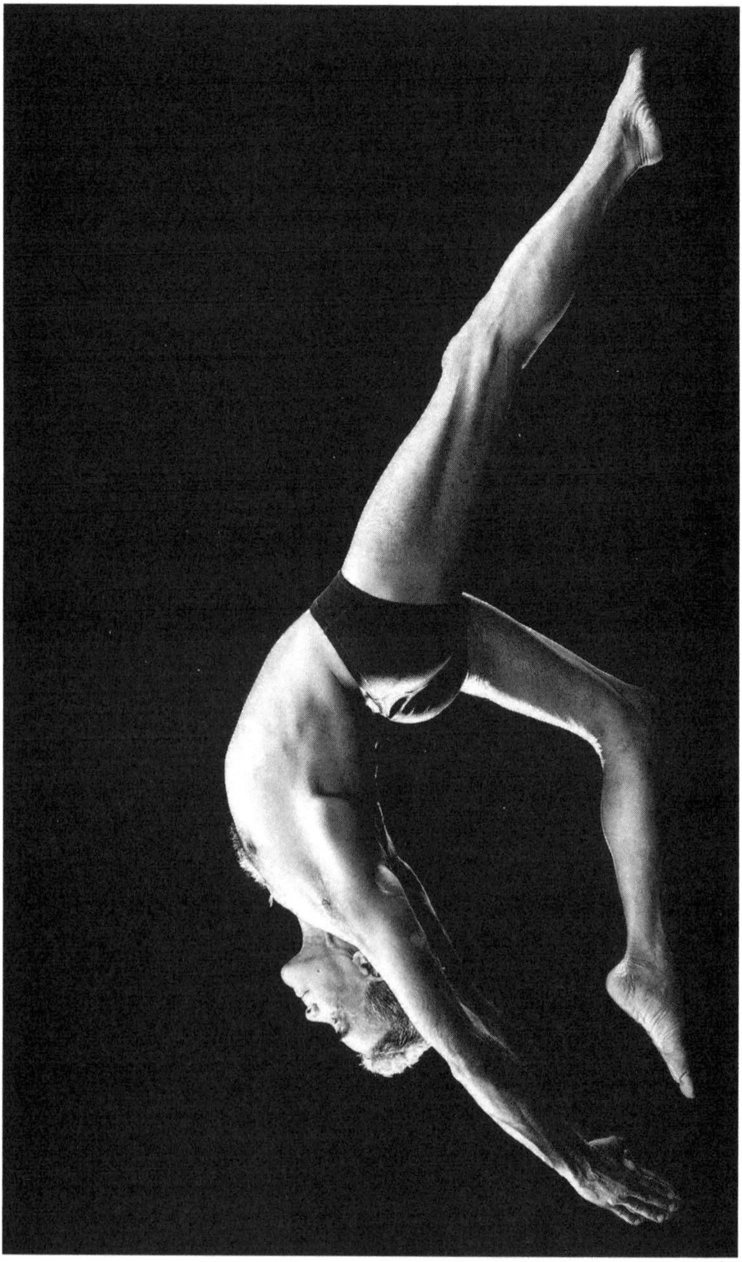

PRANAYAMA
PRATYAHARA
ASANA
DHARANA
NIYAMA
DHYANA
8 Limbs
YAMA
SAMADHI

For the Goal of Self Realization

Astanga Yoga, Yama and Niyama

Reveal Thyself to me, Oh Lord!
—Sri Dharma Mittra

What Yoga Really Is

Yoga is the highest and most efficient set of techniques devoted to Self-realization available on this planet. Designed and realized by Celestial Beings (enlightened ones), yoga is a short cut to Immortality. *Astanga* or eight-limbed yoga is not a religion, but a science that, if practiced correctly, will, within a short time, bring to the *sadhaka* (practitioner) radiant health, as well as mental and psychic powers. These attributes and abilities may then be used to succeed in the realization of the goal of life. Also, they may be applied to discover answers to essential questions such as: Who am I?, What is beyond the mind?, What's the cause of all pain and suffering?, What's the greatest of all impurities? and How can I be free from pain and suffering? Yoga doesn't mean all these fancy poses and breathing exercises -- these are just preparations or techniques that will settle the mind into silence. The source of all powers grows accessible to the steady practitioner. To succeed in all walks of life, much concentration is required. Increased ability to concentrate is a direct consequence of regular *sadhana* (spiritual practice).

Yoga practice doesn't require anything except the body. The body and the mind are purified and prepared, then surmounted through the Astanga Yoga System which is divided into eight steps or stages:

Yama	*The Ethical Rules*
Niyama	*The Observances*
Asana	*Postures -- the Exercises*
Pranayama	*Control of the Vital Life-Force*
Pratyahara	*Control of the Senses*
Dharana	*Concentration*
Dhyana	*Concentration without Interruption*
Samadhi	*Absorption with the Object or*
	Subject of Contemplation

The *yama* and *niyama* are the foundation and without them there can be no success in meditation. Imagine trying to start a fire with wet wood. Lots of smoke is produced, bringing tears to the eyes, but no true flame appears. Applying the *yama* and *niyama* purifies the mind and will help one control their passions and emotions and aid one in avoiding conflict with others. One develops compassion, reverence and love, begins to recognize sameness everywhere and feel as one with all creation. Firmly established in *yama* and *niyama*, the *sadhaka* develops a strong desire for liberation.

Along with the third limb (*asana*) and the fourth limb (*pranayama*), the yamas and niyamas constitute the outward quest. *Asana* combined with *bandhas* (locks), *mudras* (seals) and *kriyas* (cleansing techniques) brings radiant health. Remember: healthy body, healthy mind. Only a mind that is calm and steady can achieve unbroken concentration (meditation). *Pranayama* will purify the nerves, calm the mind and, consequently, allow the *sadhaka* to take control of *prana* (vital life-force) and the mind. With passion and emotions under control, success in meditation is surely in sight. *Dharana* is one of the results of *pranayama* practice, because the senses are now under control (*pratyahara*). *Pratyahara* occurs as a natural outgrowth of steady, constant practice of *asana* and *pranayama*, the two proceeding *angas* (limbs, stages or accessories). With the practice of the previous steps, meditation is easy to attain.

The deepest part of yoga practice is inward, as illustrated by the last three limbs: *dharana, dhyana* and *samadhi*. Practice of the first four limbs is known as Hatha (forceful) Yoga. Practice of all eight limbs is known as Hatha-Raja Yoga (or sometimes just Raja Yoga) and is the path illuminated by the lineage of Sri Dharma Mittra. Practice of the final three *angas* is known as Raja or Royal Yoga and practicing *dharana, dhyana* and *samadhi* simultaneously constitutes a practice known as *samyama*.

One of the purposes of meditation is to realize the things that we believe are true, because belief is not enough. We must experience "it" -- see "it" -- so we may become content and happy. Everyone believes that we are immortal souls. Still, everyone is full of doubts and is miserable. The mind needs evidence in order to be satisfied and really settle. *Samadhi* is the state of bliss-absolute, achieved when the mind is satisfied and resides in its own nature, in eternal contentment. The final stage of permanent absorption is known as enlightenment. Scholars and spiritual teachers may tie themselves up in knots trying to explain this state. It is *Turiya* (the fourth state) beyond waking consciousness, sleep with dreams and deep, dreamless sleep when one recognizes God in every shining atom of existence. Then one moves like a dry leaf, the winds of life carrying them where they will. This highest *samadhi* is beyond pain, suffering, happiness or joy. One is supremely established in that which is beyond all this.

The Yamas

There are five *yamas* or ethical restraints. Their scrupulous observance brings harmony and peace, readying the mind for Self-Knowledge. A major component of the discipline of yoga is to cultivate *yama* in daily action, as well as in formal practice.

Ahimsa is defined as non-violence in thought, word and deed. (*A* = not, *himsa* = killing or violence.) *Ahimsa* means love; "Thou shalt not kill!" This applies not only to human beings, but to every living creature. The *yogi* respects everything since *Atma* is the same in all. One needs to practice discrimination. When one comes to recognize the Almighty One equally present in all, one's compassion then moves far beyond the immediate circle of relatives, friends and pets to embrace everything and everyone. Compassion is a firm, essential step towards Self-realization. It compels the *yogi* to recognize themselves in others. When this has been achieved, it becomes impossible for us to hurt, kill or eat one another. The root cause of *himsa* or violence is *avidya* (ignorance) coupled with desirous or envious feelings. Ignorance of the True Self leaves us with no recourse but to identify with the body, senses and mind. This is the cause of all pain and suffering and is the greatest of all impurities. It is also lust, wrath, greed and violence in seed form.

The aspiring *yogi* must establish themselves in *ahimsa* in word, thought and action and come to see everything as a manifestation of the Supreme One. Then every other virtue will arise and we will emerge from every battle victorious. Hate has never been known to dispel hate; hate only begets hate. Only love has the power to conquer all. In the end, compassion is the best antidote to violence. A *yogi* is frequently strict with him or herself, but always soft and gentle in dealing with others. There is positive, angry determination that is directed to the mind and body, but never towards the Self. This mode of thought allows one to abandon useless behaviors and fruitless habits and sets the foundation for acting in a new, positive way. When anger occurs, it lasts only for an instant. Love is always present as when a teacher corrects a student or when a parent scolds a child without really experiencing anger. When one is calm and acts in harmony with karmic laws, one is beyond the pain of bad karma. Other forms of anger are harmful and happen as a result of ignorance when we perceive ourselves as being separate from others. The other four *yamas* are rooted in *ahimsa* and exist only to perfect this restraint. Without taking on the *yama* of *ahimsa*, there is little benefit to observing the other four yamas or any other aspect of the holy science of yoga.

Satya is defined as truthfulness. An aspiring *yogi* should speak truthfully. Every word, thought and action should agree. Always keep your word and, whenever possible, maintain silence. Talkative people often exaggerate. God is truth.

In order to be able to realize truth, one must speak truth. According to Mahatma Gandhi who was a man of truth: "It is better to die than to lie." Use discrimination in practicing this restraint. If someone is going to get hurt through its observance, *ahimsa* trumps *satya* and it is better to keep silent. *Vak-Siddhis* are gained through observance of this *yama*: "That which is said will come to pass." According to the great Indian epic, *The Mahabharata*, the knowledge contained within the four *Vedas*, joined even by all its supporting commentaries, is far out-weighed by *satya*.

Asteya is defined as non-stealing. Desire is the root-cause of all theft. Stealing can be understood on many levels. One may steal knowledge by not asking permission to use someone else's ideas or forms of expression. Listening to a conversation one is not a part of is a form of stealing. If one eats food without expressing gratitude or first offering a prayer, this is also a mode of thievery. Learn to say: "Thank you God for the very air I breathe." If one borrows a book with the expectation that one will return it in two days but keeps the book for three, this is stealing, as well. Leaving your belongings at someone else's house without their permission is also considered stealing as you are stealing another's space. There is also a form of stealing that causes much pain and suffering wherein one consummates a strong desire to possess the talents, skills or abilities of another. This is overcome by recognizing yourself in everyone.

Stealing caused by envy, attachments and cravings represents a serious breach of the *yama* of *asteya*. These negative qualities are symptomatic of those devoid of Self-knowledge. Inhabit the company of the wise and observe and imitate their every action and thought so that you may grow to be like them. By observing *asteya*, all wealth will ultimately be yours.

Brahmacharya is defined as continence or control of sexual energy. In classic yogic thought, *brahmacharya* represents the life of celibacy devoted to spiritual study. Sexual abstinence is prompted by the attitude that one sees Divinity everywhere. Control of sexual energy includes freedom from sexual thoughts, lust and desire for sex, except in the context of procreation with a spouse. This is the Divine plan to populate the planet. The laws of karma and reincarnation demonstrate that there are many souls waiting for a human birth with exactly the right parents and their engaging in the act of procreation gives these souls an opportunity to come into the world and strive for liberation.

One of the many reasons to observe strict *brahmacharya* is for the conservation and redirection of sexual energy. When this sexual energy is saved, it is automatically transformed into spiritual energy (*ojas shakti*) to help one advance on the path of yoga. The body then gives off a sweet smell. Loss of semen is thought to lead to early death and its retention, to enhance life. True observance of this *yama* imparts enormous will power, boundless energy, readiness for spiritual knowledge and a sense that one can move the entire world.

> *Brahmacharya is the most important virtue for Self-realization.*
> *Brahmacharya is purity in thought, word and deed.*
> *The very idea of lust should not enter the mind.*
> *No yoga or spiritual progress is possible without continence.*
> —Swami Sivananda

Continence is difficult for most people to achieve and sustain. By practicing the various techniques of yoga and by absorbing the teachings of a *yogacharya* (yogic Master-Teacher), the aspirant will find his or her way on the path to higher-consciousness. Control and change in many areas of life are possible with faith and the grace of God.

Aparigraha is defined as non-covetousness or non-hoarding. Possession of objects beyond those requisite for living represents a form of hoarding. Whenever we keep that which we don't need, this is hoarding. A simple example would be the setting aside of extra reserves of money in the bank. If one has excess wealth, it can readily be donated to a spiritual cause or organization. As in all things, cultivate discrimination. Retain only that which is required to maintain the body and a little extra, "just in case." If one lays claim to more than is required to sustain life, one is also violating the *yama* of *asteya* through the act of depriving another. Treat your life as though it were a computer's hard drive and delete everything unnecessary to make room for what's truly needed. If one is on a spiritual path, avoid receiving inappropriate gifts as they often bestow a feeling of obligation on the receiver, which disturbs the mind. To avoid this feeling, receive the gift and then give it to someone else without the original giver knowing what you've done. While it is OK to give and receive gifts that are given or received out of pure love, anonymous gifts are the best sort since they arrive with no strings attached. One must work for that which comes to you -- to do otherwise is to invite "poverty of spirit." If one has faith, everything will come in the right time, in the right way and in the right place. There is no need to worry, as that which is required will come mysteriously. Also, through observance of *aparigraha*, the memory of past lives will become available. Possess only what you need. For those who wish to enter the state of samadhi, eventually even the mind must be empty.

Never take from life more than you will need for simple and bare living.
—Swami Sivananda

The Niyamas

There are five *niyamas*: the qualities, personal disciplines and observances to be cultivated by the spiritual aspirant. As with most of the practice of yoga, the guidance of an experienced teacher is of the utmost importance.

Saucha is defined as purity. The *niyama* of *saucha* concerns both internal and external cleanliness. Externally, *saucha* is manifested in clean clothes, a clean body and a clean place of residence. *Pranayama* will purify the nervous system and postures (*asana*) will drive toxins from the body. Through the practice of *saucha*, we learn much about the physical body and, thus, ignorance is reduced. The *kriyas* (yogic cleansing techniques) purify, heal and restore the subtle systems that keep the entire body in health. The path of *bhakti* (chanting devotional songs and mantras) washes the intellect of impure thoughts. *Saucha* also relates to two other *niyamas*, for study of scripture (*svadhyaya*) will remove the greatest of all impurities, identification with the body, mind and the senses and surrender to the Lord (*Isvara pranidhana*) cleanses the intellect of impure thoughts, purifies the heart and facilitates the process of settling the mind.

Internally, *saucha* allows the mind and body to be free of all impurities so that one may reflect the highest spiritual truth. To the yogic way of thinking, the greatest impurity and primary source of all suffering is *avidya*, ignorance of the True Self. In the subtle body, asana and pranayama systematically purify the *nadis* (psychic channels), destroying *grantis* (psychic knots) created through action, thought or deed in the current or previous incarnations. Destroying these *grantis* increases the potential for yoga (Divine Union). Through the *niyama* of *saucha*, the mind becomes fit for Self-knowledge. By sympathetically observing the fullness of *yama*, everything else falls into place.

Santosha is defined as contentment. *Santosha* is contentment independent of external conditions. It is good to aspire to happiness and feel comfortable, but one must not develop attachment to these states, as they are transitory. Aspire to contentment as a means of achieving Self-realization only. True happiness does not exist on the outside, rather, contentment comes from controlling the mind and remembering the laws of karma. Everything that happens is due to previous actions and nothing moves without the will of God -- everything is perfect. "Not a single blade of grass moves except by Thy will, Oh Lord." Whatever we are presently passing through is the direct result of our past actions. One automatically becomes content when one realizes that if something bad happens (with some exceptions) it is due to one's own deeds from the past. Once one recognizes this, one is able to merely pass through experience, maintain equanimity under any circumstances and be truly happy. By this knowledge, gain control over the inner environment and elevate the mind to perceive the world free of conflict. True contentment is the result of knowledge of the laws of karma. Everything is as it should be, perfect! Swami Sivananda's advice is helpful here: "Adapt, adjust and accommodate." May we learn to be grateful for all that is, and may we cultivate contentedness by recognizing that everything is already perfect. After all, in the end, only a contented mind can meditate.

Tapas is defined as heat, austerity or burning away impurities through self-discipline. *Tapas* is the passion or fervor for any subject, sticking to it no matter what happens. It is said that *Tapas* is like a fever. Through subjecting ourselves to extremes of pleasure and pain, internal coping mechanisms are developed. After experiencing pain, suffering and disappointment in the physical world, one realizes that it is imperative to search out that which is eternal. By studying the scriptures and reading of the experiences of saints and sages, one automatically develops an inclination for spiritual things. One is then apt to do anything to find God. *Tapas* gives one the fortitude to fast for thirty days, shave one's head and renounce all material enjoyment in order to achieve the goal and realize God. Seekers on the spiritual path will therefore develop a burning desire for liberation.

Those born with insatiable *Tapas* are the old souls who have satisfied all of their desires in previous lives. These souls have already suffered through multiple incarnations and have evolved to the point that they tire of the pain, which is a defining characteristic of the world of *samsara*, the world of duality. *Santosha* (contentment) in the face of *tapas* facilitates endurance and the

ability to concentrate the mind regardless of external conditions. *Tapas* is the mother of both equanimity and steadiness.

> *By way of example, one must stay longer in the postures.*
> *It is only through doing this that one builds endurance and makes true progress.*
> *Otherwise, you will be eighty years old and in the exact place you are today.*
> *Occasionally, work with angry determination,* Ujjayi *breathing and get serious*
> *about your practice! It is through these means that one can make real progress.*
> —Sri Dharma Mittra

Svadhyaya is understood to mean Self-study and is directly
translated as "study of scripture". It is the practice of reading
and holding firmly in the mind any actual spiritual writings that
contain information that helps illumine the path to God. Examples of such texts include the Hindu *Vedas, The Upanishads,
The Yoga-Sutras, The Bible, The Koran, The Dhammapada* and *The
Bhagavad-Gita.* These works all remind us of our true nature or
Atman. This *niyama* is the study of any scripture that illustrates the
glories of God or that leads one to Self-realization. When one
"studies" something in this way, one holds it in one's attention and
comes to know something of it through intense *dharana* (concentration). To immerse oneself in scripture is to focus exclusively
on Divine ideas, thoughts and words.

Self-study does not mean psychoanalysis as we think of it in the
West. That type of study can only bring more attention to the
personality, the small self. Reflect constantly on what is real
and what is not real. The highest truth contained in scripture is
revealed to those who are fit to delve into their true nature. As
the soul evolves and refines, it begins to understand and cleave

more to the esoteric. In yoga, this includes scriptures that deal with the precise nature of the Self, the mind, the five koshas (subtle sheaths) and how to transcend them so that the True Self is revealed. At this point, the individual recognizes that God is the spirit beyond the mind. Compare God with the Supreme Self and they are one and the same. One then realizes that by surrendering the ego, the little self dissolves into the Supreme Self. That is the end of the journey.

(Another form of *svadhyaya* is Japa Yoga, the practice of mantra repetition. Through regular engagement in this form of yoga (constantly repeating a name), one learns to recognize God with form and name and can come to have *darshan* (vision) of Him or Her.)

Isvara Pranidhana is defined as surrender to the Lord and is the essence of yoga and the goal of all spiritual aspirants. Before, during and after we perform any action, we offer it to God. In this way, we free ourselves from selfish action. The perfection of action comes from the perfection of thought void of selfish motivation. Through steady practice of this *niyama*, one cultivates *bhava* or devotion. The mood of devotion will enable one to reach for something higher than the apparent limitations of the body and mind, although some study of the Self (*svadhyaya*) is required.

Devotion to God is the total surrender of the ego. Once one has knowledge of the Self, one knows that everything is God. One is then able to surrender the ego in order to achieve enlightenment. Surrender in order to obtain Divine help from within. Imagine having the hands tied behind the back: one needs help! If one surrenders to the Lord, one will be set free. By surrendering and thinking of Him all the time, one will trigger Divine attention from within and every obstruction will be cleared from the path ahead. If we perform actions without *Isvara pranidhana*, we will most likely remain bound in the ignorance of the ego. Dedicate everything to the Lord. Surrender and say:

Take me, take me; I am not the doer!
—Sri Dharma Mittra

Fix your mind on Me alone, rest your thought on Me alone,
and in Me alone you will live hereafter. Of this there is no doubt.
—Sri Krishna, an avatar of God,
speaking to Prince Arjuna in *The Bhagavad-Gita*, Chapter 12, verse 8
-- Nikhilananda translation

God is the Innermost Self,
dwelling in the center of the chest, the right side of your heart as the True Self.
Go deep within and find God. Offer the fruit of every action to the
Supreme Self. Then every action becomes even better than meditation.
—Sri Dharma Mittra

Yogic Diet

Let food be thy medicine and medicine thy food.
—Hippocrates

*It's important not to eat before teaching, particularly not cooked food,
as that can stir the emotions.
Better just to drink some juices or eat something simple and raw
if absolutely necessary.
For many years, my first meal of the day has been at 3 p.m.
after I teach at noon and it has been my experience that the body adjusts.*

*You have to be careful, or the slight "bicycle tire" around the middle can become
a motorcycle tire, which over time can grow into a tire fit for an automobile.*

*My Guru would point to the stomach and say:
"Make that your pot, my son. That delicious smell
when you are cooking is the best part of the food being wasted."*
—Sri Dharma Mittra

Introduction

If you control what you put into and what comes out of your
mouth, you have controlled much of your mind already. It follows

that without the right food, the mind will never settle itself into silence. Ahimsa (non-violence), the first *yama*, is the sure foundation of practice. Without observance of *yama* and *niyama*, there is no yoga. Through scrupulous observance of *ahimsa* in word, thought and deed, one develops compassion. It is upon this virtue that every other aspect of practice depends. How does one develop compassion? By being kind to everyone and not consuming our inferior brothers and sisters of the animal kingdom. *Your compassion must extend beyond your pets!* All the great saints ate meat in the past before they discovered a better way. As aspiring *yogis*, if we hope to realize and attain to God in this lifetime, the flesh simply must go! One can be fooled into believing that some animals are made to be loved, while others are merely food, but eating flesh is a great sin and doing so pollutes our subtle bodies (energy is literally inhibited from moving through subtle channels clogged by Astral greases). Sooner or later, the kidneys will sicken and the colon may become cancerous. If flesh is a part of the diet, it's impossible to succeed in Hatha Yoga (*asana* and *pranayama*), and without *asana* and *pranayama*, good health cannot be maintained. Thus, there can be no success in yoga.

Remember: "Healthy body, healthy mind." Consumption of animals for food is out-of-date, and indicates a complete lack of compassion towards others. Lower passions are ignited and stimulated through the consumption of flesh, and one who is involved with violence will never develop a strong desire for Self-realization. When one keeps the habit of consuming one's inferior brothers and sisters, the stomach becomes a graveyard; the kitchen, a morgue, and your meditation goes nowhere. To discover how civilized any society truly is, one has only to study how it treats animals. Forget and lose any out-of-date traditions, and open your eyes! Meditate on compassion and escape this great darkness -- the root cause of all disease and suffering. Cease to consume flesh and enjoy your short journey to Enlightenment.

Basic Principles

If you eat dead, toasted, fried or frozen food, you will feel dead, toasted, fried and frozen. It is better to consume eggs than meat, chicken or fish, etc., and cheese (dairy) is far better even than eggs. You can keep a bit of dairy at first (a little mozzarella is OK), but the flesh must go! Raw vegetables are far better for *eek* you than cooked ones. Overall, as a general rule, don't cook your food too much if at all. My Guru would always point to the belly and tell people to do their "cooking" there.

Before eating anything, give thanks to the Lord. The health of the entire body begins with the state of the colon, so eat to live, don't live to eat. Try to gradually change your diet by replacing any non-vegetables with more and more fresh vegetables, raw nuts and fresh fruit. These should never be overcooked, leftover and / or unclean. Avoid onions and garlic except for medicinal use (i.e.: to help nip sickness or disease in the bud). Avoid all foods that "hurt" (are too hot in terms of temperature), are overly spicy, too dry, salty and / or oily. When eating, one half of the stomach should be filled with solids (i.e.: food), one quarter with liquid (i.e.: fresh celery juice with lemon juice; water; or any other healthy juice), and the other quarter of the stomach should be left empty to allow for ease of digestion. This also prevents mental stress afterwards.

Fasting

Fast days should begin on days of rest and are facilitated by quietude, prayer, study of scripture, meditation, light exercise and fresh air. Fasts should not exceed 36 hours. As the body cleanses old impurities, feelings of discomfort may arise (i.e.: aches, pains, weakness and nausea). Let common sense dictate whether you break the fast or strenuous purification diet. Excessive discomfort reflects that the purification and cleansing is too rapid, and should be moderated by application of heavier foods. Fasting is best done communally and under the guidance of a teacher or preceptor. In isolation, it is perhaps best to fast just one day a month, according to capacity.

Watermelon is wonderful for breakfast, as it is a cleansing food. One may fast for an entire day on just watermelon, and feel calm and energized as a result. One may also consume watermelon to cleanse the palate after eating unfavorable foods. The best cleansing and energy-giving fruits are watermelon, pineapple, oranges, mango, papaya and bananas. If you struggle greatly with appetite, fresh-juiced lemon and warm water can be a great aid throughout the day.

What to Eat

There are a great variety of vegetables that are pleasant to the eyes and to the tongue. Avocados; brown rice with Tahini; baked potatoes with lemon juice and olive oil; various guacamoles; salads with avocados and celestial hummus; whole grain breads; vegetarian cakes and muffins; raw almond paste or butter; nuts; sprouts; soymilk; hemp nut milk; coconut; and even non-dairy ice creams. The choices available today are almost endless.

Every yogi should own a juicer and regularly make and consume fresh juices. Green juices with lemon are best, but there is also carrot, pineapple, apple, cabbage and lemon juice, etc. It's good to add one or two tablespoons of cold pressed flaxseed oil to your daily diet, especially if your diet is all or mostly live / raw. Living foods supply important enzymes and facilitate digestive, immune and metabolic function. Try to eat fruits and vegetables that come in all shades of color. These colors indicate the presence of various combinations of vitamins, minerals and other essential micronutrients required to nurture the physical body and promote radiant health.

A Dharma Yogi's Favorite Foods:

Almonds, Avocados, Oranges, Carrots, Celery, Spinach, Tomatoes, Watermelon, Lemons, Young Coconuts and Pineapple.

Basic Sprouting Instructions

Most raw seeds, nuts and beans can and should be sprouted to reap their maximum potential as food-stuffs. Doing so changes the entire chemistry of the seed, nut or bean, flooding it with the prana (vital life-force) required to turn it into a mature, healthy plant and making it easy to digest. A sprout is a complete food, and can supply the physical body with everything necessary to promote life and radiant health. Once seeds and beans are sprouted, one can place them in direct sunlight for 30-60 minutes. Then the sprout becomes a green vegetable, as well; a wondrously complete Superfood.

Soak all seeds (except almonds and peanuts) for eight hours. Drain and rinse the seeds every three to four hours until sprouted the length of the seed or slightly longer. Refrigerate and consume while fresh and potent.

Almonds: Soak 12 hours, then rinse every three to four hours for a period of 18 hours. To store once sprouted, cover with water and place in the refrigerator. (The water should just cover one half inch over the top of the almonds.) Peel the skin off before eating, as it becomes toxic during germination.

Peanuts: Soak 8 hours, and rinse every three to four hours for 16-18 hours. Cover the peanuts with water and refrigerate, just like almonds, for storage. Remove the skin before consuming, as the peanut skin also becomes toxic during germination.

Live Vegan Recipes

While making each drink, blend or meal, chant the Mantra For Purification at least three times. Please note that it is best to drink fresh juices within fifteen minutes of juicing to insure that their enzyme, vitamin and mineral content is high. After fifteen minutes, fresh fruit juices begin to convert to merely acid and sugar, and there is little value to consuming them.

Sun Salute Blend
2 large bananas or 1 avocado
1 cup of sprouted almonds (peeled)
1-2 cups of the fresh juice of your choice of rice / soy / almond milk
Agave nectar or maple syrup to taste

Mix all ingredients together in a blender until creamy.

Divine Perception Blend
16 oz. of fresh squeezed carrot juice
1 cup of sprouted almonds (peeled)

Mix all ingredients together in a blender until liquefied and creamy. Great with kale, too.

Dharma Green Cleanse Juice

1 large head of celery
1 whole cucumber
2 whole lemons
Juice all ingredients together.
May squeeze or juice the lemons
whole (after peeling).

Drink immediately for best results.
Makes approximately 32 oz.

Dharma Pure Tropical Bliss

1 ripe avocado
meat from 1 young coconut
1 fresh pineapple
1-2 cups of coconut water
1 Tbs. vanilla (or fresh vanilla bean seeds)
Pinch sea salt
May add agave nectar, honey or
maple syrup

Liquefy to a smooth, creamy consistency. This will make for a delicious,
thicker blend. Try it with some mint.

Dharma Salad

1 avocado cut in good-size chunks
2 tomatoes, sliced large
Splash of olive oil
Splash of Bragg's liquid amino's or
Pinch sea salt
Any type of sprouts

Stir all ingredients together.
(Serves 1-2)

Dharma Sprouted Almond Milk

1½ cups sprouted almonds or Brazil nuts
4 cups of filtered water
3-5 dates (or agave nectar to sweeten)
1 Tbs. vanilla (or fresh vanilla bean seeds)
Pinch sea salt, agave, honey and
maple syrup to taste

Place sprouted nuts and water in a
blender and mix until completely liquefied. Strain mixture with a nut-milk
bag or cheesecloth, squeezing all milk
from the pulp. Place liquid back in the
blender with the dates, vanilla and sea
salt. Blend, serve and enjoy. Lasts 3+
days in the refrigerator. Store in a glass
container and shake before consuming.

Dharma Super Green Juice

½ head of celery
½ head of spinach
1 cucumber
5 sprigs of cilantro
½ head of kale
1 to 2 whole lemons
1-2 inch piece ginger (optional)

Juice all ingredients together. Drink
immediately for best results.
Makes approximately 32 oz

Beet Salad

4 raw beets, grated
1 cup sunflower seeds (raw or toasted)
1 Tbs. chopped, fresh tarragon
Cold-pressed olive oil, to taste

Stir all ingredients together.
(Serves 3-6)

Carrot-Raisin Salad

2 Tbs. raisins
2 carrots
1 Tbs. lemon juice
5 tsp. raw honey, date or brown rice syrup
2 Tbs. cold-pressed olive oil

Cover raisins with hot water. Soak for 10 min. Drain. Grate carrots. Whisk lemon juice and sweetener together. Then drizzle in olive oil while whisking. Stir all ingredients together. Try it with some ginger. (Serves 2-4)

Spinach Salad

1 large bunch spinach
1 cup sun-dried tomatoes
4 oz. chopped mushrooms
1-2 tsp. sea salt
1 fresh squeezed lemon
1 tsp. cumin (optional)
olive and/or flax oil (optional)
chopped avocado and tomato(optional)
sunflower sprouts (optional)

Soak sun-dried tomatoes in warm water for about 10-15 minutes to soften. Place all ingredients in a large mixing bowl. Drain-off excess liquid and enjoy. The salad can be eaten immediately or after marinating for up to 24 hours.

Dharma's Great Guacamole

1 large avocado
2-8 Tbs. fresh, chopped cilantro
1 fresh juiced lime
1/2 tsp. or more sea salt (to taste)
1 cup fresh, shucked corn (optional)
4 Tbs. fresh chopped pineapple (optional) or
1 tomato chopped (optional)

Place all ingredients in a mixing bowl. With a fork, stir and mash ingredients together until everything is incorporated while the avocado is still slightly chunky. Enjoy alone, as a side dish with the spinach salad, with manna bread or as a dip for fresh vegetables.

Surya Burgers

2 cups sprouted sunflower seeds
1 red bell pepper, grated or diced
½ cup carrots, grated or diced
½ cup fresh basil
½ cup celery, grated or diced
½ cup fresh parsley
¼ cup Bragg's liquid aminos

Process all ingredients in a food processor. Make patties. Dehydrate at 105 degrees F. for 12-24 hours, until dry. If using Teflex sheets, turn patties over and remove Teflex after 6 hours. Can make really thin patties and they will come out like crackers, or ½ inch thick and they will be crisp outside, chewy inside. (Serves 6)

Mushroom Salad

16 oz. of fresh, chopped mushrooms
1 small lemon, juiced
1 Tbs. or less sea salt (to taste)
2 tsp. fresh cumin
¼ cup sun-dried tomatoes (optional)

Place all ingredients in a large mixing bowl. Blend with your hands,
squeezing mushrooms until they
become moist and tender. Drain off
excess liquid. Eat immediately or
after marinating for up to 24 hours.

Sprouted Almond Hummus

16 oz. sprouted almonds (peeled)
2 cups water (depends on consistency)
1 Fresh squeezed lemon (to taste)
1-2 Tbs. fresh parsley
1 Tbs. sea salt (to taste)
2 tsp. fresh cumin (to taste)

Place almonds, 1 cup of water
and all other ingredients in a food
processor or a powerful blender.
Blend on high speed until all ingredients are incorporated and smooth.
Adjust seasoning to taste and enjoy.
Garnish with olive oil and/or fresh
olives or chopped parsley.

Dharma Healthy Dips, Sauces and Soups

Ginger Tahini

½ cup tahini
¼ cup filtered water
1 tsp. juiced ginger
3 tsp. Bragg liquid
aminos
2 tsp. lemon (juice of ½
lemon)

Blend or whip vigorously
until smooth and creamy.
Use as dip or over salads
and vegetables or mix
with your hummus. Add
more water as needed to
find a consistency you like.

Happy Hummus

15 ounces chickpeas
(soaked/sprouted)
1/3 cup olive oil
1-2 fresh lemons
4 Tbs. sesame tahini
¼-½ cup water
pinch ground cumin /
coriander
fresh pepper and/or
cayenne
¼ cup or more fresh
chopped parsley
(optional)

Blend half the chickpeas
and olive oil in blender,
stopping to stir. When
creamy, add the remain-
ing chickpeas, oil, lemon
juice, tahini and spices.

Tomato Basil Soup

1 cup cubed cucumber
½ cup cubed zucchini
½ cup cubed red, orange
or green pepper
1 avocado halved
2 tomatoes chopped
1 cup spinach
½ cup basil
3 dates (soaked)
Juice of 1 lemon

Set aside ½ cup zuc-
chini, half avocado and
1 tomato. Blend the rest
of the ingredients until
creamy, then add the
remaining ingredients.

Dharma Healthy Dips, Sauces and Soups (cont.)

Tomato Sauce

½ cup sun-dried tomatoes
(soak 3-8 hours to rehydrate)
3 dates (soaked 20 min.)
4 large tomatoes
1 Tbs. olive oil
¼ cup chopped, fresh basil
½ tsp. or more Nama Shoyu or sea salt
¼ cup chopped onion (optional)
1 Tbs. ginger (optional)

Blend until well mixed but still
chunky. Great with zucchini pasta or
steamed vegetables.

Sweet and Sour Sauce

¼ cup maple syrup or dates
2 tsp. Dijon mustard
1 tsp. apple cider vinegar
2 tsp. olive oil
1 tsp. minced ginger
2 tsp. orange juice
¼ cup lemon juice
2 Tbs. Braggs liquid aminos

Stir together all ingredients. Use
on steamed vegetables and salads.

Basil Dressing

1 bunch chopped fresh basil
(2 cups chopped basil)
1 squeezed orange
1 tsp. miso paste
1 Tbs. flaxseed oil
½ cup filtered water
1 avocado
salad fixings

Mix all ingredients in small bowl
with spoon. Add avocado at end
with salad. Pour dressing over salad
and toss.

Lime Salad Dressing

2 fresh limes, squeezed
2 tsp. apple cider vinegar
2 Tbs. olive oil
¼ cup finely chopped cilantro
1 Tbs. raw sesame seeds
2 Tbs. Braggs Liquid Aminos
Pinch of cayenne

Stir together all ingredients.
Use on avocados, salads and
steamed vegetables.

Yam Noodles

4 large yams, peeled and
spiralized
3 Tbs. miso paste or raw tahini
¼ cup sesame oil
½ cup fresh cilantro
1 head of shredded cabbage
(optional)
2 Tbs. lemon juice
¼ cup Nama Shoyu soy sauce

Combine all liquid ingredients,
and then combine with
everything else. Let marinate
for 2 hours. Serves 8 people.

Delicious Vegan Desserts

Vegan Chocolate Brownies

1 cup maple syrup or agave nectar
¾ cup unsweetened applesauce
½ cup water
2 tsp. ground flaxseed
2 tsp. vanilla
1 and 1/3 cups of unbleached spelt flour or brown rice flour
¾ cup unsweetened cacao powder
¾ tsp. baking powder
¼ tsp. Celtic sea salt
1 cup non-dairy semi-sweet chocolate chips or chopped non-dairy chocolate bar
½ cup coarsely chopped pecans or walnuts (optional)

Preheat oven to 350 degrees and slightly grease an 8x8 baking pan. Combine ground flaxseed and water, and add applesauce, vanilla and agave. Stir well and set aside. In a separate bowl, combine the flour, cacao, baking powder, salt, chocolate chips and optional nuts. Add to applesauce mixture and fold to combine. Pour into pan and bake for 40 minutes. The finished result should be moist. Top with chocolate sauce, or try Raw Fudge as a topping. While baking, make chocolate sauce.

Oatmeal Raisin Cookies

2 Tbs. ground flaxseed
6 Tbs. water
1 cup coconut oil
¾ cup agave nectar or maple syrup
2 tsp. vanilla
1 ¾ cups of spelt flour
½ cup oat bran
¾ tsp. baking powder
½ tsp. salt
½ tsp. cinnamon
½ tsp. ground nutmeg
3 cups whole rolled oats
1 cup raisins

Preheat oven to 350 degrees. In a blender, mix water and flax seeds until gelatinous and creamy. In a bowl, mix oil, agave or maple syrup, vanilla, and flax seed mixture. In a separate bowl, combine the flour, oat bran, baking powder, salt, cinnamon and nutmeg. Add the wet ingredients and mix well. Stir in the rolled oats and raisins. Scoop a little dough and place on a parchment paper-lined cookie sheet. Bake until golden brown for 12 to 15 minutes.

Delicious Vegan Desserts (cont.)

Chocolate Sauce

1 cup raw cacao powder
¾ cup agave nectar or maple syrup
½ tsp. vanilla
pinch of sea salt
1-2 Tbs. coconut oil

Spread chocolate sauce on top of
cooled brownies or on each brownie
individually.

Chia Seed Cereal

1-2 Tbs. chia seeds
½ cup coconut water or tap water to
soak seeds in or 20 minutes
¼ cup of goji berries soaked overnight
2 large dates smashed
½ cup almond or cashew milk
(optional)
Sliced banana (optional)

Combine ingredients in a bowl, stir
and eat with a spoon.

Raw Fudge

1 cup rolled oats
½ cup sunflower seeds
½ cup carob powder
¼ - ½ cup raw honey
2-3 Tbs. raw almond butter
A little applesauce (optional)

Mix well by hand. Press into lightly
oiled 8" square pan. Chill and cut.
Keep refrigerated. Great as a topping for cookies/brownies/cakes.

Banana Ice Cream

3-4 bananas
1 cup young coconut water
4-6 dates
Raw carob powder, cinnamon
(optional)

Mix all ingredients in a blender.
Adjust to your taste, as desired.
Run mixture through an ice cream
maker, serve and enjoy, or freeze for
later. If you don't have an ice cream
maker, place the mixture in a plastic
container, then into the freezer.
Before serving, thaw slightly and stir.

Chocolate Mousse

1 cup non-dairy semi-sweet chocolate chips
12 oz. silken tofu (or firm)
½ cup non-dairy milk (hemp, almond, coconut or soy)
½ tsp. vanilla extract
Fresh berries and mint leaves for
serving (optional)

In a double boiler, melt chocolate chips. Blend the tofu, melted
chocolate, milk and vanilla. Chill the
mixture for one hour before serving.

Dharma Healthy Smoothies

(Liquefy in a blender to make at least 16 oz. of each drink.)

Watermelon Soup

4 cups diced, seeded
watermelon
2 Tbs. lemon juice
2 Tbs. lime juice
1 Tbs. chopped mint
(optional)
1 Tbs. Honey (optional)
1 thumb ginger

Puree all ingredients in a
blender or juicer. Chill
and garnish with fresh
mint leaves.

Digest-ease

1 ripe papaya
1 orange
1 banana
½ cup water or
coconut water
1 tsp. psyllium husks

Blueberry Nectar

2 pears
1 cup blueberries
½ lime
1 cup water or
coconut water

Coco-berry Delicious

1 cup mixed berries
2 cups coconut water
1 Tbs. soaked chia seeds
2 Tbs. coconut flakes
or ½ young coconut
meat
1 tsp. pure vanilla
extract

Green Pineapple Cloud

½ ripe pineapple cubed
½ ripe avocado cubed

Blend in a high speed
blender like a Vitamix
until light green and
cloud-like.

Ginger Coke

Meat of 1 young
coconut
1-2 cups of coconut
water
½ inch of fresh ginger,
grated

Tropical Splendor

2 ripe nectarines
1 whole banana
¼ pineapple
½ cup water or
coconut water

Mango-nana

1 ripe mango
1 whole or half banana
1 whole orange
1 cup water or
coconut water
1 inch piece of ginger
(optional)

Green Blended Meal

3 cups spinach
3 stalks celery
1 cucumber
4 sprigs – 1 bunch
cilantro
1 cup alfalfa or
sunflower sprouts
2 avocados
2-4 lemons
½ inch ginger or more
Corn kernels for garnish
(optional)

Puree all ingredients
in blender.   Chill if
desired. Garnish with
corn kernels right
before serving. Great
with crackers or over
zucchini pasta.

Dharma Healthy Smoothies (cont.)

Berry-Good
1 cup strawberries
2 whole bananas
2 cups water or
coconut water

Free-Me
¼-½ of a whole water-
melon (may add 3 sprigs
of cilantro or mint)

Coco-Kiwi
3 kiwis
1 whole banana
½ meat of 1 young
coconut
1-2 cups of coconut
water

Melon-Honey
½ cantaloupe or
honeydew
1 orange
2 tsp. honey (optional)
¼ or ½ cup water

Two Recipes From the Late Bonobo's Vegetarian Restaurant on Madison Park

Marinated Kale Salad
1 large bunch of kale
1 diced red pepper
¼ cup olive oil
¼ cup agave nectar
¼ cup lemon / lime juice
¼ tsp. sea salt

Shred by hand or cut the kale with a
plastic Chef's knife into small pieces
after thoroughly cleaning. Place the
kale and red pepper in a large sturdy
Ziplock plastic bag. Combine the
olive oil, agave nectar, lemon and /
or lime juice and sea salt in a bowl
with a whisk, then add the contents
of the bowl to the kale and red pepper waiting in the plastic bag. Shake
well and place the bag overnight in
the refrigerator. This salad will taste
even better on day two!

Popeye
1 young coconut
large handful of spinach

Thoroughly blend the coconut
water, coconut gel and spinach,
and enjoy.

Three Live/Raw Soups From the Late, Great and Missed "Exotic Superfoods" of Fresh Meadows, Queens

Once all of the ingredients are in the blender, add filtered water to the top of the ingredients and blend until smooth. Adjust spices according to the dictates of your palate. After a fast of any sort, it is recommended by many to "soup" for half the time you fasted. For example, if you were to fast on melon or watermelon, mangos, pineapple and oranges for four days, you would get the most from this austerity by "souping" for the next two. Each recipe makes at least 32 oz.

Super Green Soup
4 cups of peas
2 large handfuls of spinach
2 Tbs. chopped onion (optional)
pinch of sea salt
1 Tbs. Hemp Butter
1 Tbs. Hemp Oil
1 tsp. Spirulina powder

Super Red Soup
4 cups chopped tomatoes
1 Tbs. Red Palm oil
¼ tsp. cumin
¼ tsp. coriander
pinch cayenne pepper
¼ tsp. oregano
1 clove garlic (optional)
2 Tbs. chopped onion (optional)
Brazil Nut or Hemp Nut Protein Powder
1 Tbs. sesame butter
pinch of sea salt
1 Tbs. Goji berries

Goji Ginger
2 cups chopped carrots
1 large apple
1 avocado
1 tsp. virgin coconut oil
pinch of sea salt
1 Tbs. Goji berries
¼ tsp. cinnamon

Additional Resources To Support a Vegan/Vegetarian and Raw/Live Diet

LifeFood Recipe Book: Living on Life Force. Jubb, Annie Padden / Jubb, David. North Atlantic Books, 2003. Many simple, delicious recipes and basic general instructions to help you explore a raw/live diet. There are short passages regarding the benefits of certain ingredients / foods written in italics throughout the book.

Rainbow Green Live-Food Cuisine. Cousens, Gabriel. North Atlantic Books, 2003. This book is divided into two sections. The first is an explanation regarding the benefits of a raw/live diet to obtain "optimal health: physically, emotionally, mentally and spiritually." The second section is full of delicious and relatively easy to prepare recipes.

Living Raw Food: Get the Glow With More Recipes From Pure Food and Wine. Melngailis, Sarma. HarperCollins, 2009. A beautiful raw/live cuisine cookbook that could likely inspire most anyone. Many recipes are complicated, but the results are rewarding and especially well suited to a special occasion or for when entertaining. These recipes will have your non-vegan / non-raw friends asking to be invited to dinner.

Green Smoothie Revolution: The Radical Leap Towards Natural Health. Boutenko, Victoria. North Atlantic Books, 2009. Many great recipes for delicious, easy-to-make smoothies.

Clean Food: A Seasonal Guide to Eating Close to the Source With More Than 200 Recipes For a Healthy and Sustainable You. Walters, Terry. Sterling Epicure, 2009. Begins with how to stock the kitchen and basic cooking methods to prepare grains, legumes and vegetables. The recipes are arranged by season and there are many recipes that result in raw /live or minimally cooked dishes.

Vegan Brunch: Homestyle Recipes Worth Waking Up For -- From Asparagus Omelets to Pumpkin Pancakes. Moskowitz, Isa Chandra. Da Capo Press, 2009. All the recipes here are delicious and vegan. Whoever decided that we need milk and eggs to make a great quiche, omelet, pancake, etc? These recipes are wonderful for the whole family, especially if you are just making the transition to being a vegetarian / vegan household.

1,000 Vegan Recipes. Robertson, Robin. John Wiley and Sons, 2009. A small encyclopedia of vegan recipes.

The Vegan Table: 200 Unforgettable Recipes for Entertaining Every Guest at Every Occasion. Patrick-Goudreau, Colleen. Fair Winds Press, 2009. A broad variety of healthy and simple recipes.

The Ayurvedic Cookbook: a Personalized Guide to Good Nutrition and Health. Morningstar, Amadea with Desai, Urmila. Lotus Press, 1995. A beloved collection of 250 vegetarian and vegan recipes that is also a trusted primer on the application Ayurvedic principles to diet.

Madhur Jaffrey's World Vegetarian: More Than 650 Meatless Recipes from Around the World. Jaffrey, Madhur. Crown Publishing Group, 2002. As the title implies, the recipes are for making vegetarian food from all over the world. This book will help bring variety and wonderful flavors to your home.

Three Kitchen Gadgets
You May Find Useful:

• A high quality juicer. It's worth spending a bit on your juicer as the better it works, the more juice you are able to extract from the fruit and vegetables you are juicing, saving you money in the long run.

• A high quality blender. The Vitamix is a remarkable device to name just one.

• A food processor. It's hard to explore raw/live home preparations without one.

The Kriyas
Yogic Cleansing Actions to Promote Purification

The greatest of all impurities is ignorance of your own True Self.
—Sri Dharma Mittra

The following techniques promote internal purity on the physical and subtle levels. According to Hatha Yoga philosophy, internal purification occurs when the psychic channels are relieved of their blockages. Practice of these cleansing techniques will engender concentration and will power. Then, the *Kundalini* awakens. Most yogis only practice a few *kriyas* daily. Like much in yoga practice, the guidance of an experienced teacher is of the utmost importance.

Six cleansing duties are enumerated in *The Hatha Yoga Pradipika* and *The Gheranda Samhita*. They are referred to as either the *Shat Kriyas* (six cleansing duties) or the *Shat Karmans* (six cleansing actions). The *Six Karmans* given in *The Hatha Yoga Pradipika* are: *Dhauti, Basti* (Vasti), *Neti, Trataka, Nauli* and *Kapalabhati*. *The Gheranda Samhita* substitutes *Lauliki* for *Nauli*. These cleansing techniques are used as a preparation before practicing *pranayama* and to improve health by removing phlegm, impurities and excess fat from the physical body. (It should be noted that some of the breathing exercises have a cleansing function in and of themselves.) The balance of this chapter includes *kriyas* enumerated in *The Hatha Yoga Pradipika* and *The Gheranda Samhita*, in addition to others Sri Dharma Mittra learned from his Guru and other Yogic scriptures, all informed always by his wealth of direct, personal experience.

Kriya Techniques

Kapalabhati is a respiratory exercise that strengthens the lungs and diaphragm, oxygenates the blood and aids in the elimination of toxins and impurities from the blood and muscles. This cleansing action is also a *pranayama* or breathing exercise. When first exploring this *kriya*, inhale passively and pump the breath out vigorously through the nose for 10-15 seconds. Increase the duration of the exercise for up to two minutes per cycle as endurance is gained over time. Perform forceful exhalations at the rate of one or two per second. Exhalations should be done two to three times faster than the sympathetic, passive inhalations. Push the abdomen back vigorously when exhaling and always keep the nostrils wide open. Upon concluding a round, breathe out completely. Then, breathe in and hold the breath. Beginners do not need to apply *bandhas* (locks) if the breath is only being retained for a short time. More advanced practitioners should apply two *bandhas* during *kumbhaka* (breath retention) and hold the breath with the locks for as long as possible. The two *bandhas* to engage are *Mula Bandha* (root lock) and *Jalandahara Bandha* (chin lock). If a feeling of suffocation arises, one has held the breath beyond their capacity. This feeling of suffocation disturbs the mind and is the opposite of what one seeks to achieve through their *sadhana*. (It is recommended that those who live in cities where air pollution is a feature engage in a minimum of two rounds of this *kriya* on a daily basis.)

Dhauti is the washing of the inside of the body. A long strip of cloth or gauze three to four inches wide is soaked in warm water or milk. The wet cloth or gauze strip is then swallowed slowly and carefully while one holds onto one end. The strip is allowed to rest in the stomach for 10 to 15 minutes before slowly being pulled back out. If the cloth remains in the stomach for more than 20 minutes, it begins to pass through the digestive system. The body's gagging reflex may be activated during the first attempts, but this will be overcome with practice. In the beginning, only two or three feet of cloth should be swallowed. This may gradually be increased to 15 feet or more as the body becomes accustomed to this practice. In *Dhauti* which literally means "to wash," the swallowed cloth absorbs phlegm, bile and other impurities in the stomach. This *kriya* has many therapeutic benefits and is prescribed at yoga and *Ayurvedic* facilities in India to cure diseases caused by an imbalance of phlegm in the body.

Danta Dhauti is a *kriya* that involves cleaning the teeth, gums, tongue, ears and the frontal sinuses. Teeth cleansing by itself is referred to as *Danta-Mula-Dhauti*, and is the practice of rubbing the teeth and gums every morning. Traditionally, this practice is done using Catechu (Betel nut) plant powder, Neem or pure earth. Tongue cleansing or *Jihva-Shodhana* may be done with a metal tongue scraper, a spoon or the fingers. There was a time in the past when scooping up a clod of dirt and using it to cleanse the mouth was the best one could do with the technology then available and was better than doing nothing at all. In turn, the scriptures reflect the time during which they were written. Today, we all own a toothbrush and hopefully use it regularly.

Kama Dhauti is literally the cleaning of the ears. *The Gheranda Samhita* concisely states: "Clean the two holes of the ears with the index or ring fingers. By engaging in this practice daily, the mystical sounds (*nada*) will be heard."

Kapal Randhra Dhauti is a *kriya* by which one cleanses the frontal sinuses. *The Gheranda Samhita* directs one to "rub with the thumb of the right hand the depression in the forehead near the bridge of the nose. By the practice of this cleansing technique, diseases arising from the derangements of the phlegmatic humors are cured. The vessels (psychic channels) become purified and clairvoyance is induced." This *kriya* should be practiced daily after awakening from sleep, after meals and again in the evening.

To perform **Vamana Dhauti**, a glass of warm water with a small amount of salt dissolved in it is ingested, then three fingers are inserted into the throat and the water is vomited out. If one practices this *kriya* regularly, one may gain the physical control to throw the water back out without using the fingers at all.

Jala Dhauti. Upon first waking in the early morning to do *sadhana*, it is traditional to drink a glass of warm water with lemon and, if needed, just a little raw agave nectar or organic maple syrup. The lemon juice should be fresh: a half lemon for a smaller glass and a whole lemon for a larger glass. *Jala Dhauti* cleanses the stomach and helps one defecate upon waking. This is important if one immediately will practice *asana*, *pranayama* and / or concentration/meditation upon arising.

Basti or **Vasti**. *The Gheranda Samhita* enumerates two kinds of *Vasti: Jala Vasti* (water *Vasti*) and *Suska Vasti* (dry *Vasti*). The first is performed classically by rolling a large banana leaf into a straw, inserting it into the anus, squatting on the heels in water up to the navel and contracting and dilating the sphincter of the anus. This action draws water into the colon, at which point one holds it there for a time and churns it about. Then one releases the water by relaxing and physically opening the anal sphincter. Performing *Uddiyana Bandha* while squatting creates a vacuum in the colon and the water is then churned around by means of *Nauli*. A beginning practitioner may use a rubber hose connected to their sink water spout on one end and inserted into the anus on the other end if the necessary sphincter control has not yet been mastered to simply be able to use a straw. Use caution when experimenting with this method, as the water pressure from the faucet must be kept low and the water must not be allowed to rise too high in the colon.

Suska Vasti is performed by assuming *Paschimottanasana*, moving the intestinal tract slowly downward while in this posture, and performing *Asvini Mudra* (willful contraction of the anal sphincter). *Dry Vasti* is said to increase the gastric fire (*agni*) and be a panacea for constipation.

Neti is a practice used for cleansing the nostrils and nasal sinuses. There are two methods: *Sutra Neti*, using a catheter, linen or gauze cord and *Jala Neti*, using warm, salty water. In *Sutra Neti*, a thin catheter lubricated with antiseptic jelly is passed up one nostril until the end appears in the throat, at which time it is grasped between the thumb and forefinger of the right hand and drawn out through the mouth. In *Jala Neti*, a neti bowl (a small pot with a narrow spout) is used to pour warm, salted water through the nostrils. One should gently clear the nasal passages prior to performing this *kriya*. A quarter teaspoon of salt is dissolved into warm water in the *neti* pot, and then the spout of the *neti* pot is inserted into one nostril. The head must be tilted 90 degrees to one side so that one ear is straight above the other. The water is evenly poured into one nostril, and should pass through to the other. After all the water has passed through the opposite nostril, perform four gentle expulsions of all the air in the lungs with the head and torso hanging down in *Uttanasana* and allow the lungs to automatically refill after exhaling as in *Kapalabhati*. Be careful not to exhale too forcefully, or water may end up in your inner ear or sinuses causing discomfort and / or pain. Then the entire process is repeated on the opposite side. (*Jala Neti* is the *kriya* with the most benefit for the least amount of pain or discomfort. Aspiring *yogis* should make *Jala Neti* a regular part of their brief routine upon arising in the early morning for meditation.)

Vahnisara means fire purification. In performing this *kriya*, the navel is pressed backwards towards the spine, thereby massaging the internal organs and stimulating the internal gastric fire (the internal gastric fire is said to reside in the abdomen behind the navel). This *Agni-Sara* (fire-process (named for *Agni*, the Hindu god of Fire and father of Hanuman) is said to cure diseases of the stomach, aid in digestion and increase the gastric fire. The beginner should perform five contractions of the navel towards the spine, one each per exhalation. This *kriya* is easier to do standing with knees bent and hands on the thighs. Over time, one seeks to increase the number of contraction-exhalations to ten. *Vahnisara* is similar in execution to *Kapalabhati Pranayama* in that one consciously brings the navel to the spine, but allows the stomach to spring back out automatically. *Agni-Sara* is a good preparation for *Nauli*.

(The Rectus Abdominus is the straight band of muscle down the center of the abdomen stretching from the breastbone to the pubic bone. The ability to isolate this muscle consciously will come only after one has mastered *Uddiyana Bandha*. Assume a standing position and, while keeping the lungs empty of air, round the spine and place the palms on the tops of the thighs with the fingertips pointing in wrapped over the thighs. Apply a slight downward pressure, engage *Uddiyana Bandha* and isolate the Rectus Abdominus by pushing the band of muscle forward and holding it there as long as possible. For best results, practice in front of a mirror in the early stages of mastery.)

Nauli (Horizontal Abdominal-Rolling). *Nauli* represents the pinnacle of yogic control over the abdominal muscles and is the next stage of mastery beyond *Agni-Sara*. In this practice, the right rectus is isolated -- then the left rectus. One continues with no time between each isolated contraction, creating a wavelike motion that crosses the abdomen from right to left, and from left to right. Good form is essential and speed can be gradually increased. The number of repetitions depends on how long one can comfortably hold the breath without experiencing extreme discomfort or panic -- always stay within the boundaries of control. A demonstration will help one understand the nature of this *kriya*. Just like *Vahnisara*, it is good to practice *Nauli* standing hunched forward with the knees soft, the feet pointing slightly to the outside with the hands, fingers pointing in, resting on the thighs just above the knees. Placing a mirror on the ground will be of great help as one initially seeks to master this *kriya*.

Nauli is superb for maintaining the health of all the internal organs, aiding in the regular elimination of waste, and toning and firming all the muscles of the abdomen. The regular practice of

Horizontal Abdominal-Rolling stimulates the entire Solar Plexus region. It improves the elasticity of the lungs, the strength and mobility of the diaphragm, and massages and stimulates the liver, pancreas, kidneys and adrenal glands. There is a direct link between *Nauli* and sexual vigor, and with overcoming sexual disabilities. Regular practice provides a long-term cure for chronic constipation by assisting the peristaltic action of the intestines, the snake-like reflexive contraction of the small and large intestines that pushes food and waste through the body's digestive system under normal conditions. (Sri Dharma Mittra discovered this technique spontaneously as a child.)

Trataka. The *Tratak-Kriya* is distinct from *Trataka* as a method of *Dharana* (concentration). In application, a burning candle is positioned at eye level, about three feet away, and the flame is gazed at without blinking until the eyes begin to water. One does not stare, but looks or gazes until the eyes cease to water and eventually film over. This means looking through the eyes rather than staring through them. Eventually, the eyes tear again and the film is washed away. This *kriya* is not pleasant, but there is nothing dangerous about it. Follow *Trataka* with the Clock Exercise (rolling the eyes around like the moving hands of a clock -- make several rotations in a clockwise direction, then reverse doing the same number of rotations in the opposite direction). Conclude this endeavor by closing the eyes for a few minutes of quiet rest.

Shanka-Prakshalana is an advanced *kriya* that cleans out the entire gastro-intestinal tract. It involves drinking glass after glass of lukewarm salt water and then performing five specific exercises in an active manner. The *asanas* to be used include *Tadasana, Tiryaka Tadasana, Katti Chakrasana, Tiryaka Bhujangasana* and *Udarakarshanasana*. All are done multiple times in a dynamic fashion. After completing the exercises, one drinks another glass of lukewarm saline solution and repeats the exercises. This process is repeated until one experiences an urgent need to defecate. After one has defecated, one returns to the cycle of drinking the saltwater and performing the prescribed exercises. Again, one experiences a strong need to defecate, and should notice the consistency of the feces.

This cycle of water drinking and exercise is to be repeated until only water is expelled through the anus and the water expelled is as clear as the water that was ingested. Usually, about a gallon of saline solution will be drunk in total. At this stage, one's entire gastro-intestinal tract has been fully cleaned. It is as clean as it ever was in one's life, apart from when one was first born. Upon completing this *kriya*, the physical body is extremely fatigued. One should relax for about forty-five minutes and later consume a simple soup of lentil, green peas or any starchy grains such as kitchedi – a mild, watery soup of moong dal and rice, and then rest for the remainder of the day. It is best to consume only watermelon or fruit juices, or to fast altogether for a few days after performing *Shanka-Prakshalana*. This technique is indicated once a month for those who have a steady diet of unhealthy food. (A gentler, but as effective alternative is to consume only watermelon until when one defecates, what emerges is recognizable as watermelon. For most people, this takes at least four days.)

Nadi Sodhana Pranayama is Alternate Nostril-Breathing, which is the most efficient nerve purifier. One simply inhales and exhales gently through alternating nostrils without holding or suspending breathing. This *kriya* is also a breathing exercise, and is ideal for those with high blood pressure or those that have any sort of physical imbalance. Use the right hand in *Vishnu Mudra* and the left hand in *Jnana Mudra* and inhale slowly through the left nostril according to your capacity. Close the left nostril with the ring finger and immediately open the right nostril by letting go with the thumb. Exhale and inhale, close the right nostril, then exhale through the left. This is one complete cycle. One may begin with 12 cycles and expand their practice by one cycle daily.

Asana
As Spiritual Practice

Move the joints a little-every day. You have to find your own tricks.
Bury your mind deep in your heart, and watch the body move by itself.
—Sri Dharma Mittra

The Divine practices of yoga were revealed to the great saints of yogic lore in deep states of meditation for the perfection of all mankind. *Asana* is the third limb of Maharishi Patanjali's eight-limbed system, and its steady application bestows radiant health upon the practitioner. On a subtle level, each posture allows one to explore a complete state of consciousness when one achieves and inhabits the full pose. Take for example the Plow Pose or *Halasana*. When practiced with the proper intention and held for a long time, one begins to understand "plow" on a universal level. Then the *asana* becomes not just a tool for strengthening, toning and stretching the physical container, but a gateway to super-consciousness. (The 908 ASANAS Master Chart is invaluable in this regard, since it depicts so many varied states of consciousness. If one were to assume fully many of them, one could cut down on the need for many additional incarnations, since one would have already passed through many states and experiences in the postures.)

According to *The Bhagavad-Gita*: "At the moment of creation, a portion of Me (God) became part of the soul of every living creature." The Divine techniques of yoga exist only to help us move deep within, beyond the *maya* (illusion) that the mind and senses project of the material world, and into the heart center so that we may discover who we really are. If one is to have any success with the holy science of Hatha-Raja Yoga, every action must be according to *yama* and *niyama* (the first and second *angas* of Astanga Yoga) in word, thought and deed. Living in this fashion is yoga. Being firmly established in the first *yama* (*ahimsa*, non-violence), one begins to recognize sameness everywhere and to develop that most essential of attributes: compassion. Another dividend of this firm grounding in *yama* and *niyama* is that the *sadhaka* (spiritual aspirant) develops a burning desire for liberation. Firmly established in *yama* and *niyama*, the *sadhaka* is now ready for the physical exercises – the practice of *asana*. To make the practice of the postures even better than meditation, be sure to offer every action to the Supreme Self (God).

If we make every action an offering to the Supreme Self, the *asana* practice can become Karma Yoga (selfless or action-less action), since by offering up the result or fruit of each action, we move beyond acting with expectation of result. Doing so, the practice of postures becomes a flowing, physicalized act of devotion. Acting or non-acting in this way, our action is according to the final *niyama* of *Isvara pranidhana* or surrender to the Almighty One. Surrender to free yourself. Surrender, and you will experience a release within each posture that will allow you to begin to taste meditation right there in the *asana* practice -- particularly while remaining in those postures which are done with the eyes closed and the attention firmly fixed at the space between the eyebrows.

Like *yama* and *niyama*, asana is in actuality just a preparation. We do all these fancy poses, not so we can place both feet behind our heads, but so that we can make the body strong, flexible and healthy. As it is said: "Healthy body, healthy mind." Only a mind that is calm (healthy) can find the unbroken concentration that is meditation. Steady regular practice of the exercises will bestow upon the *sadhaka* radiant health. In turn, the exercises strengthen and tone the muscles, improve balance, increase bone mass, aid in digestion, relieve gas, constipation and insomnia, and calm the nerves. Practice of *asana* is a sure path to avoiding disease and discomfort – reason enough to practice. But, if one attains to yoga and is distracted by disease or physical discomfort, how will the mind ever truly settle into silence?

There are many things that one may learn from the faithful practice of *asana*. One learns steadiness in the face of adversity as one stays longer in the postures. It is only by this method that one truly makes progress. The body and mind are like young children -- they wish to be given comfort and treats, and have little tolerance for anything other than pleasure. Posture practice can help to train the body and mind and teach them endurance as we consciously subject them to difficulties. This is actually one of the *niyamas* and is known as *tapas* or the acceptance of pain as purification. Passing through difficulty unscathed teaches us that we are stronger than we know and invites us to move ever deeper into our practice. Work with angry determination to invoke this purifying fire. This anger is never directed at the True Self or at anyone else, but is like that which is expressed towards a child for their benefit, free of any feelings of hatred and passing almost as quickly as experienced. Also, remember that the effort involved in trying to achieve the full posture can be of greater value than actually achieving it.

To find many of these things, it is good to practice sometimes in the company of others and under the watchful gaze of one who has gone before you in experience and knowledge. Such a preceptor or teacher can be of great aid on the path which is yoga. One can also learn much by watching others and imitating their actions both physically and mentally.

> *"My Guru taught only the few main postures and, having learned them,*
> *I learned many more by watching and copying other students*
> *who came to study with him and were concurrently learning*
> *from other teachers who were active at the time.*
> *If you see someone doing something your mind says you cannot do,*
> *realize that what they are, you are also.*
> *If you try and imitate them, you will get all their tricks."*
> —Sri Dharma Mittra

It is also good to practice with others sometimes, as you develop common mind by moving in synch with others. Moving like this, as in a parade, everyone helps everyone else in their practice. Additionally, peer pressure invites the individual to stay in the postures longer, challenging themselves, and, thus, making progress. If you are home alone, it is easy to leave off holding when the mind or body says it's had enough, since there is no one there to see you break the pose.

Sometimes, the teacher may make a correction when you practice in a class. Always remember that the teacher is only correcting the body and mind to help you make progress a little faster. After all: "If the posture looks funny, you feel funny." The Real You is perfect already and needs no correction, but sometimes correcting a little at the grossest level can be of great help in every other aspect of practice.

"When a student first comes to me,
I will give them a lot of help if they need it.
Then, I will leave them alone for a while so that they can begin to find
their own way. If after six months or so they are getting no-where,
I will give them some additional help."
—Sri Dharma Mittra

It is recommended to practice on an empty stomach and, if your schedule allows, it's great to practice *asana* after noon. Any time after four p.m. is even better and after six p.m. is truly ideal. If you are a householder, you may need to do all of your *sadhana* (spiritual practice) in one sitting. Early morning is then the ideal time for the exercises. Many students feel concern if their mat is not arranged to their liking, or if they don't have the appropriate strap or cushion. Remember that one doesn't need anything to practice yoga *asana* – just the body -- that's what's required.

When doing the postures, try and move gracefully in and out of poses – like a dancer. Sometimes, it's good to imagine yourself before hundreds of people giving a demonstration. Then, you do everything carefully with great attention to detail. When you do your practice in class, be sure to always breathe through your nose so as not to disturb your neighbors. When you are home alone, use *Ujjayi* breathing (breathing through the nose with a slight constriction of the throat) to help move past any difficulty. If there is something you truly cannot do, "Fake it until you make it." Just pretend until you sort it out.

"My Guru taught me to always lead with the left side first,
except when twisting.
Then, it is recommended to always twist right first.
This is how I both practice and teach."
—Sri Dharma Mittra

It's important to repeat difficult things at least three times. You'll find that with each repetition, the difficulty lessens. Repeating something seven times is better than three times, while ten times is truly ideal. Always keep the laws of physics in mind, as they are so often the key to unlocking the physical aspect of the postures. Also, just open your eyes whenever you are in class and observe what's going on around you. You can learn so much this way.

Most traditional systems of yoga view Headstand, Shoulder-stand and Fish Pose as the main postures. Add on seven rounds of *Surya Namaskara Vinyasa* as a warm up, follow them with a forward bend, back-bend and spinal-twist, and you have a complete practice as regards *asana*. Headstand, Shoulderstand and Fish are unique among postures in that one may taste meditation right in the *asana* practice if they are executed correctly, with faith and the correct inner focus. The most efficient place to focus the inner gaze in most postures is the space between the eyebrows, also known as the Third-Eye, Seat of Wisdom or *Trikuti*. Where the attention goes, the blood goes, and where the blood goes, the prana or vital life-force follows. Fixing the attention at the space between the eyebrows stimulates the Pituitary gland deep in the base of the brain. In yoga, the Pituitary gland is seen as the true sixth-sense, so stimulating this gland is of critical importance.

Anything found can easily be lost. That's why it's so important to: "Use it or lose it." If you fought hard over a period of time to find Lotus Pose, practice it every day. If you don't do it for three days, you may have to find it all over again.

"There are some postures on the poster that I fasted for 30 days to achieve, and then could only do a few times for the picture."
—Sri Dharma Mittra

Taking a tablespoon or two of fresh raw flaxseed oil every day helps "lubricate" the joints, but you also must warm up for longer as the body ages. If you ever suffer from soreness, eat lots of fresh pineapple and/or fresh pineapple juice. If the diet is clean and you avoid "garbage" (unhealthy food), you will have less soreness and heal quicker overall.

It is recommended that Deep Relaxation be practiced at the end of *asana* practice in *Savasana* or Corpse Pose. This practice should be done for 20 minutes daily, but ten minutes is what most can manage and should be the absolute minimum. Relaxation of the muscles is as important as focusing on their development, and it is a balance of these two, which brings one to a state of radiant health. Even just ten minutes of Deep Relaxation, with the thoughts and breathing slowed almost to the point of stopping, can be as restorative as a good night's full rest. Deep Relaxation is the best antidote for impurity. It dispels tension and fatigue in the physical body and relieves depression, anxiety, headaches, cravings and desires. Deep Relaxation rejuvenates and energizes the entire system, bolstering the body's natural healing capacities and helping to normalize the circulatory system's function. When done regularly and with pure intention, one departs the body and crosses over into Psychic Sleep, briefly experiencing the Astral Plane. It is through this deep practice that one can gradually come to recognize that they are so much more than the body or the mind.

During Deep Relaxation, the mind is ever vigilant -- always aware, as one hovers somewhere between sleep and wakefulness. Some people who are not well rested will occasionally move into true sleep during this time in *Savasana*, but this is incorrect. It is important upon returning from a period of Deep

Relaxation to stretch and move gently so that the transition to a seated position is effected without returning to the state one was in prior to practice. Ideally, one returns from an experience of Deep Relaxation feeling deeply refreshed. It is a practice that must be a part of the daily routine of anyone committed to the path of Self-realization.

In conclusion, one must come to recognize that imagination is an essential element if the practice of yoga and *asana* in particular is to bear fruit. Most everything you see someone else do, you may achieve through dedication and regular practice combined with adherence to a vegetarian diet and strict observance of *yama* and *niyama*. True progress in *asana* practice is achieved by advancing slowly and steadily, according to your capacity each day. Sometimes, advance according to "No pain, no gain." Other times, be perceptive and sensitive enough to yourself to advance according to "No pain, no strain." When one ultimately achieves the full posture, one is able to rest and begin to taste a little the sweetness of the settling of the mind. Practice always the main postures and, if time permits, hold them for a long time. This is the true secret to making progress. Always remember that the True Guru, the greatest teacher, is already within you in the center of the chest, the right side of the heart as the Real You. Seek ever to move deeper within the cave of yourself and find out who you really are. In this way, you will discover the answer to every question and really begin to make real progress in yoga.

Prana, Pranayama
Mudra and Bandha

God is this great intelligence.
—Sri Dharma Mittra

Prana

The Sanskrit word *prana* comes from the root an (to breathe) and means breath of life or life-energy. *Prana* is the energy that keeps us alive. It is vitality or cosmic vibration -- the energy permeating the universe at all levels: physical, mental, intellectual, sexual, spiritual and cosmic. *Prana* is a subtle vibration and, due to *prana*, everything is able to exist and move including thoughts, names and forms. Vigor, power, vitality, electricity, magnetism, life and spirit are all forms of *prana*. *Prana* as a term is used both in regards to the all-pervasive life-force and to describe a specific current of life energy in the human body. *Mukhya-prana* or *Prana* is the Universal Life-Force, an aspect of the transcendental power of *Shakti*.

The Forms of Prana

There are ten forms of *prana*, and each has a different name according to the body function that it governs. The five primary types of life-energy are *prana, apana, vyana, udana* and *samana*.

Prana is the ascending life energy seated in the heart that motivates and regulates inhalation and all body activities occurring in the chest region including respiration.

Apana is the descending life energy seated in the anus that motivates and regulates exhalation, the bodily functions occurring in the lower abdomen and the various processes of elimination.

Vyana is the pervading life energy that motivates and regulates the various actions of the circulatory system and the distribution of *prana* throughout the entire body.

Udana is the upward-rising life energy seated in the throat region that motivates and activates both speech and swallowing.

Samana is the middle-life energy seated in the navel region that motivates and regulates bodily function in the central area of the body and is concerned also with digestion.

That which enters the body is called *prana* and that which leaves is called *apana*. *Apana* describes the part of *prana* that is concerned with the function of elimination, and provides the energy for it. It also refers to the lower belly and the toxins (waste) that can collect there when the *prana* and *apana* are not in equilibrium. An abundance of *apana* leads to problems in all areas of the body. When we inhale, *prana* from outside the body is brought in. During inhalation, *prana* descends to meet and join with *apana*. During exhalation, *apana* rises to meet with *prana*.

What happens due to this movement of *prana* and *apana*? According to the Divine science of yoga, there is a fire known as *agni* in the vicinity of the navel. The flame itself is constantly changing direction. Upon inhalation, the breath moves towards the belly, causing a draft that directs the flame downward like in a fireplace to consume any matter present here as fuel. During exhalation, the draft moves the flame in the opposite direction, bringing with it the just burned-up matter. With the next inhalation, the flame is brought back to the *apana*. If the previously burned waste has not left the body, the flame will lose some of its power. Certain asanas have a positive effect on this process, encouraging and facilitating the meeting of *agni* and the toxins. In all inverted poses, this fire is directed to the *apana*. Cleansing is further intensified when we combine inversions with *pranayama*.

There are five *upa-pranas* or sub pranas: *naga, kurma, krikara, deva-datta* and *dhanam-jaya*. *Naga* means serpent, and it activates and motivates belching, vomiting and hiccups. *Kurma* means tortoise, and it activates and motivates the opening and closing of the eyes. *Krikara* (kri, "a growling sound" and kara, "making, doing") activates and motivates hunger and thirst. *Deva-datta* (God-given) activates and motivates yawning and sleepiness. *Dhanam-jaya* means wealth conquest, and it activates and motivates the decomposition of the body.

Pranayama

It is easy to be worldly, it is difficult to be Divine.
From the heart and base of the spinal cord,
we must awaken the Kundalini so Cosmic Energy can rise to the highest.
By obtaining purification of spirit, we obtain Divine powers.
Upon obtaining awakening of the Kundalini,
set it forth on to the Road to God.
—Sri Swami Kailashananda

The main goal of *pranayama* is to unite *prana* and *apana* in the navel region and bring them up the *Sushumna Nadi*, activating all the major chakras en route so that Divine Perception can be attained. *Pranayama* is considered one of the most important spiritual practices because it deals directly with *prana*, and without *prana*, nothing would exist. Indeed, we make use of these ancient techniques so that we have an optimal intake of *prana*. To be truly effective, *pranayama* must be combined with observance of *yama* and *niyama* and the practice of meditation.

Prana means energy and *yama* means control. (The longer "ah" sound in *ayama* can also indicate expansion.) *Pranayama* can thus be translated as control of the breath, or expansion of the life-force energy or vital life force. *Pranayama* involves taking conscious control over the inhalation, retention and exhalation of breath and, by extension, the *prana* as life energy throughout the body. Inhalation is the act of receiving primeval energy in the breath and retention is when the breath is held to savor that energy. Through the practice of *pranayama*, we harness and direct the *prana* in order to restore and maintain optimal health.

Pranayama encourages the respiratory system to function at its best, automatically calming the nervous system and improving the action of the Circulatory System, without which the processes of digestion and elimination would suffer. Regular practice of *pranayama* strengthens the lungs, which increases breathing capacity and oxygen intake. With each inhalation, we bring oxygen into the body and spark the transformation of nutrients into fuel. Each exhalation discharges toxins, mostly carbon dioxide. The blood, flushed with fresh oxygen, is carried by the arteries from the left side of the heart to the cells found in every corner of the body, replenishing their source of life-giving oxygen. The heart then pumps this blood through the body at an average rate of 70 times per minute.

Pranayama can help to eradicate pain, tension and other illnesses. All breathing exercises improve gland function due to the rhythmic nature of breathing, which sympathetically balances and steadies the heart's beating and purifies the Nervous System. Once the Nervous System and senses are harmonized, cravings and desires diminish.

The respiratory system serves as a bridge between the conscious and subconscious minds, and there is an integral relationship between the state of mind and the breath. When one is calm and quiet, the breath is calm and quiet, and the resting breath-rate is sympathetically calm and quiet. When a person responds to stress stimuli, the breath-rate will climb proportionally. By controlling the breath, one is able to control his or her state-of-being at all times and begin to exert some control over the mind, as well, and then begin to tune in to the more subtle vibrations of the universe. According to *The Yoga-Sutras* of Patanjali, the practice of *pranayama* will bring the mind to a state of clarity and prepare it for deep meditation.

Employing the techniques of pranayama, *one can make rapid progress, but one must be careful and not attempt to make progress too fast. If the mind and heart are not sufficiently purified, one can become open to negative influences and psychic attacks. This is akin to the experience of the Astral Plane while on drugs. Even though you aren't ready to go into that Divine space, you experience it anyway and may damage your Astral body and psychic channels. Follow the* yamas *first -- then it is safe to raise* prana *up the* Sushumna Nadi. *Purify your heart, and you will become like a child, but beware. Without surrender to the Lord and following the* yamas, *there is no yoga!*
—Sri Dharma Mittra

"The veil is removed by practice of pranayama.
After the veil is removed, the real nature of the soul is realized.
There is no purificatory action greater than pranayama.
Pranayama *gives purity and the light of knowledge shines.*
The karma of a yogi, which covers up the discriminative knowledge,
is destroyed by the practice of pranayama."
—Swami Sivananda

Beginner Pranayama Techniques

There are three fundamental actions common to most breathing exercises:

Puraka (inhalation)
Rechaka (exhalation)
Kumbhaka (retention)

Retention may be *bahya* (external) after exhalation, or *antara* (internal) after inhalation. For beginners, kumbhakas are very short. Later on, the use of locks or *bandhas* is introduced for longer retentions to keep pressure away from the heart. Contra-indications for the practice of *kumbhaka* in *pranayama* includes heart problems, high blood pressure and asthma.

A *matra* is a measurement used for counting -- each count is one *matra*. The length of each count is roughly that of a single heartbeat. Two excellent methods for counting which boast the additional benefits of keeping the mind focused and cultivating inner expansion are counting "Om, Om, Om". For a count of 12, use Om in four groups of three or three groups of four.

For example:

Om, Om, Om		Om, Om, Om, Om
Om, Om, Om	or	Om, Om, Om, Om
Om, Om, Om		Om, Om, Om, Om
Om, Om, Om		

Kapalabhati (Skull-Shining Breath): Inhale passively and pump the breath out vigorously through the nose for 10-15 seconds to start and gradually increase to up to two minutes. Pump exhalations at the rate of one or two per second. (Exhalations should be two to three times faster than inhalations.) Push the abdomen back vigorously while exhaling and keep the nostrils wide-open. At the end of a round, breathe out completely, then breathe in halfway and hold the breath for as long as is comfortable before exhaling. Beginners do not need to know the locks if the breath is just to be held for a short time. This exercise is also a *kriya* (yogic purification technique). Its action purifies and oxygenates the lungs and blood, and tones and massages the abdominal organs.

Calming Breathing: Inhale slowly for eight counts, hold (no hand is needed) for four counts then exhale for eight *matras*. Even rhythm is essential in this exercise. Some yogis control the rate of inhalation, holding and exhalation by adjusting the opening of the nostrils. The count may be changed by keeping the *kumbhaka* ratio as half of *puraka* and *rechaka*. The counts may be 4-2-4, 6-3-6 or 8-4-8, etc. This breathing calms the mind and diminishes cravings and desires. It makes the heart pump more slowly and rhythmically, and prepares the mind for meditation.

After 20 minutes of Calming Breathing, you are ready to face a firing squad.
—Sri Dharma Mittra

Cleansing Breathing: Using the right hand, assume *Vishnu Mudra* by folding the index and middle fingers into the palm and extending the thumb, ring finger and pinky. Use the thumb to block the right nostril and the ring finger to block the left nostril. Breathe in through the left nostril and out through the right (always in left and out right). Increase the speed, similar to a locomotive, and repeat several times. If the left nostril is blocked, it is better to do *Kapalabhati*. Perform two or three short *kumbhakas* with no locks after a set of several repetitions, progressing over time to longer *kumbhakas* with locks.

Positive Breathing: Breathe through the right nostril only. Using the right hand, assume Vishnu Mudra (fold the index and middle fingers into the palm, and extend the thumb, ring finger and pinky) and close the left nostril with the ring finger. Inhale for a count of eight, hold for six then exhale for eight. For beginners, inhale for a count of four, hold for three then exhale for four. Only the thumb moves and heat is generated. Be sure to check that Positive Breathing is done only through the right nostril. This *pranayam* increases positive feelings, improves digestion and generates heat.

Sound Breathing: The color body or personal aura can be seen by those with psychic abilities -- it surrounds the physical body like an egg. But, the colors are often out of balance due to our emotional reactions to what we are passing through. It is said that the aura of one who does spiritual practice often extends far beyond the physical body, even up to six feet out in all directions. The color body is the only true defense against psychic attacks or the negative thoughts of others. A healthy, balanced aura lets the good in, but is also a mighty fortress against anything negative.

Sound Breathing

Sound	Mouth Position	Color	Mind-Body Focus/Effect
Ah	Silver Dollar size	Red	Abdominal area lowest three chakras
Yuu	Dime size	Green	Respiratory region the heart center
So	Quarter size	Blue	Thyroid region
Eee	Smiling- teeth almost touching	Different Shade of Blue	Eyes, Ears and Sinuses
Sun	Tongue pressed against upper palate	Indigo	Brain (the vibration releases impurities into blood-stream)
Sum	Lips together	Violet	Improves mental sharpness helps the elderly

Sound Breathing helps to balance the colors and focus the mind. One round consists of chanting all six sounds on the chart above. Try to comfortably sustain the sound for as long as you can and as loud as you can reasonably manage. Ideally, one should perform three rounds, but, if you are pressed for time, one round is sufficient. Sound Breathing restores and generates positive colors, exercises the vocal chords, expands the lungs, improves the voice and concentration, and calms the mind.

Bija Mantras (Seed Chants). The *Bija* Mantras are done to stimulate the major chakras or energy centers located along the *Sushumna* or *Brahma Nadi* and to improve concentration. Concentrate on each mantra while directing your attention to the chakra it stimulates. Each of the six mantras are done seven times, seven plus seven times or seven plus seven plus seven times, etc. Conclude with two long and loud chants of Om, directing your attention to the crown of the head (*Sahasrara Chakra*).

Sound	Location	Chakra
Lam	Base of the Spine	Muladhara Chakra
Vam	An Inch or Two Above the Base of the Spine	Svadhishtana Chakra
Ram	Height of the Navel in the Spine	Manipura Chakra
Yam	Heart Center in the Spine	Anahata Chakra
Ham	Base of the Throat in the Spine	Vishuddha Chakra
Om	Space Between the Eyebrows	Ajna Chakra

Brahmari: Fold all the fingers except the index fingers in to the palms, raise the bent arms with the elbows up and back and use the index fingertips to close off the entrance of the ear canal with the small flap of skin there. Exhale to empty the lungs then inhale and fill them. Make a buzzing, humming sound with the lips closed, high in the vocal range, like a female honeybee. The eyes should be closed and the inner gaze should be focused at the space between the eyebrows behind the forehead. Perform at least three rounds of *Brahmari Pranayama*, loud and long, to cleanse and purify all 72,000 astral tubes and promote single-pointed concentration.

Standing Breathing Techniques

The duration of *puraka, kumbhaka* and *rechaka* in the first four of the five Standing Breathing Techniques is a steady ratio of 8-6-8. The fifth exercise is done without *kumbhaka* (retention). The Standing Breathing Techniques are performed standing with the feet firmly grounded and about 10 inches apart. The knees may be bent slightly for increased stability.

Energizing Charging Breathing

This *pranayam* is performed to bring the earth's energy inside the body. Place the feet 10 inches apart and bring the arms up overhead with the fingers and palms of both hands turned slightly upwards. Inhale for eight *matras* from the soles of the feet through the spine and up to the fingertips. Concentrate on the fingertips while holding for six counts. Then, exhale for eight counts down the spine and back out through the soles of the feet. Do three rounds of this exercise keeping the arms raised the entire time. After three rounds are completed, one may feel that the arms have tired. If they  have not, perform up to twelve rounds of Energizing Charging Breathing. In the early stages of practice, do groups of three or four rounds, building toward a complete set of twelve.

Magnetic Breathing

Feel yourself charged with magnetic force! Hold the arms straight out to opposite sides and bend the wrists, pointing the hands and fingers down towards the floor. Inhale for eight counts from the solar plexus to the crown of the head. Focus all of the attention at the crown of the head while holding the breath for six counts. Then exhale for eight counts from the crown of the head, down the spine and back to the solar plexus. After three rounds, one may feel that the arms have tired. If they have not, perform up to twelve rounds of Magnetic Breathing. In the early stages of practice, do groups of three or four rounds, building toward a complete set of twelve.

Breathing for Inner Healing

Bring the arms parallel to the floor and straight ahead of you with the wrists bent and the fingers pointed towards the floor. Inhale for eight counts from the solar plexus up to the crown of the head, and hold the breath for six counts while focusing the attention there. Then exhale for eight counts down the neck into the arms and out through the fingertips. After the three rounds, one may feel that the arms have tired. If they have not, perform up to twelve rounds of Breathing for Inner Healing. In the early stages of practice, do groups of three or four rounds, building toward a complete set of twelve.

Spiritual Breathing

This is done to establish a connection with God in your heart. Lift the arms up overhead with the palms turned upward at an angle of about forty-five degrees. Inhale for eight counts from the fingertips to the spiritual heart located in the center of the chest, the right side of your heart. Hold the breath for six counts while focusing all of the attention at the heart center. Imagine you are still holding the energy there and exhale for eight counts back up the spine, up through

the arms and out through the fingertips. After three rounds are completed, one may feel that the arms have tired. If they have not, perform up to twelve rounds of Spiritual Breathing. In the early stages of practice, do groups of three or four rounds, building toward a complete set of twelve. It is wonderful to practice this *pranayam* out-of-doors with the sun shining overhead.

Breathing for Reservation

This exercise is performed to keep in reserve that which is required. Let the arms hang down at the sides, a little away from the body. Inhale for eight counts, while simultaneously closing the fingers gently to the palms at the exact rate of inhalation. Then, exhale for eight counts while simultaneously re-extending the fingers at the precise, even, slow speed of exhalation. This *pranayam* should be practiced for a few minutes, or until its subtle effect is achieved.

Simple Breathing Techniques

Om Breathing: This breathing exercise is ideal for the elderly or infirm and may be practiced while sitting (any comfortable position may be assumed by the hands), or while simultaneously attaining to Deep Relaxation in *Savasana*. Mentally repeat "Om" during both inhalation and exhalation without any count or retention. Keep firmly in mind thoughts of God beyond name and form. Practice Om Breathing for five to ten minutes, and you will feel calm and completely recharged as a direct result.

Deep Breath Pranayam is performed while standing. While inhaling, the arms are raised along the sides and, at the same time, the heels are raised all the way up until the hands meet each other above the head. At this point, the lungs should be completely full. After one or two seconds, return the arms and heels to the starting position while simultaneously exhaling until the lungs are totally empty. As soon as the hands meet in front of the thighs, one has completed one round of this *pranayam*. This exercise may be repeated three to seven times.

The Preparation for Complete Breathing (Segmented) is performed lying on the back. First, rest both hands on the abdomen with tips of the middle fingers near the navel. Inhale for a count of eight while consciously bringing *prana* and breath into the lower lobe of the lungs. Feel expansion exclusively in the abdominal region. Hold the breath for six *matras*, then exhale for eight counts while consciously lowering the abdomen until the lungs are totally empty. Next, employ only the middle lobe of the lungs and place the fingertips on the lowest, frontal ribs. While inhaling for eight *matras*, only the chest should move up (the sensation is of pulling the ribs up and apart with the fingertips).

Hold the breath for a count of six. Then, exhale for eight *matras* while returning the chest to its starting position. Finally, inhale for a count of eight while resting the palms on the chest with the fingers on the collarbone. As you inhale, manipulate only the upper and smallest lobe of the lungs moving the chest towards the chin as the abdomen sinks down. Hold the breath for six *matras*, and then exhale for eight counts while returning the chest back to its original position.

Complete Breathing: In this practice, one fills the three lobes of the lungs sequentially during one complete breath. First, lie down and bring the arms to rest along the sides of the body. The counts during inhalation, holding and exhalation are the same as for the preparatory exercise: 8-6-8. During the first three counts of inhalation, the abdomen goes up and expands out. During the next three counts (while still inhaling), lift the chest, and, finally, for the count of two (while inhaling a little bit more), bring the chest toward the chin. Now the lungs should be completely full. Hold the breath for six counts, then exhale for eight allowing everything to settle organically until the lungs are totally empty. Repeat the entire process three to 12 times.

Nadi Sodhana Pranayama Without Kumbhaka (Alternate-nostril Breathing Without Retention): This is the most efficient nerve-purifying *pranayam* and is used to purify the psychic channels. No retention is used, especially not by beginners. Place the right hand in *Vishnu Mudra* and the left hand in *Jnana Mudra* and inhale slowly through the left nostril according to your capacity. Close the left nostril with the ring finger and immediately open the right nostril by releasing the thumb. Exhale and inhale through the right, then close the right nostril and exhale through the left. This is one complete cycle of *Nadi Sodhana Pranayama* Without

Kumbhaka. This is an excellent breathing exercise for those with heart problems and the elderly. This exercise is a preparation for Alternate-nostril Breathing with *kumbhaka* (retention).

Nadi-Sodhana Pranayama With Kumbhaka (Alternate Nostril-Breathing with Retention): Place the right hand in *Vishnu Mudra* and the left hand in *Jnana Mudra* and inhale slowly through the left nostril while holding the right nostril closed with the right thumb. Then, close the left nostril with the right ring finger and retain the inhaled breath with both nostrils held closed. Then, open the right nostril and exhale slowly. Inhale again through the right nostril, then close the right with the right thumb, retain the inhaled breath, then open the left nostril by releasing the right ring finger and exhale gently through the left nostril. This process constitutes one complete cycle of *Nadi-Sodhana Pranayama* With *Kumbhaka.* This exercise should be practiced for at least 15 minutes daily with the following ratios for puraka, kumbhaka and rechaka before moving on to the next count: for the first month, inhalation is for 6 counts, retention is for 4 counts and exhalation takes place over 6 counts; the second month, the count is 8-8-8.

Intermediate and Advanced Pranayama Techniques

Before beginning a practice of advanced *pranayama*, some knowledge of physical anatomy and the subtle anatomy is required, as is a familiarity with the workings of the Voluntary and Involuntary Nervous Systems. This section of the manual is to be dealt with only after these subjects are understood and diaphragmatic breathing is mastered. One's diet needs to be restricted when practicing advanced *pranayama* techniques. If ever one nostril is blocked, find the location by intuition in the back of the skull, press at this point, then lay on the unblocked side until the other side clears.

Kapalabhati: Concentrate on the exhalations while performing this *pranayam* to ensure the cleansing of the lungs and nasal passages. Exhalations should be two to three times faster than inhalations. Beginners start with 10 exhalations or three rounds of 10 according to capacity. Gradually, increase the amount. Do no more than 120 exhalations-per-minute at the rate of two-per-second for up to two minutes. Most organs get massaged by the rapid movement of the abdomen. Following *Kapalabhati*, do breath retention for as long as is comfortable. Apply *Jalandhara* and *Mula Bandhas* during retention (beginners should practice only *Asvini Mudra*).

Alternate-Nostril Kapalabhati: Place the right hand in *Vishnu Mudra*. Not too much force should be employed at first, in order to prevent escaped air from moving through the ears. Alternate-Nostril *Kapalabhati* requires a vigorous, conscious exhalation immediately followed by a passive inhalation. Always begin inhaling through the left nostril and use the right thumb and ring fingers to control the opening and closing of the alternating nostrils. Inhale through the left nostril, and then exhale vigorously through the right nostril. Then inhale passively through the right nostril and exhale forcefully through the left. This constitutes one complete round. Continuously alternate nostrils for 15 seconds or ten slow rounds, then end with an exhalation through the left nostril. Inhale through both nostrils and retain the breath with the locks for about 5-10 seconds while concentrating the attention at the navel region. To conclude, slowly exhale through right nostril.

Bhastrika (Bellows Breathing): This *pranayam* creates heat. Inhale and exhale through both nostrils at the same speed, gradually increasing the speed. In other words, breathe as fast as you can, like a sniffing dog. After about 20 seconds of pumping, or for up to two minutes, inhale and hold the breath while applying *Jalandhara* and *Mula Bandhas*. Then release the locks and exhale slowly through both nostrils.

Chandra-Surya-Kumbhaka Pranayama (Moon-Sun-Holding Breathing Exercise): This is the main breathing exercise and, as such, it should be practiced with faith for at least ten minutes daily. A form of Alternate Nostril-Breathing, this exercise is also known as *Anuloma-Viloma* or Breathing With-and-Against-the-Hair or Flow-of-Energy. Through repetition, the steady practice of *Chandra-Surya-Kumbhaka Pranayama* generates tremendous heat. The left nostril is the beginning of the *Ida Nadi*, also often called *Chandra* (moon). The right nostril is the mouth of the *Pingala Nadi* or *Surya* (sun). Hence the name: Moon-Sun-Holding *Pranayama*.

This exercise begins using the dominant nostril (and ends through the same). If both nostrils are equally active, commence practice through the left nostril. The left hand should assume *Jnana Mudra* and rest with the palm facing up on the left knee or be locked under the navel. The right hand should assume *Vishnu Mudra*, and the thumb and ring fingers should remain near the right and left nostrils when they are not being used to close them off. Both nostrils are to be held shut during retention. Inhalation and exhalation are to be done soundlessly and the eyes are to be closed throughout to prevent a burning sensation. Inhale through the active nostril, hold, and then exhale out the other side. Inhale through the same side, hold, and exhale out the other. The spine should be kept straight throughout the practice of this or any *pranayam*.

For beginners, the count is 4-2-4. For intermediate practitioners, the first month the count is 6-4-6, and the second month, the count is 3-12-6. For short holds, no locks are employed. The correct ratio is actually 1:4:2 (the holding is four times longer than the inhalation and the exhalation is two times longer than inhalation). Once one advances to a ratio of 3-12-6, *Jalandhara Bandha* and *Mula Bandha* are used to seal off the torso, keep pressure away from the heart during retention, and to begin moving the combined *prana* and *apana* against the gate at the base of the spine. Over time, this gate is forced open through this action, and the *Prana Shakti* can begin to climb the *Sushumna Nadi*, activating the major chakras en route to the crown chakra (*Sahasrara*) and the dawning of Self-realization.

Increase the count to 4-16-8 once you find 3-12-6 easy, and then advance to 5-20-10. If you are serious and practice continuously, you may increase the ratios successively to 6-24-12, then 7-28-14. Some yogis are able to perform *Chandra-Surya-Kumbhaka Pranayama* at a rate of 8-32-16! For Dharma-ji, 4-16-8 proved ideal.

The teacher should advise students to increase the duration of *puraka, kumbhaka* and *rechaka* gradually and according to their individual capacity. If one is a full-time yogi, they can do six hours of *Chandra-Surya-Kumbhaka Pranayama* a day. If one perspires during the course of practice, rub the sweat back into the skin. The skin will thicken and grow shiny over time. This rubbing of the sweat firms the constitution. In the second stage of practice, the body starts to tremble as the *prana* starts to rise. In the third stage, the adept starts jumping around like a frog. When the practice grows ever deeper, the adept walks in the air.

Sukha-Purvara Pranayama (Easy, Comfortable Breathing Exercise) is Swami Sivananda's simplified variation of *Chandra-Surya-Kumbhaka Pranayama* that has no counts. Using *Vishnu Mudra* to open and close the nostrils, inhale through the left nostril, hold as long as you can and mentally repeat Om, then breathe out slowly through the right nostril. Breathe in through the right nostril, hold the breath again, and then slowly breathe out through the left nostril. Feel comfortable and practice according to capacity. If you do this with faith, you may levitate. One doesn't have to hold the nostrils closed during the holds, one can bring the hands down to rest in the lap. After 15 minutes of practice, you will feel peaceful and relaxed.

Samavritti Pranayama (Square Breathing) (*sama* = same). This breathing helps with meditation and improves concentration. It will recharge *pranic* and psychic energy, and involves the chakras. The count for beginners is four all-around: inhale for four counts, hold with the lungs full for four counts, exhale for four counts, and hold again for four counts with the lungs empty. This cycle constitutes one complete round of Square Breathing. During both retentions, contract the anal muscles in rhythm with four Om's (*Asvini Mudra*). No anal contractions are necessary during inhalation and exhalation. Keep the spine erect and tall throughout. Always hold the nostrils closed during retentions with the right hand in *Vishnu Mudra* and always keep the right hand ready.

Increase the counts as long as the new ratio remains comfortable and accessible. (The lungs are designed to hold the breath for long periods of time.) A four-count retention is ideal for beginners, six to eight counts is average length, and anything over eight counts is more advanced. Focus on repeating mentally the sound "Om" along with each count. This leads one naturally into deep mental absorption. In the final stages of advanced practice, one will be able to match the Om's to the heartbeat. Follow the numbers inside the square below from the bottom-left, clockwise:

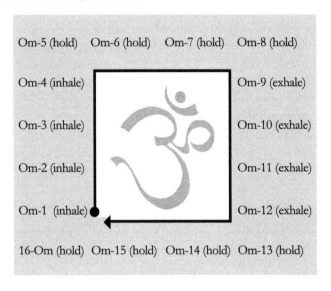

| Om-5 (hold) | Om-6 (hold) | Om-7 (hold) | Om-8 (hold) |

Om-4 (inhale)   Om-9 (exhale)

Om-3 (inhale)   Om-10 (exhale)

Om-2 (inhale)   Om-11 (exhale)

Om-1 (inhale)   Om-12 (exhale)

16-Om (hold)   Om-15 (hold)   Om-14 (hold)   Om-13 (hold)

Ujjayi means victorious or psychic breathing. It also means "that which is expressed in a loud voice" and "that which leads to success". The chest has to be lifted to fill the lungs completely. This breathing has a smooth, soft sound in the throat affected through partially closing off the back of the throat with the glottis. Inhale, lift the chest all the way up and hold for two seconds with an anal contraction (*Asvini Mudra*). Exhale while consciously constricting the throat a little and squeezing out the air. *Ujjayi* Breathing can be practiced during most postures, as well as throughout any *vinyasa* series. After two seconds, repeat the process again up to 12 times or so.

Purna Ujjayi (Complete Ujjayi) involves inhaling while making a sound in the throat through both nostrils. During retention, one lifts the chest and assumes *Jalandhara* and *Mula Bandhas* with an arrow-straight spine. Retention of the breath is for as long as one can hold without any sensation of suffocation. Exhalation is done with a strong throat sound through the left nostril with the right hand in *Vishnu Mudra* and the right thumb holding the right nostril closed. The "strong throat sound" is produced by slightly constricting the glottis in the back of the throat. No holding is done when the lungs are empty in this *pranayam*. *Purna Ujjayi* increases lung capacity and stimulates the lower chakras.

Plavini means to float. In this *pranayam*, one must swallow air until the stomach is totally filled. Small, rapid gulps of air are taken to achieve this effect. This *pranayam* is of particular help in cases where one is in water and there is danger of drowning, as Plavini enables one to float. *Plavini* is also a *kriya*.

Surya-Bheda-Kumbhaka Pranayama: *Bheda* indicates that which breaks. Assume *Vishnu Mudra* with the right hand, close the left nostril with the right ring finger, and inhale through the right nostril. Then, close both nostrils between the right thumb and ring finger, and hold the breath while applying the locks (*Jalandhara* and *Mula Bandhas*). Then, move the right ring finger off the left nostril, release the locks, and exhale out the left. Inhalation is always done through the right nostril in this *pranayam* and exhalation is always out the left nostril. This practice improves the digestive fire (*agni*) and generates heat. The *kumbhaka* should last for as long as is comfortable. Beginners should start with two to three rounds and gradually increase their practice to embrace 5-10 minutes of *Surya-Bheda-Kumbhaka Pranayama*.

Sitali: To practice this cooling *pranayam*, roll the tongue and curl the lips around it. Inhale quickly through the mouth while using the tongue like a straw. After inhaling deeply, close the mouth, bring the tongue to the upper palate, and hold it in place there, concentrating on the coolness held by the tongue. Then exhale silently out through both nostrils. Inhale again through the curled tongue the moment you feel the sensation of coolness disappear. This practice cools the entire system. Repeat 3-5 times, or as needed.

Pranic Healing: This practice requires concentration and the power of visualization. *Pranic* Healing can be directed toward your own person if you are struggling with cancer, or some other disease. Inhale slowly and deeply, and, while holding the breath, repeat Om mentally imagining the Om destroying with a positive mental attitude all the diseased cells, or putting them to sleep with lots of love. One has to use imagination and pretend that you are the Om, or imagine that you are the cancer cells being destroyed and / or leaving, combined with great love. While holding the breath, concentrate on the healing properties of the Om. If any organs or glands are not working properly, imagine all the cells that make up that troubled gland or organ returning to a normal state of balanced health and vigor. Imagine pushing out everything that should not be there, and really see the diseased areas regaining strength and beginning to function normally again. When you can't hold your breath any longer, just slowly exhale. The Om normalizes, fixes and destroys that which should not be there. *Pranic* Healing must be done with faith in order to be effective. This practice may be done as often and for as long as you like.

Distance Healing: Coordinate healing and receiving at the same time with another person. Have the receiver relax and be receptive. If possible, you should know what problems need to be addressed. Perform *Pranic* Healing as described in the previous entry, but direct the intention to the receiver if you are the healer, or imagine the process of the healing if you are the receiver. Even if you do not know where the person is located, they will receive the healing power and accompanying benefits. Whenever possible, the patient and the healer should perform their roles in the process at the same time.

The Solar Plexus as the Center of Healing Energy: The Solar Plexus is a nexus of nerves located between the spine and the pit of the stomach and is referred to as the second brain. Inhale slowly and take the energy from the Solar Plexus, and bring it (while exhaling) to an area in need of healing. (The Solar Plexus is an energy center that works closely with the Sympathetic Nervous System -- the Sympathetic Nervous System controls voluntary and involuntary functions in the body.) Involuntary functions occur even when we are not paying attention to them. The activities of the glands, for example, are involuntary. By affirmations and faith in *Brahman* (the Real Self), you can gain control over even involuntary activities of the physical body.

Mudras and Bandhas

The bandhas or locks unite *prana* (upward force) and *apana* (downward force) at the navel region. *Mudras* are seals. Together, *mudras* and *bandhas* are like the transformers and switches used when dealing with electricity. We are dealing with something subtler than regular electricity as regards *prana* and *apana*. Some advanced *pranayams* are dangerous if performed without the locks.

Jnana Mudra (Seal of Wisdom): Make a circle with the tip of the index finger and the tip of the thumb touching, and extend and straighten the remaining three fingers. This *mudra* helps to lock in energy and is used in many traditional asanas and often for one or both hands when practicing *pranayama*. It is always an option for both hands during seated concentration or meditation. The three extended fingers represent the three states of consciousness: waking consciousness, sleep with dreams, and deep, dreamless sleep. The circle of the thumb and forefinger represents the super-conscious state of Self-realization (*Turiya*).

Vishnu Mudra: With the palm facing forward, the index and middle fingers are folded completely into the palm. The index finger is thought to represent ego and the middle finger, the intellect. Both are impediments to *sadhana.*

Kali Mudra: To assume this *mudra*, interlace the fingers of both hands with the palms together, the arms straight, and press both index fingers against one another in straight lines. We employ this *mudra* in certain postures during asana practice to help facilitate the opening and stretching of the shoulders and the chest. (Note: *Kali Ma* is the Hindu goddess of destruction and rebirth. In order for new life, new ideas and fresh concepts to have room to develop and grow, something old must often be dismantled or destroyed.)

Asvini Mudra (Horse Seal or Gesture of a Horse) is the conscious contraction of the anal sphincter muscle.

Granthi Mudra is performed by placing the palms against each other and interlacing the fingers. This *Mudra* is good to perform when engaging in practice in public when you need to be locked, but having both hands in *Jnana Mudra* might draw the attention of and disturb the minds of others.

Mula Bandha is primarily a contraction of the perineum, but also involves the anal sphincter muscle and the area below the navel. *Mula Bandha* can be done with the lungs full or empty. When performing *Mula Bandha*, one should feel as if the anus and the navel are going to meet each other.

Uddiyana Bandha: The Flying-Up Lock occurs in the navel region, and should be practiced when the lungs are empty. First, breathe-out completely. Now close the throat and, with the abdomen relaxed as if you were going to inhale strongly, lift the chest a little and pull the abdominal organs up into the chest cavity. One should experience a strong sensation of suction.

Jalandhara Bandha: In the Web Lock, the chin is pressed near the base of the throat and the chest must be lifted up to meet the chin. Eventually, the chin and chest should meet (you may open the jaw to accomplish this). The tip of the tongue is pressed against the upper palate just behind the upper front teeth. Then, contract the glottis until it feels a little like you are swallowing. One should not experience pressure inside the lungs while retaining the breath. If the chin doesn't reach the chest, you may open the teeth, or place a little pillow or roll of cloth between the chin and the chest.

The following three mudras are for advanced yogis and should always be practiced together:

Maha Mudra (Great Seal) Sit on the side of the left heel so it presses against the perineum and the outer edge of the bent left knee rests on the floor out to the side. (The right leg is straight.) Lean forward and take hold of the right big toe with both index fingers. Move the shoulders and head away from the right foot and the small of the back simultaneously towards the foot, straightening and extending the spine. Take a few deep breaths, then inhale until the lungs are half full, and hold the breath applying *Jalandhara Bandha* and *Mula Bandha*. Concentrate at the space between the eyebrows. Hold the breath for 20 *matras*, then exhale gently and release the posture. Immediately repeat the entire procedure on the opposite side. One may break out in a cold sweat. Keep the spine straight throughout the process and do not over-practice this *mudra* in the beginning, as it can release too much power, and you may not be able to maintain control. It also may be done with *kumbhaka* after exhalation employing both *Uddhiyana* and *Jalandhara Bandhas*.

Maha Bandha (Great Lock) Sit on the side of the left heel so it presses against the perineum and the outside of the bent left knee rests on the floor out to the side. Bend the right knee and place the right foot on the left thigh near the left hip joint as in Half-Lotus. Place the hands on the knees, and straighten and extend the spine, breathing deeply along its length. Inhale to two-thirds capacity and apply *Jalandhara Bandha* and *Mula Bandha*. Hold the breath for 20 *matras* while focusing on the *Sushumna Nadi*. Then, exhale gently, release the posture, extend the legs forward, and massage the knees. Immediately repeat the entire procedure on the opposite side. Keep the spine straight throughout the process, and do not over-practice this mudra in the beginning, as it can release too much power and you may not be able to maintain control.

Maha Vedha (*Vedha* means penetration of the charkas by the Kundalini.) If possible, assume full Lotus, right over left, then left over right. This mudra can also be done in Half-Lotus or Sukhasana. Inhale until the lungs are half full while placing the hands down on the floor near the hips. While holding the breath, raise the seat and commence bouncing it rhythmically against the floor like a basketball for as long as the breath can be held without any sense of suffocation. This action will shake and stimulate all 72,000 nadis and may cause Prana Shakti to enter the Sushumna Nadi. When the breath can no longer be held comfortably, cease bouncing, exhale slowly and release the posture.

Yoni Mudra (Great Binding Seal): Seal-off the ears with the thumbs and close the eyes with the index fingers resting gently on the lids. Close the nostrils with the middle fingers and the mouth with the last four fingers. (The ring fingers should be placed on the upper lip and the little fingers on the lower lip.) Press the lips together, open the nostrils and inhale slowly. This can be done with or without kumbhaka, holding for as long as is comfortable. During retention, gently close-off the eyes, ears and mouth. This action shuts the "Seven Gates of the Senses" -- the two ear-holes, eyes, nostrils and mouth. When the hold is no longer comfortable, release the nostrils, exhale and inhale. This mudra increases inner perception, draws the attention inside, and brings a deep feeling of peace. It is a practice that leads to pratyahara by physically closing-off the senses. Repeat three to five times.

Yoga Mudra: Sitting in Full Lotus, interlace the fingers behind the lower back with the arms held straight. Inhale and arch back, lifting the chest with the chin up. Now, exhale and bend forward until the forehead rests on the floor. The arms should go as high as possible. Inhale, then hold the breath using *Jalandhara Bandha* (just the throat contraction and the tongue pressed-against the upper palate) and *Mula Bandha* for about five seconds. Gradually increase the duration of the hold to 20 seconds. To release, exhale, and then inhale as you gradually roll up from the base of the spine. Rest for a few breaths, and then repeat the *mudra* two more times. This mudra can also be done while assuming *Ardha* or *Sukha Padmasana*.

Khechari Mudra (Yogi Moves in the Sky Seal): This *mudra* is not accessible except to one who has the help, support and guidance of an expert teacher who has experience with this technique. It is included here for reference only, since primary, classical sources cite it as one of the practices by which one may achieve liberation, but it is neither endorsed nor recommended. The tongue has to be made to reach the space between the eyebrows outside the mouth so that it can be folded back up into the throat and swallowed. In this way the air passage to the lungs is physically blocked. The tongue accomplishes these feats as a result of having the membrane underneath permanently severed. The Guru must cut the lower tendon of the tongue with a bright, clean knife, little-by-little on a weekly basis. Salt and turmeric powder are sprinkled on the freshly cut edges of tendon to inhibit healing. The cutting is done regularly for a period ranging from six months to two years. Once the tendon has been completely severed and the yogi has learned the proper way to physically stop the breath by folding and swallowing the tongue, the practitioner gains freedom from fainting, hunger, thirst and laziness, and grows impervious to even virulent poisons. He or she is then beyond disease, decay, old age and death. Proper application of *Khechari Mudra* is said to make one an *Urdhvareto Yogin* -- a yogi whose energies have been sublimated into spiritual power. Since the breath is physically stopped, one is said to achieve samadhi instantly through application of this *mudra*. The complication arises in that one must also understand how to properly throw the tongue back out or die.

Sri Dharma has never believed in forcing any sort of result through artifice -- his path was always to advance slowly and methodically so that he was suitably prepared for the next level of experience.

Viparita Karani Mudra (also known as Sirsasana, Viparita Karani Asana and the Inverted Psychic Attitude): This practice raises the *Shakti* and, when *Shakti* rises, the aspirant gains spiritual bliss. Normally, the power of the sun rests in the Solar Plexus and the power of the moon resides in the upper palate where the nectar of life is released. When one is in Headstand, this is reversed and the aging process is suspended. This is enhanced if one visualizes the sun on the upper palate for 15 seconds followed by visualizing the moon at the navel region for 15 seconds. On the first day, pursue this process for one minute. Gradually increase the duration of practice to fifteen minutes. After six months of steady practice, wrinkles on the face and grey hair will disappear. Yogis who practice in this manner for three hours daily conquer death. As the gastric fire (*agni*) is increased, those who practice this for a long time should relax for ten minutes after coming out of the posture and take some light refreshment when the relaxation period has concluded. (Note: *Many traditions hold that this mudra is achieved by combining the visualization with Shoulderstand. Sri Dharma received it from his Guru in Headstand, and teaches that both postures are* Viparita Karani Mudra.)

The Three Main Sacred Texts

Take just one sentence of
The Bhagavad-Gita, The Yoga-Sutras *or* The Hatha Yoga Pradipika *and*
fix your mind upon it until its meaning is revealed.
—Sri Dharma Mittra

The Bhagavad-Gita

The Mahabharata is one of the longest epic poems in history and is generally attributed to the Vedic sage Vyasa. It tells the story of a civil war in ancient India between the sons of Kuru (the Kauravas) and the sons of Pandu (the Pandavas). The Pandavas, upright and virtuous, were cheated of their kingdom, Indraprastha, through a series of unscrupulous games of dice devised by the cunning uncle of Kauravas, Shakuni. The Pandavas obeyed the conditions imposed on them as losers and, after a period of banishment, returned to re-claim their land from their wicked cousins. The Kauravas refused to relinquish their false claim and the Pandavas were forced to wage war to regain their kingdom.

The best-known part of *The Mahabharata* is *The Bhagavad-Gita* or Song of God. It contains 18 chapters and some 700 stanzas in verse. *The Bhagavad-Gita* is primarily a dialogue between Prince Arjuna (the third Pandavas brother and their most skilled warrior) and Lord Krishna, his uncle, charioteer, teacher and an avatar of God. Remaining neutral, Krishna allowed one side to use his vassals in battle while the other side could have him as a charioteer (though he would not fight in battle personally). On the eve of the battle of Kurukshetra, Arjuna sees his near and dear ones arrayed against him and falters, feeling that it is not worth waging war if the outcome means killing family members, teachers and friends for the sake of the Pandavas' righteous claim. At this point in the narrative, Lord Krishna steps forward to unfurl *The Bhagavad-Gita*. He encourages Arjuna to take up arms and fight, since the battle to be waged is for a just cause. Prince Arjuna must discharge his duty as a warrior and live out his *dharma*. Lord Krishna offers Prince Arjuna the teachings of yoga (how to achieve Divine Union) and answers his many questions. These discourses and answers form the text of the *Gita*.

On the level of metaphor, the Kauravas and their supporters represent our evil impulses and the Pandavas represent that which impels us to do good. Our body is the battlefield and Sri Krishna is the portion of God in our spiritual heart that compels us to discharge our duty and do that which is right. The over-arching metaphor is of God and man, face-to-face, and fully engaged in man's process of discovery and realization of that which lies hidden in the innermost part of our hearts. It is said that when one understands the real message of *The Bhagavad-Gita*, Lord Krishna reveals himself to that person and embraces them.

The Bhagavad-Gita is the central text of the Hindu faith and one of the three texts most crucial to those that wish to attain to yoga. It reflects the received wisdom of all Vedic knowledge, simplified so as to be understood by all. *The Bhagavad-Gita's* central tenet is that one must endeavor to discharge one's duties sincerely, without regard for the outcome. "Make every action an act of adoration to the Supreme Self or God."

The Yoga-Sutras of Patanjali

Maharishi Patanjali traveled throughout India sometime between 100 B.C.E. and 500 C.E. to study the holy science of yoga as it was being practiced and taught during his lifetime. The repository of his experiences and unique insights form the text that became *The Yoga-Sutras*. Consisting of four sections or *padas* of 195 *sutras* (a *sutra* is a thread or a string) in total, *The Yoga-Sutras* is the earliest, extant document outlining the philosophy, goals and techniques of yoga. The *sutras* are laid out as bare-bones teaching points to be rendered in Technicolor and expanded upon by a teacher to their students. Each *sutras* brims with the truth of yoga.

The Yoga-Sutras guide us to understand the root of consciousness, the nature of human suffering, the gifts gained through the practice of yoga and the way to balance consciousness and soul to achieve the highest wisdom, integration and liberation. Each *sutra* contains a wealth of ideas and wisdom to guide the aspirant (*sadhaka*) toward full knowledge of his or her true nature. Maharishi Patanjali describes how through yoga practice, the aspirant can transform themselves, gain mastery over the mind and emotions, overcome obstacles to spiritual evolution and attain the goal of yoga, *kaivalya* (liberation from the bondage of worldly desires and actions and union with the Divine). One basic assumption of *The Yoga-Sutra* is that the body and mind are part of one continuum of existence with the mind being more subtle than the body.

The first chapter (*Samadhi Pada*) defines yoga and the movements of consciousness. Patanjali describes the fluctuations and modifications of thought, which disturb consciousness and then sets up the various disciplines by which they can be stilled. The *sadhaka* is advised to cultivate friendliness and compassion, to delight in the happiness of others and to remain indifferent to vice and virtue so that he or she maintains equipoise and tranquility. Through these means, the nature of the Supreme Self can be revealed to the seeker.

In the second chapter (*Sadhana Pada*), Maharishi Patanjali outlines eight means by which the *yogi* can attain union with God. As discussed in more detail in the first chapter of this manual, the eight aspects are not linear steps, but simultaneous, interwoven practices that together constitute yoga. This Eight-Fold Path to enlightenment is yoga. *Sadhana Pada* describes the external quest, and then proceeds to explain the ensuing penetration to the core of being through intelligence and bliss-consciousness. The Eight Limbs of Hatha-Raja Yoga detailed in the *Sadhana Pada* are:

>*Yama* (The Ethical Rules)
>*Niyama* (The Observances)
>*Asana* (Postures -- the Exercises)
>*Pranayama* (Control of the Vital Life-Force)
>*Pratyahara* (Control of the Senses)
>*Dharana* (Concentration)
>*Dhyana* (Concentration without Interruption)
>*Samadhi* (Absorption with the Object or Subject
>   of Contemplation)

The third chapter (*Vibhuti Pada*) speaks of the Divine effects of yoga *sadhana* (spiritual practice). It is said that the *sadhaka* who has achieved a certain level of mastery has full knowledge of past, present and future, as well as of the nature of the entire solar system. He or she understands the minds of others. These achievements can be dangerous if abused. The *sadhaka* is cautioned to ignore temptations and pursue the spiritual path. Patanjali says that once the sadhaka reaches this state, he or she acquires eight supernatural powers or *siddhis* including the ability to become small or large, light or heavy, to attain every wish and to gain supremacy and sovereignty over things.

In the fourth chapter (*Kaivalya Pada*), Patanjali goes into much greater detail in distinguishing *kaivalya* from *samadhi*. He describes the path of renunciation, the path of detachment from worldly objects and the path to genuine freedom from worldly desires. Maharishi Patanjali explains how consciousness can become pure, intelligent and ripe and free itself from the clutches of nature, enabling the *yogi* to reach the goal of absolute freedom. This is said to be the *yogi's* ultimate goal in his or her *sadhana*. The real purpose of our life is to cross the ocean of illusion. From the shore of worldly pleasures, one can then move to the other shore, the shore of emancipation and eternal bliss.

The Hatha Yoga Pradipika

This 15th-century text written by the sage Svatmarama is the oldest significant surviving manuscript devoted specifically to the exposition of Hatha Yoga. Earlier texts all contain material that predates the foundation of Hatha Yoga, which was not established as a separate form until sometime around 700-1000

C.E. by the great sage Matsyendra and his student, Gorakhnath. An earlier text written by Gorakhnath himself and called simply *Hatha Yoga* was available in Svatmarama's day and parts of it are reproduced in his *Pradipika*. Unfortunately, the earlier text is lost to history.

Pradipika means "to shed light on" in Sanskrit. *The Hatha Yoga Pradipika* does precisely that for the subject of Hatha Yoga through compact, terse, *sutra*-like stanzas that are ready to be expanded upon and used as teaching topics. *The Hatha Yoga Pradipika* is an esoteric handbook detailing the means to achieve Divine Union through physical mastery – the outward quest that is Hatha Yoga.

The Hatha Yoga Pradipika consists of 390 verses divided into four sections as follows:

Asanas: Basic positions for meditation and spinal flexibility or deep relaxation. This section also includes a few dietary guidelines

Pranayama: *nadi suddhis* to purify the subtle *nadis* (astral tubes) and seven *kriyas* to cleanse the physical *nadis* (nerves or tubes)

Mudras: In-depth description of 10 *mudras* (seals)

Samadhi: Three additional *mudras* (*Sambhavi* and two related techniques) and elaboration on the advanced technique of *Khechari Mudra*. There is some emphasis on the various sounds (nada) that arise in *Sushumna Nadi* as the *prana* begins to move in that channel. These sounds help focus the mind and provide *yogis* with feedback on their progress towards *samadhi*.

Conclusion

Read *The Bhagavad-Gita*, *The Yoga-Sutras* and *The Hatha Yoga Pradipika* carefully and meditate upon them constantly (*svadhyaya*). Reflect upon their meaning. Through regular reading, unconsciously, deep in the mind, you will be examining every facet of your daily life. Realizations will not emerge until obstacles are removed and impurities of the mind and heart are swept clean. Let's say you don't like a person or a race or possess anger, excessive ego or harbor jealousy. These conditions block the psychic channels and life's meaning cannot be realized. Through contemplation of *The Bhagavad-Gita*, *The Yoga-Sutras* and *The Hatha Yoga Pradipika*, one can achieve realizations that remove fear, even the fear of death.

Om, Lord Shiva
and Other Classical Yogic Concepts

The aspirant needs three qualities in abundance to succeed in yoga:
ability to keep silence, ability to fast and lots of patience.
—Sri Dharma Mittra

Om, the Pranava

The Almighty One doesn't have a name and is beyond form. In order for us to call out or address our prayers to Him, we require a name. Most of us continue to perceive reality through the vehicle of the mind and the senses. Because we are still dealing with the mind, we must contend with the material world of name and form. Without a name, how can we reference Him to one another or gain insight into His true nature ourselves? God is omnipresent, omniscient and omnipotent, yet truly lacks any concrete attributes for the mind to latch onto. To solve this seemingly unsolvable problem, the ancient ones (the Celestial Beings whose insights are gathered in the *Vedas*) set about discovering a name for Him. It had to be rich and powerful; containing all sound, notes, colors and be totally complete and beautiful. The name they realized in deep states of absorption was "hum"

-- a humming sound that couldn't be expressed by the human mouth. Thus it became "Om" or, more accurately, "AUM."

Om's vibrations, whether sung aloud or experienced mentally, stimulate the Pituitary Gland, eventually activating it. The Pituitary Gland is understood by yogis to be the sixth-sense. Om is the mantra of the third-eye and its power turns a *bhajan* or spiritual hymn into a mantra just through its inclusion at the outset. Repeating Om for a long time, correctly and with faith coupled with strict observance of *yama* and *niyama*, triggers Divine Perception. One may then become intoxicated with spiritual bliss.

Om is the sound of the vibrating universe.
It is the sound that came before and will exist long after.
One has only to quiet the mind and listen; it is always there.

Lord Shiva

God is beyond all thought or understanding, yet as we move along the path toward understanding, it is a great help to have a name and form to fasten the mind upon. For those who walk the path of yoga, Lord Shiva represents the omnipresent, omniscient and omnipotent essence of the Supreme Self in name and form as we inch slowly toward moving beyond name and form.

Many devotees from assorted faith traditions and spiritual disciplines become hopelessly enamored with and attached to the object of their devotion. Ninety-nine point nine percent of the time, this in itself can become an obstacle to ultimately realizing the True Self. At the same time, the earnest devotee cultivates devotion, reverence, love and compassion through their attachment. All of these qualities are essential for one who attains to yoga (Divine Union).

Lord Shiva is God in name and form. Through earnest supplication directed towards Him, the aspirant hits every other god since He sits in the heart of all beings, even the gods. To achieve the final goal, even the Guru and God in name and form must be abandoned. This will provoke deep sadness at first, but the final settling of the mind into silence grants one direct knowledge of the true nature of the Supreme Self. Once that knowledge is gained, one has moved beyond suffering and death to immortality while still living.

(Note: there is much information both written and online concerning the names and forms of Lord Shiva from the perspective of the Hindu faith and that of yoga. If you are curious you can lose yourself in such, but keep firmly in mind that what God truly is, is beyond all this.)

The Laws of Karma

Everything that you are currently passing through is a direct result of your deeds from the past. Until one comes to recognize this simple fact as absolute truth, the mind can never truly settle into silence. Many people live their life with the mistaken notion that they are born into this world with a one-way ticket and that upon death they are bound to spend the rest of existence in heaven, hell or some other such place. The *yogi* understands that after many incarnations and much karma being worked-out, the soul, Astral body or "that which is Eternal" evolves enough to be born as a human being. Only a human being has a chance at achieving immortality, since only a human being is born with the possibility of realizing the nature of the Supreme Self and piercing the veils of illusion that obscure God beyond name, form and time. Action, thought, word and deed leave an imprint on the subtle bodies, and it takes many incarnations to resolve the fruit of various selfish actions. This is why it is so crucial to offer the fruit of every action to the Lord -- so that one can act free of the bonds of karma and serve everything that lives. Be patient, develop a burning desire for liberation, do your spiritual practice and seek out the teacher who can help you on the path. It is through all these means that one may move beyond the laws of karma, perhaps even realize the Self in this very lifetime and become a "light unto the nations," leading others to discover the True Self.

The Guru

A true teacher is one who never says they are a teacher, but is always a student until devoid of ego and stuffed with correct knowledge and conduct. At this stage, they perceive the Supreme Self, eternal within themselves. Seek out a person through whom God manifests a little more clearly and make such a one your teacher. After all, you can't talk to God, but you can speak to another human being.

When you find the fountain of living waters,
drink deeply and often there, and only there.
By this means, you will surely achieve radiant success in yoga!
—Swami Sivananda

The science of yoga has traditionally been learned under the guidance of a preceptor. Nearly every master had a guide or preceptor who was charged with their safety. The term Guru is defined as one who dispels darkness. It is the Guru who girds one in strength against their lower nature, all obstacles and difficulties. A true Guru is never concerned with what people think of them and possesses all the *siddhis* (yogic powers). He or she reveals these only to a close disciple in private.

Sit at the feet of the Guru and follow his or her guidance. Copy the Guru, both physically and mentally, be loyal and reverent, and there is no doubt that you will make rapid spiritual progress. Except in the exceedingly rare case where one is born already completely dwelling in the spiritual heart, usually as the result of intense *sadhana* in previous incarnations, a Guru is an absolute necessity.

Spiritual knowledge is a matter of *Guru-parampara* -- it is transmitted from Guru to disciple. The disciple is bound to follow the Guru's guidance with sincerity and deep reverence. Yoga is complete obedience to the teacher, and true spiritual knowledge can only be imparted psychically. The Guru's grace enables the disciple to perceive the latent, spiritual power within, revealing the doorway to Super-consciousness. The true Guru unlocks the door to liberation, but it is the disciple who must step through the revealed doorway. The Guru illumines the spiritual path by casting his or her internal light towards the aspirant so that he or she can begin to see with the inner-eye due to the awakening and rising of spiritual energy. Additionally, the Guru takes on the task of guiding the soul away from identification with the material world. In the Guru, the disciple comes to recognize the ideal of liberated perfection in human form -- a concrete, human example upon which to base one's life. The Guru is everything.

Swami Kailashananda a.k.a Yogi Gupta,
Sri Dharma Mittra's Guru.

Mantra Initiation

The Guru Mantra is the means to cross the ocean of the world.
It is the specially energized thought of the Guru placed into your
possession for your protection and,
should the need arise, it will manifest before you in invisible form
and protect you from the harmful consequences of your life.
—Swami Kailashananda

Mantra initiation is a spiritual marriage between the disciple and the Guru and is not restricted by the laws of time and space. Mantra initiation is the Guru's formal acceptance of an aspirant once the student has shown sincerity of heart to serve humanity and to work diligently towards their own Self-realization. The link that is formed between Guru and disciple through initiation is eternal and cannot be broken. Even if the student breaks from the Guru, the Guru will never break from the disciple.

At the time of mantra initiation, the Guru accepts responsibility for that disciple's spiritual life and well-being by bringing him or her into his or her spiritual family. Initiation transforms the mind and creates a psychic link between the Guru and the disciple. The Guru Mantra is specifically charged with the thought of the Guru for the disciple's protection. This mantra's precise number of syllables carries a vibration which will act on the individual disciple, vaulting his or her progress forward. The results of the practice are already there in the mantra. This Guru Mantra is for life and by its repetition, the disciple inhales and exhales in a certain rhythm which creates changes in the physical and Astral (spiritual or psychic) bodies. When practiced with purity of heart and fierce determination, the Guru Mantra brings illumination to the disciple. The student must have certain feelings for the teacher to reap the benefits of initiation. This is a spiritual partnership and a disciple must follow the instructions of the Guru and be ever-ready to provide for his or her needs, comfort, well-being, projects and programs.

> *The right teacher will attract the right students who obey all the rules.*
> *These rules are known as "tradition."*
> *By way of example, for the practice of pranayama to be effective,*
> *one has to be nice, reverent and possess good qualities.*
> *It depends on where one starts from*
> *and on what kind of teacher one aspires to follow.*
> *In the case of my Guru, they would never allow people to see the Guru*
> *unless one took classes with the disciples first for many months.*
> *In order to be initiated, I had to do two years of selfless work (Karma Yoga)*
> *and attend every class, everyday.*
> *Only then the Swami in charge said: "I think he's serious enough about it.*
> *We will introduce him to the Guru and tell him about initiation to the Guru."*
> *So you see, initiation is not for everyone.*
> —Sri Dharma Mittra

Diksha is a subtle transfer of the Divine energy of a Guru into the heart, body and soul of a disciple. This pure energy initiates a process of change in the recipient which ultimately leads to the destruction of all negative tendencies and spurs the formation of creative, positive thoughts which encourage him or her to strive for the highest and best in both the spiritual and material fields of endeavor. *Diksha* can assume any form: spoken words in the form of mantras, subtle radiation emitted from the eyes or gentle warmth from a touch on the forehead with the thumb. Spiritual energy is also transmitted by the Guru during formal initiation through the vehicle of a personal mantra, but the Guru is not limited to these means. He or she can also transfer energy across continents and give *Diksha* through the medium of a telephone or a photograph. *Diksha* is not as easy to receive as the proceeding words might lead one to imagine. First, one has to find a real Guru who can transform one's life, and then one has the responsibility to devote oneself to benefit from the diksha. One must do just as the Guru says and make great efforts.

The Gunas

The *gunas* (primary qualities of nature or *prakriti*, the material world) are *sattva* (purity or peace), *rajas* (action) and *tamas* (inertia). All beings are subject to all three *gunas*, as they are part of *prakriti* (nature or matter), and are responsible for our illusions and suffering on earth. *The Bhagavad-Gita* aims to free us from these qualities by helping us gain an understanding of the nature of these qualities and how they keep us in bondage and illusion. The purpose of describing the three qualities is not to encourage us to become *sattvic* or to eliminate the other qualities -- even cultivation of *sattva* is not an end unto itself. *Sattva* is only the means to overcome passion and ignorance, thereby achieving Self-realization through purity of mind and heart. One should go beyond the three *gunas* to attain immortality and freedom from birth, death, old age and sorrow.

The *gunas* exist in all beings in various combinations and concentrations. Depending on their relative strength and concentration, they determine the nature of a being, its actions, behavior, attitude and its attachment to the world it lives in. The primary purpose of the *gunas* is to create delusion through desire and attachment. Under their influence, human beings cannot recognize the presence of God. Through understanding the three qualities and through right worship, study, knowledge, speech, devotion, faith, behavior and sacrifice, a process of purification occurs and one becomes established in tranquility. The quality of sattva then manifests in abundance. One can then realize the Supreme Self by attending to one's duty without desire or attachment, offering the fruit of all actions to God.

Sattva (peace, purity, harmony) is a quality void of impurity that is illuminating and free from sickness. It binds the soul through attachment with happiness and knowledge. *Sattva* names the pure state, leading to liberation. Moderation is observed in all actions, performance of spiritual obligations comes naturally and developing virtues is a priority. The *sattvic* state is balanced and does not last a long time due to sensitivities to the changes in life and impressions from the past -- it can quickly turn into *rajas*. When one is able to reach *samadhi*, tranquility can endure because it is connected with the true nature of the Self that does not change. *Sattva* is a perfect mirror to reflect spiritual bliss -- *sattva* is the dominant quality of a yogi. One who attains this state has good discrimination, worships higher beings, does regular spiritual practice and eats living, raw, vegan foods bursting with *prana*. Regular *sadhana* leads to the development of virtues: consciousness ascends, the chakras open a little bit, some knowledge of how to attain Self-realization is attained and retained, and one enjoys some spiritual bliss. Spiritual bliss is Supreme Bliss -- there is no feeling of "I" (the doer). *Samadhi* draws within reach as the *sadhaka* advances in self-control, action is perfected and one draws close to liberation.

Rajas (action) is a quality full of passion born of thirst, intense desire and attachment. It binds the soul through attachment with action, and attachment in all forms leads to pain and suffering.

Conversely, freedom from attachment leads to liberation. *Rajas* is restless, intense, constant activity. *Rajasic* individuals often consume food that is spicy, hot, salty and/or sour, which disturbs the digestive system, and consequently leads to an agitated state of mind. This type of state leaves one dependent on the senses for stimulation and gratification, initiating an endless and hard to break cycle.

Tamas (inertia) is the quality of darkness and crudeness born of ignorance, indolence and delusion. The lowest of the *gunas*, it binds the soul through recklessness, heaviness and sleep. *Tamas* signifies all that is heavy, dull, inactive and inert. Those in whom the quality of *tamas* prevails eat food which is dead, frozen, stale, twice-cooked and fried. An abundance of alcohol, flesh and other poisons in the regular diet leave one feeling dead, cooked, frozen, fried and lifeless.

When *sattva* is predominant, all the gates of the human body illuminate knowledge. When rajas is predominant, greed and the striving for selfish activities appear. When *tamas* predominates, darkness, inactivity, recklessness and delusion are evident. At the time of death, a *sattvic* person attains higher worlds and, when reborn, takes birth among pious people. After death, a *rajasic* person remains in the middle worlds and, when reborn, takes birth in the family of those who are attached to actions. The *tamasic* person sinks to the lowest regions and is reborn among the ignorant and deluded.

When an individual overcomes the three *gunas*, he or she neither likes harmony, illumination, activity or delusion when they are present, nor dislikes them when they are absent. He or she remains unshaken and unconcerned, knowing that the *gunas* are carrying out their actions. Alike in pleasure and pain, remaining the same towards a piece of gold or a lump of clay, towards the desirable and the undesirable, equal in defamation and self-adulation, alike in honor and dishonor, the same to friends and foes, without any egoistic effort in performing actions.

He whose mind is not attached to anything,
who has subdued his heart and who is free from all longing --
he, by renunciation, attains supreme perfection, which is freedom from action.
—The Bhagavad-Gita,
Chapter 18, Verse 49 -- Nikhilananda translation

The Kleshas:
Obstructions, Obstacles or Impurities

Patanjali enumerates five major obstacles that stand between the self and Self-realization. They are *avidya* (ignorance of the True Self), *asmita* (identification with the ego), *raga* (attachment), *dvesha* (aversion) and *abhinevesha* (clinging to life).

Avidya, ignorance of your own Self, is the greatest of all impurities and the root cause of all pain and suffering on the material plane of existence. *Asmita, raga, dvesha* and *abhinevesha* all exist as a result of *avidya*. Discrimination and meditation are the undoing of the kleshas, as the beautiful techniques of yoga are the key to overcoming *avidya*. When the mind is calm, it can see beyond itself and the illusion it projects. When the mind grows calmer still, the veil of illusion is rent in two, and the realization dawns that all name and form is illusion. One then realizes non-duality and recognizes that there is no small self. All is one without second.

Asmita is egoism. Its by-products are envy, hoarding and greed, and all depend on the separation from God which *avidya* creates. When we are blinded by avidya, we identify the self as the body and the mind, failing to recognize that the little self is but a pale reflection of the Supreme Self.

Raga is attachment. *Raga* is that which helps reinforce the bonds which keep us from recognizing the root cause of all pain and suffering. There is sometimes attachment to the idea of heaven, a name and form of God, happiness or *samadhi* which can prove to be an impediment.

Dvesha is aversion. This *klesha* sprouts directly from attachment since when one comes to realize that happiness, dependent on external objects, people, pleasure and conditions, is always doomed to end in misery, one begins to feel aversion for these objects of attachment. This is inevitable, as everything in this world of *samsara* (the repeated cycle of birth, misery and death determined by our actions from the past) is merely *maya* (illusion of the mind projected through the vehicle of the senses) and subject to the ravages of time. Everything external we love and cling to will ultimately die or disappear. You may love food and derive much pleasure from eating, but the moment you are done eating, you feel miserable again. As the body ages, you can't even enjoy the foods you love anymore and then you really suffer!

Abhinevesha is fear of death. This deep fear informs every aspect of life and is always in the background as a motivating force behind action, leading inexorably to more pain, suffering and fear. When one lacks the discrimination to perceive what they really are, life seems ever tremulous and fragile, and every effort is made to extend and preserve life. The classic image is of a mouth above water, desperately gasping for air. The tremendous effort to stay alive consumes and fully occupies the mind, even in the midst of living life. Those that lack belief in re-incarnation suffer greatly from this affliction.

The **kleshas** are very much linked to the laws of karma, since the self-motivated action they call into being binds one to the body, mind and senses. Observe *yama* and *niyama*, and you are already well on your way to dissolving the *kleshas*, as the *yamas* and *niyamas* stand as a mighty bulwark against them. As you advance in practice and gain a little insight and spiritual knowledge, you may come to believe in the binding nature of *kleshas*. But, belief is not enough. Knowledge is the key to moving beyond the *kleshas*, and knowledge is the fruit of the tree whose roots are the ethical precepts of yoga. As the ethical rules come to govern all action, combined with surrender to the Almighty One, there is no more desire. It is only through the accumulation of knowledge that one may ultimately realize the nature of the True Self. The gaining of knowledge leads to the development of a strong desire for liberation. This desire for liberation acts as a shield, repelling suffering. Then, the pain diminishes. One must refine their discrimination (*viveka*) through the practice of yoga until it is a mighty sword which can be used to rend the veil of illusion and reveal the universal truth of God.

Karma Yoga

Karma Yoga is the yoga of selfless-service and skillful action. This is the yoga of action outlined by Sri Krishna in Chapter III of *The Bhagavad-Gita*. This yoga blossoms with deep spiritual knowledge. By selfless action, one can attain knowledge of the

Self. Do selfless work, and don't even think of the spiritual benefits. Repeat, "I am doing it because it has to be done for you my Lord." When the heart becomes pure, one is fit to become one with the Lord or Highest Self. A real yogi doesn't desire anything. Knowing well that he or she is the Eternal Self, he or she is always content (*santosha*). This concept is hard to realize in one lifetime!

Work is worship, work is puja and work is meditation.
Do not forget this!
You will have to evolve spiritually through work and meditation combined.
Feel that the whole world is your home: one big family.
Work that is done without expectation of fruit
can never bind one to karma or samsara.
Do not expect anything when you serve or give.
Those who serve the world, truly serve themselves.
Do not lose any single opportunity in helping and serving others.
Perform regular, selfless-service daily with the thought,
"I am serving God in manifestation."
When you serve, remember that you work for God.
You will soon grow spiritually.
　　　　　　　　　　　　　　—Swami Sivananda

Collective Mind

When a wildebeest breaks from the pack out on the African veldt, they run the risk of being eaten by lions. In a school of fish, all the fish move together, but no one is truly leading or following anyone else. We read in *The Bible* of a stoning that is to happen, but of everyone hesitating to be the first to throw a stone and break from the non-action of the group. The police and the angry mob stand facing each other across a barricade, but no one moves until the first person breaks formation and acts. A group of people practice meditation together, and when one person breaks concentration, everyone starts to break. Everybody thinks and then acts together.

When people are together cooperating, they tend to mentally share in everything with one another psychically. Someone is always doing something, but for the sake of achieving collective mind, as *yogis* we must learn to renounce our individuality and allow ourselves to merge with everyone and everything around us. There is a spirit of cooperation that informs any group endeavor. Students of yoga violate this spirit every time they break with the class to do their own thing. Even if the teacher is asking you to do something you feel may not be correct, honor his or her request so as to keep the collective mind of the group intact. Cooperation is really just an aspect of love, and lack of cooperation and sharing reveal lack of compassion. Where there is cooperation, there is also enthusiasm. Then, the teacher feels very happy.

When people come to a table to eat together, everyone brings along their own dish, but everyone must learn to share in everything. If one comes to the table with a dish and doesn't share, then they also receive no benefit. Imagine that everyone has their own unique color, but when they get together, they all share. Then all the colors bleed together into one, and there are no differences or distinctions between colors any more; there is just sameness everywhere.

The Etheric Records

Thoughts before they materialize as words have tremendous power. Tune your mind to the Celestial Musicians, and merge into the Universal Collective Mind in the subtle form of the Etheric Records, the complete repository of all knowledge past, present and future that is accessible to those who are receptive to it and pure enough to serve as vessels. When this knowledge passes through a human channel, it inevitably is filtered through the mind, time and culture of the vessel. Thus, *The Bible, The Dhammapada* and *The Bhagavad-Gita*, etc. all contain the same knowledge, but through the distorting lens of name, form and time that are inescapable when dealing with the maya or illusion of the material world. Tuning the mind to the Universal allows one to gain access to the highest knowledge over which there is no ownership. There is here no sense of "mine" as in "my song" when inspiration seemingly strikes and a song is "written" or "composed". this is a Celestial Song that the mind is pure enough to have channeled from the source of all music. When this becomes possible, the practitioner is tapped into the mind of everything.

All of human knowledge is available to those who have purified
their physical, mental and spiritual bodies to the degree
that the highest knowledge becomes accessible to them anytime.
As you think something and then say it,
it immediately becomes part of the Etheric Records.
It's already there as your karma and everyone else's colliding and interacting.
Everything is already preordained,
but you can't tell people that or they won't make any effort.

—Sri Dharma Mittra

Holy Satsang

Satsang is the yogic practice of spending time with like-minded individuals in the presence of a spiritual preceptor or Guru to receive traditional teachings. These teachings are of infinite value to one who thirsts for knowledge of the True Self or God. These gatherings often include *kirtan* (call-and-response chanting of spiritual songs that help develop bhakti or devotion in the participants) or study of scripture replete with esoteric knowledge to support or amplify the master's discourse. The un-liberated self is lost in the *maya* or illusion that the mind and senses project of the material world. This maya obscures the portion of God that dwells in the spiritual heart of every living creature. The true Guru is the one who has achieved *moksha* or liberation while still in the flesh. Such a preceptor has the power to help the sincere aspirant pierce the veil of illusion that shrouds and obscures the Real Self. *Satsang* is a vehicle through which this process is greatly aided and abetted. The Guru's grace guarantees a shortcut to immortality.

Subtle Anatomy

All is within. Psychic things (like prana*)*
are those you cannot perceive with the physical senses.
—Sri Dharma Mittra

Introduction

In addition to physical anatomy, the *yogi* is concerned with what is commonly referred to as the subtle anatomy, also known as the Astral, Spiritual or Energy Body. Knowledge of the subtle body helps the *yogi* to transcend the experience of existence while living within the physical body. The ancients discovered, catalogued and mapped the psychic channels and energetic anatomy with great precision. Each *yogi* discovers this spiritual anatomy for themselves through exploration and practice.

Yoga Nadis

Nadi means stream or channel. As regards the physical or gross body, *nadi* can mean tube, vessel or nerve. In the context of the subtle body, the *nadis* are viewed as a series of subtle channels running throughout and sometimes beyond the physical body that are not visible to the physical eyes. Some are 1,000 times thinner than a hair and there are at least 72,000 of them. Also known as psychic channels, their main function is to act as channels for energy to pass through. There are ten main yoga *nadis*: three of primary importance and seven of slightly lesser importance. The three main *nadi* are **Sushumna** (middle, main, central -- the royal highway to God), **Ida** (associated with the left nostril, moon, negative, cool, Parasympathetic Nervous System, channel of comfort) and **Pingala** (associated with the right nostril, sun, positive, heat, Sympathetic Nervous System, tawny current).

The **Sushumna Nadi** is the most important of the yoga *nadis*. *Sushumna Nadi* runs down the center of the spinal cord and is intersected at regular intervals by the other two major nadis: *Ida* and *Pingala*. The seven major chakras are found at each point where *Ida* and *Pingala* cross and intersect with *Sushumna Nadi*.

One key place that **Ida and Pingala Nadi** intersect is at the base of the spine. A gate here blocks the entranceway of *Sushumna Nadi*, blocking and preventing *Prana Shakti* from entering and coursing up the body's main energy channel. Engaging *bandhas* (locks) during retention of breath in *pranayama* forces *prana* and *apana* to combine at the navel region, which is then forced against the gate at the base of the spine. Performing this action regularly with great determination coupled with strict observance of *yama* and *niyama* will eventually force the gate to open. *Prana Shakti* may then flow up through *Sushumna Nadi*. As this happens, the major chakras along the spine open and ignite like the blooming petals of a flower and begin spinning like a CD playing in a CD player. Consciousness can then rise and transform everything.

The seven lesser *nadis* are: **Ghandari** (ends at the left eye),

Hastijihva (ends at the right eye), **Pusha** (ends at the right ear), **Yashasvini** (ends at the left ear), **Alambusha** (ends in the mouth), **Kuhu** (situated above the sexual organ), and *Shamkini* (in the **Muladhara** or anus region).

The Chakra System

Chakra means wheel. A Chakra or energy center exists at each place where at least two *nadis* intersect. The Chakras are vortexes of spinning energy saturated in high intelligence that manifest through various states of consciousness. They hold influence over the function and health of the glands and organs located nearby in the physical body. As the Kundalini (seen in deep meditation as a snake looped three-and-a-half times at the very base of the spine and representing potential feminine energy) rises, each Major Chakra located along *Sushumna Nadi* is pierced. Most of the time, energy is expended at level of the first three chakras, as we are consumed with matters of food, survival, sex, fame and acquisition of power. Occasionally, awareness rises to the level of the Heart Chakra, but it can always sink back down. When awareness reaches the base of the throat in the spine (*Vishuddha Chakra*), the aspirant becomes deadly serious about spiritual matters. Even this stage is not permanent, as energy keeps moving from one place to another according to one's previous and present actions, thoughts and deeds. Through the practices of meditation, *pranayama*, surrendering to the Lord (*Isvara pranidhana*) and steady purification of the heart (*Tapasya*), consciousness can eventually reach the Sixth Chakra (*Ajna*). Only then will it remain permanently raised. Divine Perception is gained by the mind at this stage and once acquired is never relinquished.

The 7 Major Chakras:
Whirling Psychic Centers of Consciousness

It is said that the main purpose of *pranayama* (conscious control of the *Prana* or Vital Life Force, the breathing exercises) as a *sadhana* or spiritual practice is to awaken the Divine Cosmic Power. This power, known as *Kundalini*, is conceived of as a sleeping coiled serpent that lies dormant at the base of the spine, the *Muladhara*, Basal or First Chakra region. Through steady application of specific yogic techniques, this power is made to travel up the spine, penetrating all the Major Chakras in its path, eventually reaching the highest Chakra -- the *Sahasrara* just above the physical skull, where it unites with the Supreme Soul. As soon as the Major Chakras are pierced by *Kundalini*, the ordinary consciousness is raised to a specific state of consciousness. Until one's consciousness evolves to the point of the *Ajna* or Sixth Chakra opening and activating, the consciousness always moves between Chakras as a result of one's deeds from the past and what one is currently passing through. Once one's consciousness arrives at the Sixth Chakra, it never descends again.

While there is a relationship between the Glandular System and the Major Chakras, the Chakras are truly part of the Subtle or Psychic Anatomy. Only those blessed with psychic powers or abilities can actually see them -- not even the most powerful electron microscope can. As for the many artistic diagrams and images you can see online or in books devoted to the subject, these only represent in some small way the basic nature and characteristics of these whirling centers of psychic power. It's less important what they really look like, what is truly of help is actively engaging the powers of the imagination to grasp what they truly are, and then to use this knowledge to help make real progress in yoga.

The Major Chakras and Their State of Consciousness From the Base of the Spine to the Crown of the Head and Beyond

The First Chakra, Muladhara At this level, an individual acts in darkness, devoid of discrimination as a savage, and views the world in a very cruel and materialistic way. Lacking the discrimination to tell right from wrong, the individual hurts himself and others. In this state, the Divine Energy is at its lowest degree of strength. Imagine a caveman: someone so primitive that they are only concerned with the most basic acts of survival. Their responses to the outer world are painted only with the broadest of brushstrokes as in fear, anger, joy, etc. When rage is experienced, there is no discrimination or control as regards the resultant action. Although we all pass through this state of consciousness as young children, most move beyond as they age and evolve. The beautiful techniques of yoga help to keep us from residing in this state even if we occasionally pass through it.

The Second Chakra, Svadhisthana Here one thinks only that the world is brought about by the union of male and female -- that sex is the basis of everything. Holding such a view, this poor soul endowed with little understanding wastes all its semen and sexual power in vain, sympathetically slowing down its spiritual progress. An individual lost in this state is easily hooked on sex, and it is hard for them to ever really break free. The more one's cravings are satisfied, the larger they grow and the faster they multiply. This craving (longing or lust) is no doubt a form of suffering, especially when virility comes to an end with old age. Of course, when exercised properly, with moderation and without attachment, then the suffering inherent in this state is lessened.

The Third Chakra, Manipura In this state, one seeks for power and achievement. Here one works hard for name, fame and position – even their religious observances are related to these aims, giving rise to arrogance. Ostentation, rudeness, etc.:

Giving themselves up to insatiable desires, full of arrogance, pride and hypocrisy, they hold erroneous views through delusion and act with impure resolve.
—The Bhagavad-Gita,
Chapter 16, verse 10, -- Nikhilananda translation

Striving hard only to amass wealth for the satisfaction of their passion, one says: "I'm happy and prosperous.
I'm rich, special and whom else is equal to me?"
Motivated by selfish actions, one offers sacrifices, gives and rejoices.
Haughty, self-honored, arrogant and intoxicated with pride, one feels sure that this is all. Everyone's worship is self-motivated.
—The Bhagavad-Gita
-- these verses also apply to the first two Major Chakras to a lesser degree.

They rise for the destruction of the world.
—The Bhagavad-Gita

The Fourth Chakra, Anahata At this level, one begins to transcend the ordinary human emotions partially described above. One acts with pure resolve and with conscience. Ordinary love is now constantly being transformed into compassion, and it purifies the mind and heart, increasing spiritual perception. This may be the beginning of the end of sin.

The Fifth Chakra, Vishuddha Here one strives hard for spiritual fulfillment. Virtues such as self-denial, self-control, austerity, steadfastness, uprightness, renunciation, dedication, truthfulness and tranquility are highly cultivated. This may be the end of sin. So, the savage is turned into an angel.

The Sixth Chakra, Ajna After long and painful spiritual practices such as self-purification, the mind, heart and intellect are purified and the consciousness is expanded to the level of Divine Perception. One sees the Spiritual World or has a complete vision of God.

The Seventh Chakra, Sahasrara This is the end of the journey, one returns home again. As the air from a bubble becomes one with the ocean of air around it after bursting, so here pure consciousness, existence and bliss are freed from their veil or bubble (ego, individuality, perception of duality, maya) and become one with the Homogeneous Mass of Existence, Complete Knowledge or Bliss Absolute.

After attaining Me, these great souled men are no more subject to birth,
which is transitory and the abode of pain,
because they have attained the Highest Perfection.
—The Bhagavad-Gita

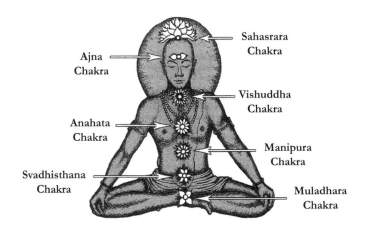

Chakra	Location	Element	Yantra	Deity
Muladahara (Root or Anal)	Perineum/Anus between the anus and genital organs at the base of spine.	Earth	Yellow square with a red triangle inside and four red petals.	Ganesha or Brahma and Dakini
Svadhisthana (Sex)	Sacrum, behind the pubic bone; the height of the sex organ.	Water	A white, crescent moon in an orange circle with six vermillion petals.	Kali Ma or Vishnu and Rakini
Manipura (Navel)	Behind the navel.	Fire	Downward-pointing red triangle in a yellow circle with ten dark blue petals.	Rama or Rudra and Lakini
Anahata (Heart)	Heart Center	Air	Smokey gray six-pointed star in a circle with 12 deep red petals.	Krishna or Isha and Kakini
Vishuddha (Throat)	Throat	Ether/ Space	A white circle inside an inverted red triangle inside a circle with 16 smoke-colored petals.	Shiva or Sadashiva and Sakini
Ajna (Third Eye)	Between the Eyebrows (Pituitary Gland).	None	Snow white circles inside circles and two indigo petals.	Feet of Shiva or Command Eye of Brahman and Hakini
Sahasrara (Crown)	Crown-of-the-Head, back beyond and above (the Pineal Gland).	None	Thousand-Petaled, Violet Lotus.	Lord Shiva or Shiva and Yakini

Visualization	Bija	Mantra
Square room with no ceiling. Walls yellow with a square window in each. Red triangle on the floor and Sri Ganesh atop the red triangle tossing red flower petals onto the triangle.	Lam	Ganesha Namah Om, Ganesha Namah Om, Ganesha Namah Om, Jai Jai Ganesha
Dark blue lake with a bright white crescent moon over it. Black Kali Ma sitting on the crescent with light emanating from her Yoni. A crescent sword is held in her raised, right hand, while your head is held in her left hand.	Vam	Jai Jai Ma / Kali Ma
Dark blue river Ganga with the sun rising over the water. Standing in the cold water at the height of the navel, a red triangle within you.	Ram	Hare Rama, Hare Rama, Rama Rama, Hare, Hare /Sita-Ram, Sita-Ram, Sita-Ram, Sita-Ram, Sita-Ram, Sita-Ram, Sita-Ram, Ram, Ram
Deep, dark green field at night with silver Lord Krishna radiating silver light from above.	Yam	Sri Krishna Govinda Hare Murare, He Natha Narayana Vasudeva
Lord Shiva sitting inside a white circle with blackness surrounding the circle. Focus on the Bindi-point on Shiva's head.	Ham	Om Namah Shivaya, Om Namah Shivaya, Om Namah Shivaya, Shivaya Om Namaha
White feet of Lord Shiva resting on the third eye, tapping lightly to awaken the sleeper.	Om	Om Namah Shivaya, Om Namah Shivaya, Om Namah Shivaya, Shivaya Om Namaha
White Lord Shiva covered in ashes seated on a lotus flower with a white crescent moon on his forehead at the third-eye point and a white moon behind him. Amrita drips from the crescent while he tosses red flower petals. There are brilliant rays of pure white light - the light of pure consciousness.	Om	Om Namah Shivaya

The Koshas

Deep within the heart of every being dwells a portion of God (*Atman*) -- the luminous, Divine Self. Through the practice and techniques of the classical yogic system, the *yogi* is finally able to recognize this portion of God dwelling within. A practice that greatly aids this endeavor is the study of the *koshas*, the Five-Fold Sheath. The concept of the *koshas* is the metaphysical theory that defines the individual as divided into five selves. The theory appears to derive from the layers of the self described in *The Taittiriya Upanishad*. The five *koshas* are defined as five sheaths that cover over and obscure the True Self, much like a sheath covers over a brilliant sword. These sheaths are successively finer starting from the outer periphery of the body and moving steadily inward towards the core of the self, and each layer is contained within its predecessor.

Beginning with the outermost, grossest layer and moving progressively to the innermost, most subtle layer, the five *koshas* are the *Annamaya Kosha* (the Physical Sheath or body), the *Pranamaya Kosha* (the Vital Life-Force Sheath), the *Manomaya Kosha* (the Mental Sheath or lower mind), the *Vijnanamaya Kosha* (the Intelligence Sheath or higher mind) and the *Anandamaya Kosha* (the Bliss-Sheath).

By studying and coming to understand the nature of the different sheaths, the *yogi* can begin to discriminate between the different layers, and learn to draw him or herself into the subtle and causal bodies which reside closer to *Atman* and mirror a more accurate reflection of the Real Self.

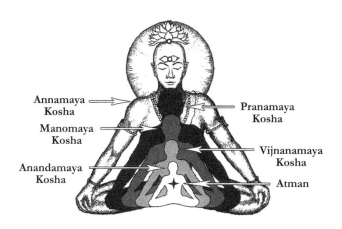

The grossest, outermost layer or sheath is known as the **Annamaya Kosha**. The *Annamaya Kosha* is the first of the five *koshas* and primarily consists of the physical body. Its component parts include blood, flesh, bones, skin and hair -- all the physical components of the body that depend upon food and oxygen for survival. A *yogi* who resides predominantly in the *Annamaya Kosha* believes that he or she is only the physical body, and he or she is deeply attached to and involved solely with the state of the physical form. It is through the knowledge and realization of the subsequently finer sheaths that the *yogi* can realize that the physical body is not the Real Self. Also, this body lives only as long as it can assimilate food and oxygen. Without them, the body perishes, so it can't possibly be the True Self (which is permanent and unchanging).

The next layer or sheath inward is the **Pranamaya Kosha**. The *Pranamaya Kosha* is the second *kosha* and consists of the Vital Life-Force, otherwise known as *prana*. This sheath animates the *Annamaya Kosha* (the Physical Sheath). The *Pranamaya Kosha* contains all the five forms of *prana* or energy, including *prana*, *apana* (downward-moving energy or elimination), *vyana* (which governs blood circulation), *samana* (which governs digestion) and *udana* (which governs diaphragmatic action), as well as the organs of action. This *kosha* is associated with feelings of hunger and thirst and the processes of evacuation and regeneration. This sheath is more important and subtler than the first sheath since without *prana* the body would cease to function. *Prana* enters the body at the moment of conception and leaves it at the hour of death. By experiencing this aspect of existence, the *yogi* may believe for a time that he or she is this finer energy animating the physical form. But, by delving deeper into the core of the self, he or she will soon discover that this sheath is merely another illusion covering the Eternal Self.

The next and third *kosha* is the **Manomaya Kosha,** and is defined as the lower mind or mental sheath. In reality, there are two aspects to the mind and this *kosha* is actually the lower aspect of it. The *Manomaya Kosha* consists of the volitional, emotional aspect of the mind which is governed by the five sense organs: touch, taste, smell, hearing and sight. The yogi residing in this layer has thoughts and desires which identify with form and name, position and qualitative evaluations. He or she experiences pain, pleasure, longing, doubt and fear -- the many tides of human emotion. But, the lower mind lacks the cognitive ability to reason and does not engage in discrimination. By way of example, imagine that you see your spouse or partner hugging another person. The *yogi* residing in the *Manomaya Kosha* (without any discrimination) might become angry, and start screaming and fighting with them. However, as a *yogi* established in the next sheath, the *Vijnanamaya Kosha* (with discrimination), you would immediately discern that your spouse or partner in fact is hugging a relative and doing nothing wrong at all. The *Manomaya Kosha* is clearly still not the Supreme Self, because it is in a constant state of flux.

The **Vijnanamaya Kosha**, the Fourth Sheath, is defined as the Intelligence Sheath (vijnana means knowing). This Fourth Sheath is the wisdom that lies beneath the processing, thinking aspect of the mind. This aspect of the mind or intellect "knows", decides, judges and discriminates according to the information being processed. One reason for a yogi to do regular sadhana is to gain access to this kosha. The Vijnanamaya Kosha is the realm of higher wisdom, wherein one commences to seek truth by diving within toward the eternal, glowing center of all consciousness. The yogi who rests in the Vijnanamaya Kosha is more sattvic overall and manifests more golden qualities due to this layer's closer proximity to the Transcendent Self. However, as with all the koshas, the yogi soon realizes that even the highest aspect of the mind cannot be the Real Self, as it is a feature of the material world and therefore bound by its rules and definitions. Even the higher mind is not eternal.

The innermost and finest of all the koshas, and the one closest to the pure consciousness of Atman, is the **Anandamaya Kosha.** The Anandamaya Kosha is known as the Bliss Sheath or Body of Bliss. This "bliss body" is the causal body and it permeates and influences all of the other koshas. The yogi who resides in the Bliss Sheath experiences absolute peace, joy and love. The Anandamaya Kosha is a perfect reflection of Atman, suffused with a spontaneous and effortless joy that is independent of any reason or stimulus that could cause a mental reaction. The subtlest of the five koshas, the Anandamaya Kosha may be seen as the Self in the silence of deep meditation, but beware! This too is only illusion and not the Supreme Self. Although the Body of Bliss is a perfect reflection of Atman, it still remains a covering over the True Self. The yogi established in the Anandamaya Kosha may become deluded in thinking that he or she has already achieved his or her goal in reaching the absolute state of bliss. Soon the yogi will realize that the Bliss Sheath cannot be the Self, because he or she is still able to witness the bliss through the activities of the mind. When and if one achieves Self-realization, the Anandamaya Kosha will fall away along with the other four koshas, as they wither away in the brilliant light of pure discrimination.

The great goal of yoga, the Divine Science of Self-realization, is to directly experience and realize Atman. By doing so, the yogi merges completely with the Divine. Atman is omnipresent, omniscient and omnipotent, and to even attempt to describe its true nature is impossible. Atman is beyond consciousness, form, name and time -- Atman is indescribable. Through sincere and constant study of the mystical Five-fold Sheath, the yogi makes rapid progress, finding a shortcut to immortality by quickly realizing the truth within his or her own heart.

The Three Bodies

The adhesive force by which all three bodies are held together is desire.
The power of unfulfilled desires is the root of all man's slavery.
—Sri Yukteswar Giri,
quoted in *Autobiography of a Yogi*

The physical body consists in its entirety of the Physical, Astral and Causal Bodies and the five *koshas* or Mystical Sheaths.

The Physical Body is the crudest of the three bodies and is the container that *Atman* (the True Self) resides within. The first three stages of Astanga Yoga (*yama, niyama* and *asana*) strengthen and purify the Physical Body.

The Astral Body exists within the Physical Body, but is of a more subtle nature and extends a few inches beyond it. It cannot be seen or touched except by those with *siddhis* or *yogic* powers who may see the Astral Body as an aura of swirling colors, although it can be sensed by others, as well. The Astral Body includes the *nadis, chakras* and *prana,* and it is *prana* which binds the Astral and Physical Bodies to one another. The Astral Body is said to carry the basket of karma from previous incarnations into the current one and to retain the current incarnation's impressions to bring along into the next. The Astral Body is strengthened and purified by the middle three steps of Astanga Yoga: *pranayama, pratyahara* and *dharana.*

The Causal Body exists within the Physical and Astral Bodies, but is even larger, more subtle, and of a higher vibration. The Causal Body bears the seed state of the Real Self or *Atman* from one reincarnation to the next. The Causal Body is devoid of individuality or personality, and is experienced during the final two *angas* of Astanga Yoga: *dhyana* and *samadhi.*

Mantra and Bhajan

Kirtan is constant remembrance through chanting.
—Ismrittee Devi

Now you have a weapon in your hand!
(said after teaching the Maha Mrityunjaya Mantra)

Clap your hands and sing with great enthusiasm! Imagine you are
established in a state of bliss singing in the hearts of all living beings.
—Sri Dharma Mittra

As there are different people with different temperaments, there
are different techniques in yoga that are appropriate to them. It is
best to experiment with many approaches under the guidance of
one who has a little experience with them, and then to commit to
a regular practice of those that seem to work best. One must start
from where they are, and it is ideal to begin *sadhana* with that to
which the mind is attracted. If one begins in this manner, there is
the chance that one will become attached to this new endeavor and
be true to it. *Kirtan* (call-and-response chanting of the names of
God) is an example of a deceptively simple-seeming *sadhana* that
may be practiced by anyone, irrespective of their physical condition
or ability to concentrate. This style of chanting is one of the devotional practices common to the Bhakti Yoga (path of devotion) of

both Hinduism and yoga. *Kirtan* may be done solo, but is generally done in *sangha* or community of like-minded individuals who come together to do *kirtan* or sing *bhajans* (*bhajan* refers to singing prayers or hymns rather than the repetition of God's name). Sung or chanted prayer is an attribute common to most religious and devotional practices. Through the chanting of the names of God, one practices *dharana* (concentration) in a way that is pleasant and demands little effort, but has great potential to help one to eventually taste a little of the bliss of *samadhi*. One learns to concentrate with one-pointed focus (*ekagrata*) on the names being sung and become absorbed in the communal endeavor. It becomes meditation when the concentration is uninterrupted. The key is to clap and sing with great enthusiasm. Otherwise, if God were to visit, why would He stay?

It is said that if one were to chant a name of God even a single time with pure devotion and single-minded focus, one would achieve the highest *samadhi* in that very instant. *Mantra japa*, one of the main techniques of Mantra or Japa Yoga, is said to be ideal for one to whom *dharana* does not come easily. Repetition of a mantra in an undertone or just in the mind is like firmly anchoring a swaying ship, because it gives the mind an object to firmly focus upon.

If there is no *kirtan* where you live or what's available is not to your taste, you can always buy a recording of something you like, learn it and practice on your own. Swami Sivananda says it's good to sing a little before engaging in spiritual practice. Most are familiar with chanting the *Pranava* and perhaps a little mantra at the start of an asana class and, perhaps, the Om and the three *Shanti's* at the conclusion. It's traditional to invoke Ganesh, the elephant-headed remover of obstacles, before practicing the breathing exercises, and it's good to chant the Om and the Mantra For Purification any time, anywhere. It's also good to invoke Lord Shiva, since through offering devotion to this name and form of God, you include all the other names and forms of God. Remember though that what God really is, is beyond name and form, and that chanting with devotion can be wonderful for cultivating reverence and love. Become established in *yama* and *niyama* and chant a little the names of God. You just may find that it works for you.

Some Traditional Mantras
and Bhajans of This Lineage

Om is the best of all mantras. It begins with an "Ah" sound in the throat, is sustained loud and long on "Oh," which gracefully changes two-thirds of the way through to "Mm" with the lips together, fading slowly away to silence. In the silence, one continues to hear the echo of the cosmic vibration. (The "A" represents the physical, the "U", the mental and the "M," the spiritual. The silence following the "M" is the best part. It represents Super-Consciousness -- that which is beyond all this. Chanting the *Pranava* stimulates the Pituitary gland, the master gland, activating the yogic sixth-sense of Divine Perception.)

Jai Ganesha
Jaya Ganesha, Jaya Ganesha,
Jaya Ganesha Pahimaam;
Sri Ganesha, Sri Ganesha,
Sri Ganesha Rakshamaam.
~ Hail to Ganesha, save me! Your holiness, Ganesha, protect me. (Lord Ganesha, the elephant-headed remover of obstacles and son of Lord Shiva, is traditionally invoked before practicing *pranayama* or before commencing a series of mantras or prayers to various aspects of God.)

Om Namah Shivaya

Om Namah Shivaya, Om Namah Shivaya,
Om Namah Shivaya, Om Namah Shivaya!
~ I bow to Lord Shiva again and again;
I bow to the inner light -- the Supreme Self.

The Ram-Nam

Om Sri Ram, Jaya Ram, Jaya Jaya Ram;
Om Sri Ram, Jaya Ram Jaya Jaya Ram.
~ Om, salutations to the incarnation of Vishnu.
(Ram is the seventh incarnation of Lord Vishnu, whose exploits
are celebrated in the *Ramayana*.)

Sita-Ram

Sita-Ram, Sita-Ram, Sita-Ram, Sita-Ram,
Sita-Ram, Sita-Ram, Sita-Ram, Ram, Ram.
~ Sita is the essence of feminine perfection and Ram the ideal
man. Combined, they are "one without second," or perfection.

Guru Mantra

Gurur Brahma, Gurur Vishnu, Gurur Devo Maheshvara;
Guru Sakshat, Param Brahma, Tasmai Sri Guravei Namaha.
The Guru is God in the form of Brahma, Vishnu and Lord Shiva.
~ He is illuminating light, the highest expression of truth. To that
supreme truth, we prostrate ourselves. (This *bhajan* is often recited
at the conclusion of the ceremony of lights known as *Aarti*.)

Sri Krishna Govinda

Sri Krishna Govinda Hare Murare
He Natha Narayana Vasudeva.
~ His Holiness Krishna or Govinda is lord of all.

Hare Krishna Maha-Mantra

Hare Krishna, Hare Krishna, Krishna Krishna, Hare Hare;
Hare Rama, Hare Rama, Rama Rama, Hare Hare.
~ Chant the glory of Krishna, chant the glory of Rama.
(This is known as the *Maha Mantra*, meaning "Great Mantra." It is
said to be the most powerful in this Iron Age (*Kali Yuga*). It brings
purity to the mind and heart and signifies that God is everywhere.)

Maha Mrityunjaya Mantra

Om Tryambhakam Yajamahe
Sugandhim Pushtivardhanam
Urvarukamiva Bandhanan
Mrityor Mukshiya Maamritat.
~ Om, we worship the Three-Eyed One (Lord Shiva) who is
fragrant and who nourishes all beings. May He liberate us from
death for the sake of immortality even as a cucumber is severed
from its bondage (to the creeper). As our ancestors did, I worship
the ever-expanding energy of the fruit of the vine. To its root
it is bound; from death, may I be free. (Chant seven, 12 or 108
times. This great death-conquering mantra comes from the *Rig
Veda* and is of great importance to this lineage as we are a Shiva
lineage.)

Om Namo Narayanaya (The Mantra for World Peace)

Om Namo Narayanaya
~ The mantra of Lord Narayanaya (Vishnu, the preserver of
the universe) is chanted to invoke His all-pervading power of
mercy and goodness. Repetition of this mantra confers infinite
love, prosperity, power, glory, wisdom and total liberation.
(This mantra is often given in this lineage to practice *japa* on a
mala. It is done for the purpose of bringing a state of peace into
the entire world and to cultivate reverence for the teacher.)

The Maha-Vakya
Asato Ma Sat Gamaya,
Tamaso Ma Jyotir Gamaya,
Mrityor Maamritam Gamaya
~ Lead me from the unreal to the real, from darkness to light, from mortality to immortality.

I Have No One Else But You (by Sri Dharma Mittra)
I have no one else but You, only You, my Lord.
I have nothing else but You, only You, my Lord.
Oh, my Lord, come, come to me!
Oh, my Lord, come, come to me;
Oh, my Lord, come, come to me!

Dedication Song
Twameva Mata Cha Pita Twameva,
Twameva Bandhuscha Sakha Twameva;
Twameva Vidya Dravinam Twameva,
Twameva Sarvam Mama Deva, Deva.
~ Oh God of Gods, You alone are my mother, father, relative, friend, learning, wealth and everything.
(This mantra is traditionally recited during *Aarti.*)

Gayatri Mantra
Om Bhur Bhuva Svah Tat Savitur Varenyam
Bhargo Devasya Dhimahi Dhiyoyo Naha Prachodayat
~ Oh Lord, You are the protector of life and of breath, dispeller of miseries and bestower of happiness. You are the creator and the most acceptable Intelligence. May your qualities and your inspiration pass to us. (This is one of the most widely recited mantras in India, where it is usually recited at sunrise and sunset.)

Om Namo Bhagavate Vasudevaya

Om Namo Bhagavate Vasudevaya, Om Namo Bhagavate Vasudevaya.

~ The mantra of Lord Krishna is chanted to remind us of all his wonderful teachings, which bestow happiness and spiritual realization and assure success in all undertakings.

SoHum

Sohum, Sohum, Sohum Shivoham;
Sohum, Sohum, Sohum Shivoham.

~ I am That, That I am; I am Lord Shiva Himself.

("That" is God. According to Sri Swami Kailashananda and the *Upanishads*, *Sohum* is the greatest of all mantras.)

Guru Chant

Jaya Guru, Shiva Guru, Hari Guru Ram,
Jagad-Guru, Param Guru, Sat-Guru Shyam.
Sri Guru Charanam, Sri Hari Sharanam.

~ Hail to the Guru -- the Guru is Shiva, Hari and Ram.

The Guru is the entire world's teacher who resides in truth and bestows auspiciousness. His holiness is our fortress and our protection.

Shiva Mahadeva

Shiva, Shiva Mahadeva, Namah Shivaya, Sadha Shiva;
Shiva, Shiva Mahadeva, Namah Shivaya Sadha Shiva.
Durga, Durga Mahamata, Namah Durgayei, Namo Namah;
Durga, Durga Mahamata, Namah Durgayei, Namo Namah.
Kali, Kali Mahamata, Namah Kalitei, Namo Namah;
Kali, Kali Mahamata, Namah Kalitei, Namo Namah.

~ Shiva, Shiva, great God; I bow to Shiva, true Shiva. Durga, great mother, I prostrate myself before you. Kali, great mother, I bow to you.

Chant For Willpower (By Sri Swami Sivananda)

Om Om Om, Om Om Om;
Om Om Om, Om Om Om.

Om Om Om, Om Om Om;
Om Om Om, Om Om Om.

Soham, Soham, Soham Shivoham;
Soham, Soham, Soham Shivoham.

Soham, Soham, Soham Shivoham;
Soham, Soham, Soham Shivoham.

Bhajo Radhe Krishna, Bhajo Radhe Shyam;
Bhajo Radhe Krishna, Bhajo Radhe Shyam.

I am that I am, I am that I am;
I am that I am, I am that I am.

I am not this body, this body is not mine;
I am not this body, this body is not mine.

I am not these emotions, these emotions are not mine;
I am not these emotions, these emotions are not mine.

I am neither body nor mind, Immortal Self am I;
I am neither body nor mind, Immortal Self am I.

Om Namah Shivaya, Om Namah Shivaya;
Om Namah Shivaya, Om Namah Shivaya.

Bhajo Radhe Krishna, Bhajo Radhe Shyam;
Bhajo Radhe Krishna, Bhajo Radhe Shyam.

Swami Kailashanda Affirmation

I am not this body, I am not this mind.	(3X)
I am witness of three states.	(3X)
I am knowledge absolute.	(3X)
God is truth, God is bliss.	(3X)
God is peace, God is knowledge.	(3X)
God is love, God is light.	(3X)
God is Bliss-Absolute.	(3X)

Bhaja Govinda

Govinda Bhaja Govinda;
Govinda Bhaja Govinda.
Radhe Radha Govinda, Govinda;
Radhe Radha Govinda, Govinda.
~ God, adore God!

Lokha Samastha Sukinoh Bhavanthu

Lokha Samastha Sukinoh Bhavanthu.
~ May all beings be free and happy.

Om Mani Padme Hum

Om Mani Padme Hum
~ I am the jewel in the lotus. (One of the main mantras used by Buddhists everywhere, it has a strong association with the Bodhisattva of compassion.)

Prayer Before Meals #1

Brahmarpanam, Brahmahavir, Brahmagnau,
Brahmanahutam, Brahmaiva Tena Gantavyam,
Brahmakarma Samadhina.

~ Brahman (God) is the oblation, Brahman is the melter. A butter (ghee) offering by Brahman is the oblation poured into the fire of Brahman; Brahman will definitely be reached by him who always sees Brahman in action.

Prayer Before Meals #2

Om Anna Poorene Sadhaa Poorne
Shankara Praana Vallabe
Jnaana Vairaagya Siddhyartam
Bhikshaam Dhehee Cha Paarvatee

Mataa Cha Paarvate Devee
Pitaa Devo Maheshwaraha
Baandhawaa Shiva Bhaktaahaa
Swadesho Bhuvana Trayam

Hari Om Tat Sat Brahmaarpanamastu
Lokah Samasta Sukinoh Bhavantu

Om, beloved Mother Nature, You are here on the table as our food, You are endlessly bountiful, benefactor of all; Please grant us health and strength, Wisdom and dispassion to find permanent peace and joy.

Mother Nature is my mother, my father is the Lord of All. All people are my relatives, the entire universe is my home.

I offer this unto Om, the Truth which is Brahman (universal). May the entire Creation be filled with peace and joy, light and love.

The Mantra For Fullness

Om Purnamadah Purnamidam,
Purnaat Purnamudachyate;
Purnasya Purnamaadaayah,
Purnamevaa Vashishyate;
Om Shanti, Shanti, Shantih.

~ Om, the world there is full; the world here is full; Fullness from fullness proceeds, After taking full from the full, It still remains completely full. (From *The Brhadaranyaka Upanishad* 5.1 in translation by Patrick Olivelle.)

Shanti Mantra (the Final Strophe)

Om Shanti, Shanti, Shantih.

~ Om Peace, Peace, Peace. (The final strophe of any number of Peace Prayers from *The Upanishads* is often used to bless and conclude Vedic rituals or consecrate the sacred practice of yoga.)

Pratyahara, Dharana and Dhyana

When you close the seven gates of the physical senses, you are then able to look deep inside at the great "I am" right at the center of the "house".
—Sri Dharma Mittra

Pratyahara or sensory-withdrawal is the fifth *anga* or limb of Maharishi Patanjali's Eight-limbed Path. *Pratyahara* is a natural outgrowth of regular practice of the previous two *angas*: *asana* and *pranayama*. *Pranayama*, in particular, is a great aid in the process of learning to control any reaction of the mind to sensory input. *Pratyahara* is literally emancipation of the mind from the senses. By following the path of Hatha Yoga, one automatically achieves *pratyahara* as the senses cease to chase after external objects and *prana* (rhythmic vibration or life-force) becomes king over the mind.

Through regular *sadhana*, the mind steadies, impurities are burned away and a firm foundation is established. The fascination with the outer world begins to seem less important than the eternal truth that dwells within. Sight is the strongest sense, and learning to work comfortably with the eyes closed for long periods of time in both long-held postures and during sustained breathing exercises begins to bear rich fruit. Learning to simply turn off the attention devoted to sensory imput is essential to move into the final three stages of Astanga Yoga: *dharana, dhyana* and *samadhi.*

Mouna (Observing Silence) The nature of most people's minds is to be ever active, like a monkey leaping from tree to tree. The trick to gaining mastery over this aspect of the mind is to be unconcerned with the thoughts that constantly rise and fade away. Through the seemingly simple act of keeping silent, energy is saved and stored within, and the Divine qualities of the Atma or soul begin to saturate the conscious mind as it begins to slow down. The psychic connection with all of creation strengthens beyond measure, and contemplation eventually becomes almost automatic. Through the practice of keeping silence, one can withdraw from the external noisy and restless world, and instead can be drawn closer to our real nature – the Real Self or Atma.

Mouna is a very flexible technique. You don't need to sit, you don't need a special place to practice it -- you don't even need to stop your normal activities. It is a practice that you can try either by yourself or in the presence of others. At first, you may wish to try it for one day during a weekend, then continue to engage in the practice on a regular basis, once a week or once a month. You will feel fresh and relaxed at the end of the day on which you maintain silence. Your relaxed mind will be able to fulfill the tasks of the week with accuracy and speed in a natural and spontaneous way. *Mouna* should be approached with a positive attitude and a clear sense of purpose. Only tension and frustration will result if it is undertaken through force or compulsion. If you experience some turmoil arising during the practice, don't worry -- a natural process of purification is taking place on the mental plane.

Dharana or concentration is the holding of attention on one point without break for a determined amount of time (about 12 seconds). Concentration (dharana) becomes meditation (*dhyana*) when it is sustained, without break, for 12 consecutive units of concentration (about two to three minutes). Please note that these time intervals were given by Swami Sivanada in an effort to give beginning practitioners some concrete guidance. In application, there are those who sit for the first time to practice concentration and in twelve seconds they are able to slip into a deep state of meditation. For most others, developing the ability to sit and focus the mind on one point without interruption demands time, patience and steady work. If one loses their steady focus during concentration, the interruption should not exceed three seconds within any single twelve second interval.

There are simple exercises to develop concentration such as gazing at a candle flame, observing the breath or concentrating on a mantra. A practitioner developing the ability to sustain *dharana* has awareness that he or she is the one engaged in the act of concentration; he or she is aware that the object of meditation exists, and also remains aware that the mind is taking action to induce concentration. There is always awareness of these three things – the mind, the object and the act of meditation in *dharana*. In meditation (*dhyana*), one eventually loses awareness of even the act of meditation. In *samadhi* (bliss-absolute), all of these things disappear and the sadhaka becomes the object. To discover the state of *dharana*, begin by concentrating on external objects. Later, when the power of the mind is harnessed, one can work through *pratyahara* (sense-withdrawal) with internal objects to go deeper into the states of *dhyana* and *samadhi*. Concentration is like poured water viewed under a strobe light -- each individual droplet is distinct from one another. Meditation is like poured oil in that even if viewed by strobe light, it pours in one continuous, steady flow.

What to Sit On The ancient ones discovered when sitting on the bare ground to attend to their sadhana that their minds were disturbed by the magnetic field and vibrations of the earth beneath. To insulate themselves from this, they would sit atop a tiger or deerskin laid out upon a mat of woven kusa grass. One can attain this same result today by sitting on a wool blanket or a rubber yoga mat.

Dharana Preparation and Seated Poses

The following positions for concentration and meditation practice are listed in increasing order of difficulty. Choose a comfortable position or just sit in a chair.

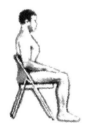

Egyptian Pose
Sit up straight and tall in a chair. Your hands should rest flat against the top of the thighs in *Jnana Mudra* (thumb and first finger touching). Rest the feet flat on the floor; the ankles may be crossed or not. Make sure you are comfortable, in a vertical position with the nape of the neck tall and the shoulders relaxed downward.

Sukhasana
Easily cross the legs while sitting on the floor. The knees are bent and the ankles are crossed. *Sukhasana* (Easy Pose) is sometimes called Indian-style or Cross-legged Sitting Position. One may

elevate the buttocks by sitting on a cushion if the hips are tight to make the pose more comfortable.

Vajrasana
Also called "Thunderbolt Position" or "Simple-Sitting Pose." This posture is comfortable for shorter meditation periods, and is the basic pose assumed by those who cannot sit cross-legged. Kneel on the floor and sit on the heels with the tops of the feet on the floor. To make it Thunderbolt, place the hands on the knees. Hands may also be clasped or in *Jnana Mudra*.

Virasana
"Hero Pose." Kneel with a pillow between the feet and sit on the pillow with the heels at the sides of the feet. Join the hands in some way to conserve your energy.

Sidhasana
"Adept's Pose." Cross the legs, place the right heel so it presses against the perineum and sit a bit on the side of the foot. Traditionally, the left foot rests atop the inside of the lower portion of the right leg or is tucked behind the back of the right knee. If this is uncomfortable, the lower part of the left leg may simply lie on the floor near the right. To make the pose even more comfortable, sit on a firm cushion. This pose is named for the adepts who have traditionally assumed it, as it is thought to help one achieve success in keeping the *yama* of *brahmacharya* (abstinence).

142

Padmasana

"Full Lotus" is the most beneficial seat for meditation. Sitting on the floor with the knees bent, place the right foot first by the left hip joint, then the left foot by the right hip joint with the lower left leg against and on top of the lower right leg. If your knees and hip joints are not flexible, simply cross the legs closer to the ankles. Then choose a hand *mudra* or position to lock in the energy. (Note that *Padmasana* is not always readily accessible to Western practitioners who have sat in chairs almost since birth. To work up to the full pose, practice bending alternate knees and rub olive oil into the knee which is bent.)

General Guidelines
for the Practice of Dharana

Observe silence and learn to speak only when absolutely necessary. Reduce watching TV and / or following the news. Choose to watch movies from which one can learn something spiritual. Try to cultivate the absence of fickleness, refrain from making nervous gestures and generally work toward an overall economy of movement. Be sure to get enough sleep, eat only light meals after 6 p.m. and try to go to bed on an empty stomach. If one is full of doubt, it is due to ignorance of reality. Invest in yourself by finding out about the essence of the Self through reading *The Bhagavad-Gita* and other essential holy books. Develop the ability to distinguish what is real from what is unreal. An overall state of calmness will be induced through an increase in spiritual knowledge, as gaining esoteric knowledge imparts a sense of calm independent of any other aspect of practice.

Dharana Techniques

Japa (recitation) of OM. Verbally, slowly repeat the sound of Om. You will be calling the name of God and employing the sacred, three-part syllable He most readily enters into, the *Pranava* (the Sanskrit name for the Om). You will be bathed in the high, spiritual vibrations of this sound or mantra, considered to be the highest mantra of all: it is the sound vibration that represents God. Start chanting as few as three Om's, and work-up to five minutes of sustained recitation. This practice will affect the heart rate and calm and quiet the senses. Combining *Japa* of Om with Calming Breathing or other soothing *pranayama* exercises is recommended for excellent results. (While chanting the *Pranava* aloud is wonderful, doing so in an undertone has even greater benefit. To hear the *Pranava* with the inner ear alone is thought to have a powerful effect on the physical and subtle bodies, as well as on the mind.)

Candle Flame Trataka. Place a candle three feet in front of you at eye level. It is important to practice this form of *trataka* or gazing in a room where the air is still so the candle flame will remain steady. (Please note that this form of *trataka* is distinct from the kriya or yogic cleansing technique described in that section of the manual.) Concentrate your gaze on the flame while keeping the eyelids slightly lowered. Gaze for one to two minutes at the flame, firmly capturing the image in your mind. Then close the eyes and try to re-experience the candle flame in your mind, clearly seeing it at the space between the eyebrows projected upon the movie screen on the inside of the forehead. As soon as the image of the candle flame fades, open the eyes again and re-capture it, like taking a picture. Beginners should practice this form of *dharana* for about five minutes or so. Once you become accustomed to this technique, the duration of practice can increase first to ten, and then to fifteen minutes.

Crystal Ball Trataka. Gaze steadily at a crystal ball. Then, after two to three minutes, try to experience the image with the eyes closed. Imagine that the eyelids are transparent and everything remains the same except that the eyelids are opening and closing. Mentally try to see everything you were physically observing when the eyes were open.

Beautiful Flower Trataka. This *dharana* technique is a form of *trataka*, but the object concentrated on is a beautiful flower. Observe with care every detail of the object: petals, colors, the various qualities of the flower. It is as if one were to take a picture of the flower, then view the picture just taken in the mind. By way of example, when one captures an image with a digital camera, one can see the picture captured right away, and then store it to view anytime. In this exercise, the eyeballs are the camera and the brain is the hard disc wherein the picture data is stored. The space behind the forehead is the LCD (the camera's small monitor where one may view the images captured and stored in the camera's memory).

Om Symbol Trataka. Use a picture or a statue of the Om symbol, the Sanskrit symbol for the *Pranava* as the object of contemplation. Continue gazing at the symbol and keep the image deep in the mind while considering the meaning of Om and what it represents. Close the eyes and draw the symbol and its meaning into the mind, then open the eyes again and gaze on the physical representation of the *Pranava* to cement the image. Then close again the physical eyes and retain a mental picture of the symbol along with its meaning. This practice will bring bliss-absolute by remembrance of the qualities of the omnipresent, omniscient and omnipotent; the All-Prevailing One: God.

Enlightened Being Trataka. For those who are more spiritually inclined, use the image of a Saint as the object of *dharana*. Or, if you know of an illumined Guru who inspires you, use that image. Gaze upon the image (which can be a picture of face, feet or full body, or a statue), and try to visualize it with your mind's eye. Then, gradually, just like channeling, try to feel the qualities of the enlightened being as you concentrate on his or her likeness. Of course, the Lord is formless. The eye, however, wants something tangible to gaze upon. You may choose Jesus, Ram, Shiva, Buddha, Krishna, Moses, Sri Swami Sivananda, Sri Swami Kailashananda or whomever you wish. In thought and action, seriously visualize or pretend that you are that being with all his or her Divine qualities. You will soon become one with the being -- the object of contemplation, and share in all of his or her wisdom.

Moon Trataka. The moon here serves as the object of concentration. This technique is recommended for people who are emotionally sensitive. The moon rules the sign of Cancer, a lunary water symbol. Look upon it in all its brightness and milky light. See its refection upon the ocean, if possible, and concentrate on the moon's qualities of steadiness, depth and calmness.

Sound Meditation. Sound now replaces the image or concrete form as the object of concentration with the mind solely becoming focused on information gathered through the ears, as opposed to the eyes. If you have access to a stream or river, listen to all the sounds as they merge into an eternal, unbroken Om. Or, focus on listening to the leaves in the trees rustling in the breeze; a waterfall; birdsong; or the rain falling upon the surface of a lake. Also, if it's quiet enough, one may simply listen to the sound of one's own breathing. Sit with the eyes slightly open or fully closed and fasten the mind to the sounds of nature. God is right there. (Note, one may also practice this form of dharana on a ticking clock or watch, a consistent recorded or live musical drone like that produced by a tamboura, or upon any consistent sound to which the ear is attracted.)

Walking Meditation. This *dharana* technique is practiced in India and throughout parts of Asia. The practice involves walking a little with the gaze just ahead of the feet and the hands together with the arms straight and loose in front of or behind the torso. One begins with the left foot, peeling it off the ground as slowly and deliberately as possible, the mind fascinated by every detail and sensation. The weight shifts to the right foot and the left foot eventually leaves the earth, travels in slow motion through space, and one part of the foot at a time regains the soil just ahead of the right foot. Without pause, the weight then shifts to that foot and the process repeats on the opposite side. To conclude after ten to fifteen minutes of deliberate, continuous motion, one brings the feet together and stands with the eyes closed for a few slow, steady breaths. As the mind becomes fully absorbed, the breathing slows and the thoughts die away.

Japa and Mantra Meditation with a Mala

A true, spiritual *mala* necklace has 108 beads (plus one), a number that is of special importance in a variety of spiritual traditions. The extra bead is the Guru, *Sumeru*, *Nehru* or Head Bead and, as the Guru stands supreme beyond the laws of time and space, this bead stands apart from the other 108 and is not counted. It is thought on a simplistic level that one gains knowledge of all 108 *Vedas* through the practice of *Mala Mantra Japa* (the practice of performing a complete set of 108 mantras as one moves each bead towards oneself, one at a time, to keep track numerically). 108 is the most sacred number in the entire Vedic system, as it is thought to be the number upon which the entire universe is based. Wrist *mala* are 27 plus one beads, so one must do four rounds of mantra on them to achieve the complete 108. Smaller necklaces have 54 plus one beads, and one must do two rounds of mantra on them to arrive at the requisite 108. In *Mantra Japa* on a *mala,* always begin next to the Head Bead. One method of *japa* on a *mala* is to use the thumb and middle finger of the right hand above the height of the navel, and to move the beads towards you, one-by-one. Repeat one mantra mentally for each bead. The beads are to be moved along by the right thumb and middle fingers in rhythm with the breathing as dictated by the subtle vibrations present in the mantra. Perform the action with devotion, dedicating each action to the form of *Isvara* or God to whom the mantra is directed, repeating the Holy name over and over. If one completes a round of 108 rosaries and wishes to immediately do another, simply turn the *mala* at the *Sumeru* bead and begin to count anew with the bead just counted. (At the height of Sri Dharma Mittra's practice, he would sometimes perform seventy rounds of *Mala Mantra Japa* a day.)

Complete rounds of *Mala Mantra Japa* are like money deposited in a spiritual bank account to be used, as needed, especially in an emergency. One may "save" and "bank" the latent power of undedicated rounds of mantra for future use. Say most for yourself in the beginning, and some you can give away. It is important to help yourself first -- then you will become strong enough to help others. This will help move you toward Self-realization. As the mind purifies, you will be able to understand more about the true nature of reality.

God is beyond explanation, and true knowledge of Him can only be imparted psychically to those who are pure in mind and heart. One can only understand through surrender to the Supreme Teacher within. By using the *mala* with a personal mantra, one establishes a psychic connection with the Guru. This is a private telephone number which may be "dialed" to call for help whenever the need arises. The Buddhists go to a special place and do mantras for world peace for all beings and creatures that are suffering. As their minds get purified through this action, they become one with the Buddha.

The practice of *japa* on a *mala* or rosary helps develop the ability to focus on meditation and prevent distractions from disrupting the steady flow of single-minded absorption. In the classical tradition, one recites silently their personal Guru Mantra with love and devotion as a way to honor and connect with the preceptor and gain spiritual benefit. One may also recite a general mantra, such as: "Om Nama Shivaya" or "Om Namo Narayanaya" to great effect.

A *mala* should never be placed on the ground, as it will immediately lose its charge as a result. After charging your *mala*, it is good to wear it, at least for a short time. A *yogi* should always have a *mala* around their neck or in their pocket according to Sri Swami Sivananda. In this way, the *mala* may function like a forget-me-not and spur the aspirant to remember their practice and always think of God.

There are many types of *mala* beads made from different types of wood, seeds and precious stones, each having special properties that subtly affect the subconscious mind. These materials have been infused by God the Creator with different medicinal, meditative and astrological benefits. In addition to the following, there are many other types of stones and beads used to form *mala*, such as red or white coral, pearls, lotus seeds, Hermatite and turquoise.

Sandalwood Beads are made from the wood of the rare sandalwood tree, currently becoming extinct. They are highly pure, *sattvic* and have a pleasant fragrant scent. *Japa* on sandalwood *mala* enhances calmness, a positive state of mind and supports meditation.

Rudraksha Beads are known as the "Tears of Shiva." They are holy seeds from a tree, and come in many varieties with different facets. The different varieties of *Rudraksha* beads possess varied healing properties. The Tears of Shiva are devotional in nature, and are used by those who worship Lord Shiva. The single-facet *Rudraksha* bead is considered the rarest, and can be very expensive. A four-facet *Rudraksha* helps with mental problems, memory loss and mental blocks. A five-facet *Rudraksha* protects the health and aids in digestion. It is a charm against poisons and destroys physical problems. The six-facet *Rudraksha* is beneficial in remedying blackouts, hysteria, mental problems and women's diseases.

Tulsi Beads are made from the wood of the holy basil plant which is *sattvic* in nature. *Tulsi* has a purifying and normalizing effect on the nervous system. It is revered as a sacred plant in India, and has an exonerated status in *Ayurveda*. Hindus view *Tulsi* as a goddess in the form of a plant, bestowed with great spiritual healing properties and powers. In India, each family home or garden still grows *Tulsi*. Devotional beads made of *Tulsi* wood are perfect for Karma Yogis involved in spiritual practice. The *Tulsi mala* is also favored by devotees of Lord Krishna.

Navgraha Mala or the Nine Planet Rosary has different precious and semi-precious stones that each represents one of the nine major celestial bodies studied in Vedic Astrology. The different stones summon beneficial forces to counteract any negative impact of the astrological bodies on the wearer. Performing *japa* on them and then wearing the *mala* afterwards is an even greater aid to warding off the negative impact of the planets upon your astrological chart. For general reference, the nine planets studied in Vedic Astrology are: *Surya* (Sun), *Chandra* (Moon), *Chevvaai/ Mangal* (Mars), *Budhan* (Mercury), *Guru/ Brihaspati* (Jupiter), *Shukra* (Venus), *Shani* (Saturn), *Rahu* (North Lunar Node) and *Ketu* (South Lunar Node). These nine celestial bodies do not all correspond to the nine planets in our Solar System.

Crystal Beads are usually made of crystal from the Himalayas. The beads are carved from the purest available crystal, and the high vibration of the composite material helps neutralize negative influences. They are naturally energizing

Rosewood Beads are a dark brownish-red and are good for improving circulation, strengthening one's aura and warding off negative energy.

Rose Quartz Beads are clear pink crystal beads associated with the emotions and the heart. They can be used to help reduce aggression and negativity, promote inner peace, love, compassion and aid with diseases of the heart, skin and circulatory system.

Citrine Beads are clear yellowish-gold beads that help the wearer attain psychic abilities, financial success and a positive outlook on life. There is a relationship between Citrine beads and the Solar Plexus and Mantra Mala Japa performed on a Citrine mala is thought to promote stomach and digestive health.

Dhyana

Press the nape of the neck back and all the nerves will fall into place along the spine. Try not to collapse.
Pretend you are Lord Shiva or Lord Buddha, and your face will change --
you will look serious!
The technique of imitation is applied by a yogi to gain complete knowledge.
For example, to find out how a monkey feels,
copy him physically as regards his body language.
As it is said: "Blessed are those who can copy the teacher physically.
Twice blessed are those who can copy the teacher physically and mentally."
During meditation practice, heat is generated.
You can go up into the mountains or some other cool place to find relief.
If the head gets hot, rub the top with oil.
—Sri Dharma Mittra

Dhyana is meditation. Everyone is different. Some can concentrate easily as a direct result of their spiritual progress in past lives. As one attains success maintaining concentration for two to three minutes, one enters the state of meditation and begins to identify with the object of concentration. The mind will subsequently enter a state of steady flow. This state of consciousness is continuous, like water flowing slowly from a gently tipping pitcher. After about thirty minutes of sustained *dhyana*, even the flow disintegrates into *samadhi*. The pitcher from which the water is poured falls into the vessel receiving the poured water, and there is no more distinction between the water in the pitcher and the water that was already poured. Over time, with constant practice and unwavering dedication, the Witness begins to emerge. One develops the capacity to stand outside the self watching and observing as the body eats, drinks, meditates, enjoys a movie and generally engages in the dance of human activity. Who is watching? The mind, of course. But, as one develops this capacity to stand apart while the mind and body are involved in the cycle of living life, one develops sensitivity to the fact that there exists something eternal and constant, separate and distinct from the body and mind. This ability to stand aside and observe is known as witness-consciousness.

Another fruit of deepening practice is the ability to achieve *ekagrata* or one-pointed consciousness. In daily life, the mind of most people is in constant motion like a monkey jumping from tree to tree. As one advances in *sadhana*, particularly in Raja Yoga, one develops the capacity to achieve and sustain *ekagrata*. Swami Sivananda cites the example of the scientist who bends the full force of his or her mind to the task he or she has set out to accomplish. *Ekagrata* is the state in which the scientist focuses single-mindedly on the task at hand. The best way to realize one-pointedness is to focus all of the attention at the space between the eyebrows. "As the physical eyes close, the Spiritual Eye opens and the light of truth shines forth."

General Guidelines for the Practice of Dhyana

Meditate in a positive place which is clean and free of clutter. Light incense to purify the Astral plane and recite the Mantra for Purification. It is best to have a corner in the house reserved for concentration and meditation. Do not practice *dharana/dhyana* in the kitchen, as thoughts of food may arise in the mind and disturb practice. A church, temple, synagogue or shrine is an excellent place to practice, as it is a place where people come to pray, and the associated devotional vibrations infuse every nook and cranny. It is best to meditate at the same time every day. Later, with practice, one should be able to concentrate any time one desires. To insure success in *dharana/dhyana* when practicing with seed or focusing on an external object, chose one that attracts the mind. Work with an object for 30 consecutive days. If there is limited or no progress during this time, switch objects for the next 30 days. If at all possible, meditate for four sittings a day: one during the "Hour of Brahma," one at midday, one in the late afternoon and one more an hour before retiring for the evening. Start with five to ten minutes at each sitting. The best time to do *sadhana* is between 4 and 6 a.m. This two-hour period is known as *Brahmamuhurta*, or the Hour of *Brahma* and is the most sattvic time of day. The mind is calm upon waking, and one slips easily into meditation. Do not think that sleep is being sacrificed, as meditation imparts far greater benefits than sleep.

(A photographer who observed the rooms of Buddhist monks in Thailand documented that there were no beds in the cells, only a square platform just big enough for sitting. These particular monks never slept. Instead, they spent their time in a constant state of meditation, meditating from ten to twenty hours a day. Because these monks meditated constantly, they did not require much sleep.)

The more one practices, the faster progress is made. It is entirely due to the great effort applied to Hatha Yoga *sadhana* that one will achieve success in meditation. Through being able to sit quietly for a long time, every answer will be revealed. Through *samadhi*, one will come to realize immortality. When eternal awareness is realized, one merges with all, and all is God. Upon this realization, real sadness wells up for the loss of enjoyment in the mind and the senses. This grief is short-lived. When the mind realizes it does not have support anymore in material quests, it will turn exclusively to spiritual truth.

In life, whenever one tries to attain something, one encounters obstacles. Personal karma, habits and health problems get in the way. Just like when Moses went to the desert and heard voices that spoke of temptations, the mind devises tricks. If one makes a decision to fast and just read the scriptures for 30 days, the mind will play tricks during that time. The tendency of the mind and senses is to want only pleasure. The mind is so powerful, it will discern a little headache so that one can start to make excuses for not practicing. One might say: "I'll start in the New Year" over and over. Then the New Year passes, and one is still over-indulging and generally carrying on as before. One feels that one cannot stop and change behavior, and delays the decision until their birthday. In a short time, it's the new millennium. So it goes as you continue to do the things you do not really choose to. One acts automatically due to past habits. Then one day, you are 80 years old and it is too late. It is best to make a contractual promise. Write and sign the document, then give the promise to someone in whom you believe to help insure that you stick to your word and follow through with right action.

Dhyana Techniques

Eternal Question Meditation. Sit comfortably and ask an important question such as: "Who am I?", "Is there re-incarnation?" or "What is eternal?" This form of *dharana/dhyana* can be practiced at all times: while riding the bus or walking down the street. If the question is reflected upon with sincerity and great faith, every answer will be revealed.

Positive Quality Meditation. Fix the mind firmly on a quality essential to one who yearns to achieve *moksha*, or liberation. Choose a quality such as reverence, steadfastness, devotion, humility, patience or compassion. Bring the entire intellect to bear as you seek single-mindedly to try and understand every aspect of the chosen quality. Like the Eternal Question Meditation exercise above, this process can be initiated anytime, anywhere, and the fruit of knowledge will help to bring one ever closer to the goal.

Third-Eye Meditation. Sit comfortably and bring all of the attention to the space between the eyebrows. This area is known as *Trikuti*, the Third Eye or the Seat of the Mind. You may see brilliant lights, colors, mental images and/or be visited by Divine visions. One may become intoxicated -- stuffed with spiritual bliss. Remain unconcerned, and maintain a steady, inner gaze fixed on the space between the eyebrows behind the forehead.

Focusing all of the attention here will stimulate the Pituitary Gland, which controls the Sixth-Sense, deep in the brain. In this way, one eventually activates the Yogic Sixth-Sense, drawing closer to achieving Divine Perception.

Spiritual Heart Meditation. Bring all of your attention to the center of your chest, the right side of the heart, your spiritual heart. Dive deep within the cave of your Self, and become one with God. At the moment of creation, a portion of God became part of every living creature. Go within and really try to feel God's presence at the heart center. Really see the Divine Spark glowing in the spiritual heart. If you can't initially see it there, pretend for as long as is needed until it is revealed to you.

So-Hum Meditation. Sitting comfortably with the eyes closed, bring all of the attention to the breath. Listen for or imagine that during every inhalation the sound "So" is heard, and within each exhalation, the sound "Hum." So is already an integral part of each inhalation and Hum is an organic part of each exhalation. *Sohum* is Sanskrit for "I am that, that I am" -- the "that" being God, the Supreme Self. *Sohum* is the greatest of all mantras, as it is already contained within the breath of all living creatures. Human beings unconsciously recite this mantra some 21,000 times every day. So, concentrate on the breath, but leave it by itself as in deep sleep. Always remember the meaning of the mantra: "I am you, you are me," and feel as though you are face-to-face with God. Surrender all ego and become one with God.

Study of the Self. Sit comfortably and watch the mind. Leave the body by itself, and leave the breath by itself. Witness the thoughts that rise like bubbles of gas in liquid and remain unconcerned as they float to the surface and pass away. Observe all the activities of the mind and their effect on the body and the senses. Who is watching? The mind, of course. This is a very powerful form of concentration / meditation that is prescribed by Lord Krishna to Prince Arjuna in *The Bhagavad-Gita*. One can spend an entire day reflecting in this manner, drinking mainly green juices and holding a private retreat from the world. It's better than a trip to India or bathing 1,000 times in the Ganges, and you don't have to spend time and energy traveling anywhere.

The highest state of meditation is samadhi
where there is no "I" or ego anymore.
No doubts, no "me", no "you", no notion of time,
no eating, no talking, no walking, no working and not doing anything at all,
except realizing that the Self is action-less.
—Sri Dharma Mittra

Samadhi and the Fourth State

After reaching samadhi, *you are like a dry leaf moving in the wind.*
Imagine a dreamless sleep-state when the mind has stopped.
The mind has to do with the personal state
that disappears along with doubts, pain and suffering in deep sleep.
You realize that the reality we conceive of as real is not real.
Only the great "I am" consciousness is real – the Self is real.
All of nature, this play of life which includes both suffering and pain
has the purpose of purifying the mind.
One goes beyond the five bodies and beyond the bounds of time.
Whatever you see seems subject to time – even the gods who evolve
as part of creation exist for a time then pass away along with everything else.
All that truly remains is the great "I am."
—Sri Dharma Mittra

Samadhi is the eighth and final step of Patanjali's Eight-Limbed Path wherein there is absorption with the object or subject of contemplation (the object of meditation and the mind focused on it have merged). Imagine a bubble floating in the air, and that the air both within the bubble and outside of it is all God. The bubble bursts, and there is no longer any distinction between the air that was within the bubble and the air outside. This is *samadhi* -- a level of consciousness induced by deep meditation.

The great sages Vyasa and Patanjali outline three stages or depths of *samadhi*:

Laya Samadhi is the latent, potential level of *samadhi* that begins in deep meditation. This is a joyous and peaceful state and can be recognized when one feels spiritually inspired after meditating. During this first stage of *samadhi*, the mind remains aware of the action of meditation, the object of meditation and the meditator.

Savikalpa Samadhi (Formative *samadhi*) is the initial, temporary state of full *samadhi*. The conscious mind is still, but the self has not fully surrendered its desires. There remains a degree of self-awareness, which is an erroneous identification with the little self, rooted in the material world. In this second stage of *samadhi*, the mind remains aware of the action of meditation and of the object of contemplation, but any awareness of the meditator him or herself has fallen away.

Nirvikalpa Samadhi (Formless *samadhi*). There are no more "forms," because the mind is finally under control. Upon entering *samadhi*, the differences among objects and people of the material world have faded and everything becomes one. In this state, nothing remains but pure awareness. Just before attaining this state, there is great sadness, as one must let go of everything cherished to this point. Even the idea of God and Guru are discarded, as they are still rooted in name and form. In this third stage, only the object remains. No one can locate "you" anywhere, as you are now everywhere. All that remains is the Fullness, as you become one with everything.

When the Mind Settles Into Silence

Turiya is the fourth state of consciousness after waking, dreaming and deep sleep. We learn in *The Yoga-Sutras* of Patanjali that yoga is the settling of the mind into silence. All these beautiful techniques, all this theory and philosophy have been developed to bring us to that place where we move beyond *all this*. "All this" embraces the material world of name, form and time that we experience through the vehicle of the mind and its appendages, the senses. It is the mind that meditates and the mind that experiences the bliss of *samadhi*. There is no true knowledge of the Absolute until the mind is perfectly still. Then we have the chance to discover what we truly are.

Many in the West experience yoga merely as the physical postures. Yoga is really so much more. It is a complete series of Divinely -realized techniques designed to give the practitioner direct knowledge of God. Patanjali uses the term *Isvara* for God, which is wonderful as this term can function like a blank space to be filled in by the seeker. If the practitioner sees God as Shiva, Jesus, Buddha or Allah, then this is what Isvara can come to mean to them. They can cultivate such essential qualities as reverence, love and devotion by dedicating every action to their *Ishta-Devata* while slowly coming to understand that what God really is, is beyond name, form or time. This is exceedingly hard to grasp, as we live in a world of name, form and time, but don't worry. As you advance along the path, you will come to be less concerned with name and form and, perhaps, even less bound by time.

Imagine that the entire world as we know it is constructed upon the spinning blades of a propeller. After the mind has been purified through steady observance of *yama* and *niyama* and one has realized the Supreme Self or God while still embodied, it's as though one steps off the speeding propeller and stands in stillness while still endowed with awareness of the meditator, action and object. One watches the blades of the propeller turn, recognizing the true nature of the entire mechanism and the force that drives it, immediately becoming aware of the fact that the blades can't be seen anymore due to motion or illusion. One then realizes that the only reality is that Fullness beyond motion, forms and names. This is the state of *samadhi* just before *Nirvana Samadhi*, the final, highest *samadhi*, when the physical body perishes. The embodied soul and the mind experience exceeding bliss from that point forward, and this is just a touch of that Fullness. After the fall of the body (death or *Nirvana Samadhi*), one steps-off the propeller altogether and stands supreme in stillness, instantly merging in that Fullness. All that remains is Fullness -- one without second, beyond duality. This is far beyond enlightenment.

There are many dedicated students who achieve a small taste of the bliss and it is remarkable to note how that mere taste affects their practice and their life. In the beginning, it is but a brief taste -- a few shining, perfect moments. Over time, it can come to last for days on end. The final step is one that few will take, as it involves taking leave of everything, even the teacher, concept of God and the construct of self. In this letting go, there is great sadness. What remains is this great "I am," which is omniscient, omnipresent, omnipotent and without limit. Then one's body and mind become like a dry leaf moving in the wind. As in a dreamless, sleep-state, the mind is stopped, and that which is gained can never be lost. This has been called *Turiya* or the Fourth State, and is beyond waking consciousness, sleep with dreams or deep, dreamless sleep. It is that state where, with the mind stopped, all is revealed. Embarking upon this journey requires patience, devotion and surrender. Find someone who has some experience who can guide you and dedicate yourself to practicing every day without fail. Become established in the *yamas* and *niyamas*, be nice to everyone and dedicate the fruit of every action to the Almighty One. In doing these things, you will already be well on your way.

Guidelines For Developing
a Personal Practice

Yogis that take the search for freedom into the innermost part of their soul
are called sadhakas.
Surrender to Isvara *(the Lord) is a certain path.*
Realize that God is already within -- The Spiritual Sun already blazes within.
God abides as the Antaratma – *the Innermost Self.*
Harmony between you and the Lord within is the destination.
—Sri Dharma Mittra

These guidelines are intended for someone with limited time each
day that is seeking to build into their lives a regular practice that will
over time move them toward realization of the Supreme Self. For
these suggestions to prove effective, they must be combined with
scrupulous observance of *yama* and *niyama* and the fruit of every
action should be offered to the Lord. Remember also that your
meditation will go nowhere if you are involved in any way with
violence. So, if you are still consuming the flesh of our inferior
brothers and sisters of the animal world or practicing cruelty towards anyone, stop all this as soon as possible and begin to make
real spiritual progress. Then every action will be even better than
meditation and you will surely achieve radiant success in yoga.

If you can engage in *sadhana* only once a day, the ideal time for practice is between 4:00 and 6:00 a.m. Most important is to choose a time that works for you and your schedule so you are sure to practice each day and are able to attend to your other duties. Try to practice on an empty stomach – three hours after a full meal and one hour after a light snack at a minimum. (One may always add to these bare bone instructions if there is additional time available on a given day.) Be sure to drink fresh green juices every day, eat light food (fresh juices, fruits, salads) if at all after 6:00 p.m., try to match action to that which is thought and said, and be nice to everyone. Om *Shanti, Shanti, Shantih.*

Kriya: drink warm water with fresh-squeezed lemon juice upon arising in the morning. It can be sweetened with a little raw honey, raw agave nectar or pure maple syrup, as needed.

Bless the Practice: bow to the Lord and ask for blessing. Chant three Om's, loud and long with your whole heart. If you know it, do the Mantra for Purification.

Asana: perform seven rounds of *Surya Namaskara Vinyasa* or one round of *Surya Namaskara Vinyasa* and one of *Shiva Namaskara Vinyasa* to warm up. Then, do Headstand, Shoulderstand, Fish, a Back Stretch (Forward Bend), Cobra, Bow and a Spinal Twist (the essential skeleton of the Dharma I-IV *asana* sequences).

Relaxation: do ten minutes of Deep Relaxation in Corpse Pose.

Pranayama: two rounds of *Kapalabhati* is recommended for those that live in cities and ten minutes of Alternate-Nostril Breathing is recommended for everyone everywhere.

Dharana/Dhyana: spend at least five minutes practicing seated concentration/meditation. Watch the breath and focus the inner gaze at the space between the eyebrows.

*If there is additional time, study *The Bhagavad-Gita*, *The Yoga-Sutras* or *The Hatha Yoga Pradipika* and / or do *mantra japa* with a *mala*. Once you've mastered the Psychic Development sequence, do it twice a week for it to have an effect, and try to do at least ten minutes of Karma Yoga each day. And, above all else, be receptive to the grace of God.

168

Deep Relaxation

Lie now like a corpse.
Relaxation is the best antidote for impurities.
Leave the body by itself, leave the breath by itself, and rest.
Let the body rest completely.
If the body rests completely,
there is the chance that you might lose body consciousness
and have the chance
to lose all body awareness, moving beyond the body, beyond the mind.
—Sri Dharma Mittra

Guided Dharma Deep Relaxation

Deep Relaxation is most often practiced at the end of asana practice, but it can be done as a practice unto itself. Deep Relaxation is done in *Shavasana* or Corpse Pose, lying on your back with legs and arms straight, the feet relaxed slightly to the sides a little wider than the hips, the arms slightly away from the sides with the palms facing up and the eyes closed. This practice should be done for 20 minutes daily, but ten minutes is what most can manage and should be the absolute minimum. Relaxation of the muscles is as important as focusing on their development, and it is a balance of the two that brings one to a state of radiant health. Even just ten minutes of Deep Relaxation with the thoughts and breathing slowed almost to the point of stopping can be as restorative as a good night's full rest. Deep Relaxation is the best antidote for impurity. It dispels tension and fatigue in the physical body and relieves depression, anxiety, headaches, cravings and desires. Deep Relaxation rejuvenates and energizes the entire system, bolstering the body's natural healing capacities and helping to normalize the circulatory system's function. When done regularly and with pure intention, one departs from the body and crosses over into *Yoga Nidra* or Psychic Sleep, briefly experiencing the Astral Plane. Through this deep practice, one can gradually come to recognize that they are so much more than the body or the mind.

Once one has assumed *Shavasana*, one relaxes the body in stages, directing the focus of the mind to one unique area at a time with about five to fifteen seconds devoted to each region or specific body part. Sri Swami Kailashananda (Sri Dharma's Guru) always led with the left side first when teaching asana (with the exception being Spinal Twists, when we always twist right first). We, in turn, follow his example in both practice and teaching. Sri Dharma often concludes the verbal portion of Deep Relaxation with a guided visualization to relax the mind, using specific images that have associated colors. This has the added bonus of being a Color Meditation, which clarifies and strengthens one's Color Body or Personal Aura.

The following is an example of the manner in which Sri Dharma often guides students in the practice of Deep Relaxation. It is approached in this order to sequentially relax the different parts of the physical body.

• Left foot: left big toe, the next toe, middle toe, next toe, little toe, ankle, calf, knee and thigh.

• Right foot: right big toe, the next toe, middle toe, next toe, little toe, ankle, calf, knee and thigh.
• Relax the pelvic region.

• Everything below the waist, dead-like -- no sensation.

• Left hand: thumb, index, middle, ring, pinky, palm, wrist, forearm, upper arm and shoulder.

• Right hand: thumb, index, middle, ring, pinky, palm, wrist, forearm, upper arm and shoulder.

• Entire back sinking down.

• Abdominal region, loose.

• The chest, loose, but light -- not heavy.

• Suggest to the internal organs to relax: the lungs, heart, liver, kidneys -- then all the rest.

• Relax the neck and scalp.

• Relax the face: forehead, eyebrows, eyelids, cheeks, nose, upper lip, lower lip, chin, throat, ears and the brain.

• Now remain absolutely still.

• Leave the body by itself now; leave the breath by itself.

• Observe the body as in deep sleep. Keep watching the body in deep, dreamless sleep.

• Go within your heart and become one with God.

• In the meantime, let the body rest.

Relax for eight to ten minutes, as time permits.

The following is an example of the manner in which Sri Dharma guides students in the practice of Deep Relaxation when there is less time available. There is a pause made after each instruction is offered:

1. Lie on your back – we're going to relax now.
2. Left hand, arm, shoulder.
3. Right hand, arm, shoulder.
4. Left foot, leg, knee and thigh.
5. Right foot, leg, knee and thigh.
6. Your back, heavy.
7. Abdomen and the chest.
8. Neck and face.
9. Leave the body by itself now.
10. Try to find your Self inside – where are You?
    (silence for an additional five plus minutes)

Prepare to Come Out: Start to notice again the breath, the face, the hands, arms, feet, legs and the rest and stretch, as needed. (The Great Stretch is when one reaches the arms overhead, hands clasped, legs together or ankles crossed.) Pull and stretch the body out, lengthwise in both directions. One may turn the body to one side, rest in a fetal position, and then slowly come to a seated, meditative pose.

During Deep Relaxation, the mind is ever-vigilant, always aware as one hovers somewhere between sleep and wakefulness. Some people who are not well-rested will occasionally move into true sleep during this time in *Shavasana*. This is incorrect. Softly touching their feet will bring them back to the task at hand without startling them or disturbing their neighbors. It is important upon returning from a period of Deep Relaxation to stretch and move gently so that the transition to a seated position is effected without returning to the state one was in prior to practice. Ideally, one returns from an experience of Deep Relaxation feeling deeply refreshed and rejuvenated. Deep Relaxation is a practice that must be a part of the daily routine of anyone committed to the path of Self-realization.

* These are four examples of music that Sri Dharma Mittra plays softly while guiding the students in this practice:

Pachelbel Canon in D Major

Roads of Blessing: Vajra Chants "Offering Chant" by Lama Gyurme and Jean-Philippe Rykiel

Clarinet Concerto in A, K. 622 Second Movement, Adagio by Wolfgang Amadeus Mozart

The Divine Gypsy: Instrumental Arrangements of Selections From Paramahansa Yogananda's Cosmic Chants "They Have Heard Thy Name" by Monks and Lay Members of SRF (not used during the past few years)

Teaching a Dharma Yoga Basics Course

Move stiffly, like a beginner.
—Sri Dharma Mittra's request
of advanced students of *asana* when he asks them
to demonstrate a yoga position for the class.

Preparation: The best way to prepare to teach a Basics series is to be as comfortable as possible with the series and the poses it contains. Even if your daily practice has included other level series, you would do well to do at least the *vinyasas* daily until you no longer have to think about the sequence or which variation of each posture is part of the series. A teacher cannot take students any farther than she or he has personally ventured, so, as a teacher, you owe it to your students to teach from your experience.

Always dedicate the fruit of all action and remember that you are not the doer!
—Sri Dharma Mittra

Opening Session: Dress neatly and wear a clean Dharma Yoga shirt. Light an incense stick to purify the space and chant the Mantra For Purification prior to commencing any transmission of yoga. Help the students to set up their mats with appropriate spacing in the yoga temple or studio. Begin by introducing yourself briefly, being sure to include your experience with the sacred science of yoga and connection to Sri Dharma Mittra and Dharma Yoga. Then you may ask the students to introduce themselves, briefly stating their exposure to yoga and reason for taking the six-week course. After everyone has spoken, methodically guide them on how to find a comfortable seat with a straight spine, the shoulders back and down, the chest open, the eyes gently closed and a relaxed expression on the face. Explain that they will be breathing almost exclusively through their nose and that their mouth will remain closed throughout the practice to follow. Direct them to maintain attention on slow, rhythmic breathing with attention to the present moment.

Before chanting the three Om's with your new class, take a few moments to explain what the *Pranava* is and why it holds such a prominent place in Vedic culture. Explain how to shape the lips so that the sound begins with "Ah," moves almost immediately to "Oh" and the final third (the best part) decrescendos gradually into silence on "Mmm." Tell them that the Om should be loud and long and sung or chanted with enthusiasm.

Ask the students to come to *Pranamasana* at the front of their mats, and briefly explain what *Surya Namaskara Vinyasa* is and why we begin practice with it. Guide them through a complete cycle, taking time to demonstrate, explain and assist each posture. It is good to give each posture's Sanskrit name immediately followed by the English translation. Remember when demonstrating that it is important to demonstrate in a way that the students can absorb and imitate. Sri Dharma often asks advanced students demonstrating for him in his classes to: "Move stiffly like they are a beginner," so that the beginners in the class can understand and re-create what they're seeing. Also, move slowly and gracefully in and out of any asanas you demonstrate and the students will copy your actions as directed. If you are demonstrating, show how to go in, maintain and come out of a complete posture.

After you have completed *Surya Namaskara Vinyasa*, give the students a few breaths in *Pranamasana* so they can observe the effects of this opening *vinyasa* series. Then give a few sentence overview of Sri Dharma's *Shiva Namaskara Vinyasa*, and break down and teach the series in the same manner as the classical Sun Salutation.

If it is an hour-long class, one may need to move immediately to Deep Relaxation, *pranayama* and *dharana* at this point, possibly skipping pranayama. If one has an hour-and-a-half or more, one may be able to cover some of the stationary asanas in the first session, being sure to skip ahead to *Sukha-Ardha-Matsyendrasana* as the final pose before Savasana. It is crucial to budget eight to ten minutes for Deep Relaxation, regardless of your overall timing. Deep Relaxation is the practice which will prime your students for concentration and, later, meditation, and really begin to cultivate in them receptivity, the hallmark of our lineage. Be sure to refer closely to the script provided in this manual for guiding Deep Relaxation as Sri Dharma seldom deviates from its overall format and it is a complete practice. As with leading the posture series, be sure to give a brief explanation of Deep Relaxation, *pranayama* and *dharana* as you present them. Instruct the students to look at you while you lead them through the opening round or two of the breathing exercises as some new students will struggle to form the *mudras* or have difficulty discerning right from left. Close class with one Om followed by three *Shanti's* exactly in the manner received from Sri Dharma.

Closing: At the close of the first session, always instruct the classes to consider viewing this six-week commitment as a daily affair, and suggest that they choose at least one thing that spoke to them during the class and practice it each day for at least ten minutes. It would also be beneficial for them to view the spiritual discourses on Sri Dharma's Level I *Maha Sadhana* DVD. Tell them that this will greatly enhance their experience of Dharma Yoga, since "The secret to success in yoga is constant practice." At the conclusion of the succeeding sessions, give a brief explanation of some aspect of the classical philosophical or ethical precepts. Be sensitive to the class and what their needs appear to be. You may always tell the students that you will be available for a few minutes after class if anyone has any questions. People generally are grateful to have the opportunity to receive additional information to support their practice.

After the final two classes of the series, it is good to offer advice as to next steps after the six-week Basics course concludes. This is a question especially eager students will come to you with by the third week, so it's a good idea to have thought through the answer in advance of the question. For some students, moving into a regular Dharma I class will be the ideal follow up to a Dharma I Basics course. Others may benefit from taking another six-week Dharma I Basics course or may be ready to pursue a Dharma II Basics course if one is available to them.

Assisting: For some, assisting comes naturally and to others, physically assisting students can be a great challenge. It is of great importance to recognize that a true beginner will find certain *asanas* difficult and proprioception (the ability to sense the position, location, orientation and movement of the body and its parts) may not come easily to them. Gently reminding the students to look at you when you demonstrate once in a while, and inviting them to watch each other and try to move together, will often bring the class into *sangha* (community of like-minded individuals) -- sometimes even in the opening session. When physically assisting, recognize you want to help the student find their best version of the posture for their body, and not force them into your ego-driven ideal of where you think they should be. The main focus should be on helping them find a version of the posture that allows energy to move more freely throughout the physical and subtle bodies. If you are blessed to be teaching a large class, you may not always be able to fix everything all the time. Keep mental track of what you see and try and work your way through the class as you can, always keeping in mind that next week is another chance to help the students move forward.

The Divine Mood: The Scriptures state and Sri Dharma often reminds us that yoga needs to be practiced in *bhava* -- the Divine mood or state. Keep this very much in mind when selecting music for your class, setting the lighting if that is within your control, and by allowing yourself to be a vessel for the teachings to pass through. We all have personalities and experiences that shape who we are and influence the manner in which we transmit the sacred science of yoga, but it is of paramount importance that we recognize that teaching should never devolve into performance. There are sometimes external pressures when we are auditioning for a job in teaching these classes or if we are being paid based on the enrollment numbers, but it is crucial to trust in the inherent value of the teachings themselves, and the fact that these series evolved out of over four-and-a-half decades of Sri Dharma's personal practice and long-time teaching experience. Regarding music, be sure that your selection of material and personal taste do not overshadow the crucial role music can play in enhancing or detracting from the journey inward. In doing *sadhana* and leading others, we seek to come face-to-face with God. If this is what we attempt, then the music should aid this endeavor. Be sure, also, that the volume level is low and the tempo of the music fits the overall sense of quietude we are trying to create. According to Dharma-ji: "Traditionally, yoga was practiced in silence, but in India, there might have been the sound of a flute playing somewhere in the distance as one practiced." Consider this when making your musical selections or organizing your play-lists.

Lighting can also enhance the atmosphere, but please be aware that Sri Dharma does not favor students practicing in the dark in a class setting. During the daytime, natural light is ideal, if available. In the evening, make sure that if the light is soft, it still allows all students to see without strain or effort.

Week Two and Moving Forward: In the second week, one moves through the opening and *vinyasas* with a little less verbiage and a little more speed. This will allow more time for the stationary poses that follow the *Shiva Namaskar Vinyasa*. Be sure that whatever poses you add, there is still time for the appropriate counter-poses -- and always move to *Sukha-Ardha-Matseyendrasana* before *Savasana*. An example would be doing *Shiva Namaskara Vinyasa* then the stationary postures through *Matsyasana* then skipping to *Sukha-Ardha-Matseyendrasana*, and concluding with *Savasana*.

Depending on the make-up of your class, you will probably be able to run through the entire series by week four, provided you move through the opening *vinyasas* at a reasonable pace. One may still review posture directions and make corrections at this time. Speak less in successive weeks of each six-week series. Give the students the opportunity to focus more inside and distract less from that process.

Week 1: *Vinyasas, Vrkshasana - Matsyasana,*
      then skip to *Sukha-Ardha-Matsyendrasana.*
Week 2: *Vinyasas, Vrkshasana – Sukha-Purvottanasana,*
      then skip to *Sukha-Ardha-Matsyendrasana.*
Week 3: *Vinyasas, Vrkshasana - Parsva Savasana,*
      then skip to *Sukha-Ardha-Matsyendrasana.*
Week 4: Entire series, as written.

The Final Class: It's great if you can leave a few minutes at the end of the final class to form a seated circle in the center of the room close together. You may want to lead them through three rounds of the Mantra for World Peace (*Om Namo Narayanaya*), introducing and presenting it first, followed by the Om and three *Shanti's*. Then take just a few minutes when they are particularly receptive to urge them to make this six-week session the beginning of something wonderful for the rest of their lives. Urge them to make daily *sadhana* a fixed and vital part of their life.

Dharma Yoga Basics II follows the format of Basics I in that one begins by teaching the *Shiva Namaskara Vinyasa* in detail the first week and little time is usually then available to cover many of the stand-alone postures. It is important to again skip to *Ardha-Matsyendrasana* after whatever free-standing poses you do get through, even over the next few weeks. Depending on the students, you may wish to modify certain poses or offer easier variations. *Vrkshasana*, for example, seems quite beyond some beginning students, and telling them that they can experiment with the raised foot on the side of their calf or ankle or that they may support themselves against a wall is a welcome accommodation for those that are struggling.

Week 1: *Shiva Namaskara Vinyasa.*
Week 2: *Shiva Namaskara Vinyasa, Vrkshasana - Sirshasana,*
    skip to *Ardha-Matsyendrasana.*
Week 3: *Shiva Namaskara Vinyasa, Vrkshasana - Matsyasana,*
    skip to *Ardha-Matsyendrasana.*
Week 4: Entire series, as written.

(Note: If time permits the first week, one may teach *Sarvangasana, Halasana* and *Matsyasana* out of sequence just to start building these crucial postures into the students' vocabulary as early as possible. In week 2 if time is short, skip around to bring in this series including *Sirshasana* in this way, as well. By week 3, it's usually possible to include it within the class as written.)

In offering any spiritual words at the conclusion of class, be receptive to the needs of the students. Students clearly thrive on brief introductions to the core concepts of *The Bhagavad-Gita, The Yoga-Sutras* and *The Hatha Yoga Pradipika.* However, with other groups it's more appropriate to leave them in silence at the conclusion of the formal class. It's always important to be sensitive to the specific needs of each group.

In Conclusion: Spend some time thinking about what it means to attempt to lead others to Divine Union before you teach your first class. Dharma Yoga is more than just a system -- it is a holistic approach to the holy science of yoga with the ultimate objective of drawing those you teach to God. If you are a seasoned teacher in a different style, you may have to consider what taking on this new method will require you to give up. If you are relatively new to teaching, you have the easier task of just learning the series as best you can and of working to always copy the teacher as you now begin to teach yourself.   Do your best to be above reproach in your conduct both in and out of the yoga studio, school or temple, and try to strive ever to be receptive to the grace of God.   In this way, you will come to serve others with a pure heart, without ego and with the simplicity and earnestness born of thinking, speaking and acting always on the truth.

Hand-Drawn Charts

Om. May we practice yoga so that our bodies and minds are purified.
O Luminous One, may we find a Guru (spiritual preceptor),
hence to receive the right guidance and knowledge.
O Imperishable, Incomprehensible, Infinite One (Brahman),
may we cross (by Thy Grace) this ocean of birth and death.
May detatchment be our boat and strength (acquired by the practice of yoga),
be our speed (of the boat) and the Guru be our guide,
Thy light, our destination. Thus, safely we cross this ocean (of pain and delusion)
and get home again. May we never leave home again. Hare Om.
—Sri Dharma Mittra
from the Sun Salutation Yoga Course Chart

Sri Dharma Mittra has been involved with artistic creation on my many levels throughout his life. At the Yoga Gupta New York Center, Sri Dharma was asked to create drawings to illustrate a book by his Guru called *The Third Eye* that, unfortunately, was never published. In the 1970's when Sri Dharma had a school near Carnegie Hall, he spent a considerable amount of time and energy creating individualized course charts for his various students at the time, so they could make rapid spiritual progress. He also created charts and posters to help everyone better understand basic Yogic concepts. On the following pages appear a few examples.

You go as far as you can imagine.
—Sri Dharma Mittra

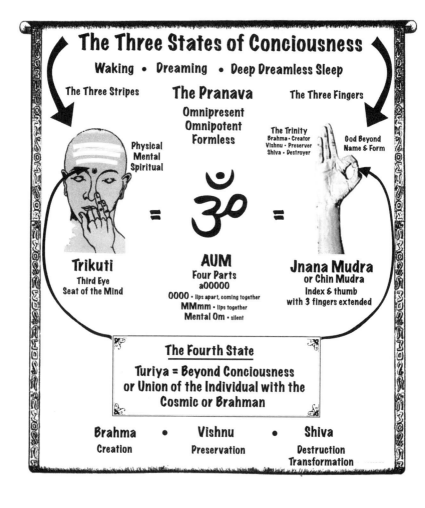

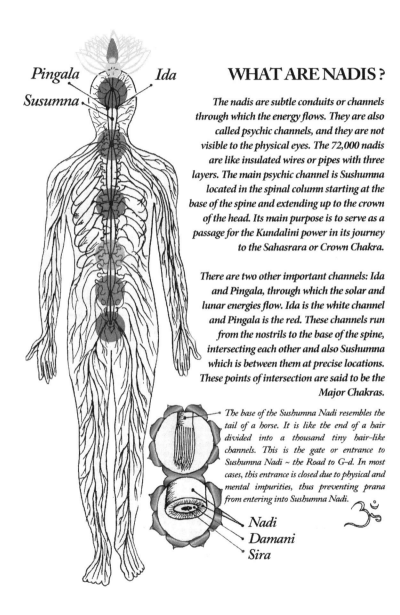

Pingala Ida

Susumna

WHAT ARE NADIS ?

The nadis are subtle conduits or channels through which the energy flows. They are also called psychic channels, and they are not visible to the physical eyes. The 72,000 nadis are like insulated wires or pipes with three layers. The main psychic channel is Sushumna located in the spinal column starting at the base of the spine and extending up to the crown of the head. Its main purpose is to serve as a passage for the Kundalini power in its journey to the Sahasrara or Crown Chakra.

There are two other important channels: Ida and Pingala, through which the solar and lunar energies flow. Ida is the white channel and Pingala is the red. These channels run from the nostrils to the base of the spine, intersecting each other and also Sushumna which is between them at precise locations. These points of intersection are said to be the Major Chakras.

The base of the Sushumna Nadi resembles the tail of a horse. It is like the end of a hair divided into a thousand tiny hair-like channels. This is the gate or entrance to Sushumna Nadi ~ the Road to G-d. In most cases, this entrance is closed due to physical and mental impurities, thus preventing prana from entering into Sushumna Nadi.

Nadi

Damani

Sira

Sitting Positions
for Breathings and Meditation

YOGA ASANA CENTER

egyptian pose

Choose any of these:

1 — EASY LOTUS
2 — HALF-LOTUS
3 — FULL LOTUS
4 — CHAIR

5 — SIDDHASANA
6 — HERO

JNANA MUDRA

A PILLOW MAY BE USED

(NOT IMPORTANT) WOOL BLANKET

KUSA-GRASS DEER SKIN
NOT IMPORTANT

TIGER SKIN

Of course! The skin is from animal that naturaly died —

The spine must be extremely erect and in a vertical position.
If available, a wool blanket or deer skin over a kusa grass or a tiger skin should be placed under, in order to diminish the magnetic earth currents that tend to pull the mind to material perception.
— Most yogis don't use them —

How to Handle the nostrils

RETENTION

1 — THESE FINGERS REST HERE OR THEY MAY BE FOLDED. SEE ILLUST 3.

2 — BOTH NOSTRILS BLOCKED

3 —

4 — THUMB
2ND FINGER

5 —

Right Hand

Mudras-Bandhas

ABDOMINAL LIFT 3

RAISED LOTUS 5

MAHA MUDRA 2

CHIN-LOCK 7

Their main purposes are to unite Prana and Apana, and the Bandhas to seal their union. Here are the main Mudras: 1 - Yoga Mudra, 2 - Maha Mudra, 3 - Uddiyana Mudra (abdominal lift), 4 - Sirsasana, 5 - Tolasana, 6 - Baddha Padmasana, 7 - Jalandhara Bandha, 8 - Uddiyana Bandha, 9 - Mula Bandha (anal cont.).

BANDHAS - Techniques

Chin-Lock (Jalandhara Bandha)
To be observed during inhalation, retention and exhalation. Lower head and gently press chin against the breast bone just between the collar bones.

Abdominal Contraction (Uddiyana Bandha)
To be observed during retention after exhalation. With lungs completely emptied, pull abdomen back toward the spine and suck or pull it up by using the diaphragm muscles. Get the feeling that the abdominal organs are being pushed up in the chest region.

Anal Contraction (Mula Bandha)
To be executed during retention after or before inhalation. Here the region between the anus and the navel are contracted including the anal muscles. The pranayamas described ahead require the application of the Jalandhara and Mula Bandhas only.

Jnana Mudra
To purpose of this mudra may be to prevent the dissipation of the body's vibrations. The index finger represents the individual soul and the thumb the universal soul; their union represents knowledge. The others fingers symbolize the three states of life: Creation, Preservation and Transformation (or it may be Destruction). Techniques: Just join the tips of index and thumb, then extend the others (fingers together)

HEAD STAND 4

6

BADDHA PADMASANA

ABDOMINAL CONTRACTION

8

1 **YOGA MUDRA**

JNANA MUDRA

Glossary of Key Terms

Abhyasa: perseverance.

Adhara: support, prop.

Adho-Mukha: face-downwards.

Agni: fire personified; the god of fire. Symbolic of the digestive fire located at the height of the navel and corresponding to the Manipura Chakra.

Agnisara Dhauti: literally "purging by cascading the fire." One of the six Kriyas, Agnisara Dhauti consists of a rapid series of abdominal lifts or Uddiyana Bandha. This technique builds great heat (Tapas) in the body while it strengthens the muscles that support the viscera. The heat is a result of impurities burning away in the abdominal area.

Ahamkara: ego, sense of "I".

Ahimsa: "non-harming"; the first Yama or restraint of Patanjali's Astanga Yoga system. Showing respect to all creation; not harming any being by action, word or thought.

Ajna Chakra: "Wheel of Command." Also known as Trikuti or the Third Eye, Eye of Shiva, the Seat of Wisdom or the Seat of Command. It corresponds to the nerve plexus between the eyebrows and is the sixth major Chakra or energy center along the Sushumna Nadi. Lord Shiva is usually depicted with the Third Eye open to indicate his Divine Sight.

Akasha: where everything begins; the origin of all creation. Subtle beyond perception, it is activated by Prana and can assume names or forms that can be perceived by the seer. Also referred to as ether, space and openness.

Alamba: supported.

Anahata Chakra: "Wheel of the Un-struck (sound)." The fourth major Chakra or energy center, located near the spiritual heart along the spine.

Ananda: bliss.

Anandamaya Kosha: the fifth sheath, the "Body of Bliss"; a perfect reflection of the True Self or Atman.

Ananta: endless.

Anga: limb, point.

Angustha: the big toe.

Annamaya Kosha: the grossest of the five sheaths, the physical aspects of the body.

Antara Kumbhaka: breath retention after inhalation.

Aparigraha: "non-hoarding," the fourth Yama or restraint of Patanjali's Astanga Yoga system.

The Aranyakas: the Aranyakas are sometimes called the "Forest Texts," because ascetics retreated into the forest to study the spiritual doctrines alone, or sometimes with their students. The Aranyakas were transitional between the Brahmanas and the Upanishads, in that they still discuss rites and have magical content and some hymns from the Vedas, as well as the early speculations and intellectual discussions that flowered in the Upanishads.

Asana: "seat" or "comfortable position." The third of Patanjali's Eight Limbs of Yoga. The word originally referred only to the various sitting positions for meditation. In Hatha Yoga, it has come to embrace all the various physical postures and their variations.

Ashram: A spiritual community of like-minded individuals generally organized around a specific person or ideology. The residents of an Ashram typically live under a cooperative economy or are supported by donations from the larger community outside.

Ashrama: often reduced to Ashram in modern Indian languages, Ashrama refers to any of the four stages in the ideal life of a classical Hindu namely: Brahmacharya, Grihastha, Vanaprastha and Sannyasa.

Ashta: eight.

Astanga: "Eight limbs", the eight "parts" or "stages" into which Maharishi Patanjali divided Yoga when he traveled throughout India about 200 B.C.E. Patanjali studied everything he could that went by the name of Yoga, then prepared a treatise presenting a structural and functional analysis of the techniques and philosophy that came to be known as the Yoga-Sutras.

Astanga Yoga: Eight-Limbed Union; the Eight-Fold Yoga of Patanjali consisting of moral discipline (Yama), self-restraint (Niyama), posture (Asana), breath-control (Pranayama), sensory inhibition (Pratyahara), concentration (Dharana), meditation (Dhyana), and ecstasy (Samadhi) leading to liberation (Kaivalya).

Asteya: "non-stealing", the third Yama or restraint of Patanjali's Astanga Yoga system.

Asvini Mudra (Aswini Mudra): the "Seal of a Horse" or "Gesture of a Horse". A rhythmically repeated contraction and release of Mula Bandha (root lock) used to strengthen the anal sphincter muscle in preparation for applying this Bandha.

Atharva Veda: the final Veda, Atharva, is in a different category than the previous three. For a long time, many referred to only the first three Vedas by which complete ceremonies could be conducted using the Rig for reciting, the Sama for singing and the Yajur for performing rituals. The Atharva Veda is composed of hymns containing magic spells and incantations. The line between prayer and magic, and between black and white magic, was usually drawn by ethical considerations, as the spells were used with both light and dark intentions. The Atharva Veda is associated with Atharvan, a famous fire priest who is remembered as having been a master of magical rituals.

Atman: the initial Sanskrit root is "At" meaning "to move" and the second root "An" means "to breathe" or "to live." Atman is "the breath that moves" or the "moving spirit." In other words, a living, breathing, moving being or person. In everyday speech, Atman simply means "person" or "self" in the same way they are used in English. In the esoteric language of India used in Yogic scriptures, both in a religious and philosophical context, the word Atman refers to the Self in a way similar to the English concept of spirit or soul. Neither the word spirit nor soul properly conveys the meaning of Atman, as there is no direct counterpart in English. Atman is the essence of each person as distinguished from their form and name.

Aum (Om): the Pranava. The mystical syllable which represents, among other things, all that is, was and ever shall be.

Avidya: ignorance of who we are; the first of the five Kleshas (obstacles) and the greatest of all impurities.

Ayama: length, expansion, extension.

Ayurveda: the Vedic science of sacred health or medicine considered to be an outgrowth of the esoteric knowledge contained within the Atharva Veda (the textual authority underpinning Ayurveda). Yoga and Ayurveda have always been closely aligned, but Yoga has been more concerned with physiology (both gross and subtle), while Ayurveda is more concerned with pharmacology (both magical and scientific).

Baddha: bound.

Baka: crane.

Bahya Kumbhaka: breath retention after exhalation.

Bandha: "to bind" or "tie back". In Yoga, the word refers to the various muscular contractions or locks used to retain breath containing Prana or energy within a given area of the body.

Bandha Triya: the "Triple Lock," consisting of Mula Bandha, Uddiyana Bandha and Jalandhara Bandha, performed together so as to seal off the upper and lower ends of the Sushumna Nadi, forcing Prana into the Manipura Chakra where it is purified and prepared to be sent up the Sushumna Nadi to the Crown Chakra. This process is also known as "Raising the Kundalini". The goal of performing this lock is that Shakti (the female principle) which resides as the coiled serpent Kundalini at the Root Chakra can perform in union with Shiva (the male principle) at the Crown Chakra where it rides the great white swan of the liberated Self.

The Bhagavad-Gita: the Bhagavad-Gita is the essence of all Vedic knowledge and is thought to have been composed by the sage Vyasa, the legendary author of the Mahabharata. The Bhagavad-Gita is primarily a dialogue between Prince Arjuna (the third Pandavas brother) and Lord Krishna, his charioteer and an avatar of God. Krishna, who is the uncle and friend of the Pandavas, gives Arjuna the teachings of Yoga, offering-up a vision of how to achieve Divine Union with God. The Bhagavad-Gita's central teaching is to the point: to be alive means being active and, if we want to avoid difficulties for ourselves and others, our actions must be benign and beyond the grip of ego.

Bhakti Yoga: one of the Nine Forms of Yoga, characterized by ecstatic celebration and worship of the Divine particularly through the medium of Kirtan, Mantra-Japa, Puja and intense faith.

Bhastrika Pranayama: Breath of Fire; Bellows Breath.

Bheka: frog.

Bhuja: shoulder; arm.

Bhujanga: serpent, cobra.

Bija: seed.

Bindu: "seed" or "point"; the creative potency of anything where all energies are focused. The Third Eye.

Brahma: God the creator. His divine consort is Saraswati, the goddess of learning and knowledge. Brahma is usually conceived of by Hindus as a bearded, four-faced, four-armed deity. The four faces symbolize that Brahma is the source of all knowledge necessary for the creation of the universe. The four arms represent the four directions and thus represent the omnipresence and omnipotence of Lord Brahma. The white beard denotes wisdom and its length conveys the idea that creation is an eternal process. The crown on the head of the Brahma implies that he has supreme power and authority over the process of creation. Brahma is also a symbol of the individual mind and intellect. Brahma's major work of creating the universe being essentially finished, he is not much interested in human affairs and therefore is neither widely nor devoutly worshipped.

Brahmachari: a "student of God." In practice, it means "one who is celibate."

Brahmacharya: The first Ashrama or stage of life in classical Indian thought, embracing the years of childhood, learning as a student and apprenticeship. Brahmacharya is the fifth Yama or restraint of Patanjali's Astanga Yoga system.

Brahman: the root "Brih" means "to grow, increase or expand". The root "An" means "to breathe or live". Brahman is the "spirit" or "breath" which expands. The "life principle" which has "expanded to become an entire universe." The Vedas speak of the day and night of Brahman, referring to the unfathomably long periods of time during which this Universal Life Principle is either manifest (like now, being the "Day of Brahman") or un-manifest (like before The Big Bang when there was nothing except a singularity; when the entire universe was shrunk to less than the size of a neutron, known as the "Night of Brahman"). According to the ancient texts, this cycle goes on forever. Ninety-five percent of the universe is not matter like we see around us, but is matter that can't be seen or "ether". It's of a type that mystifies astronomers and cosmologists. Two-thirds of this is apparently an even more puzzling type of matter known as "dark energy" which is thought to be responsible for our universe's accelerating growth. Brahman is also sometimes used as a variant of Brahmin.

The Brahmanas: the Brahmanas were written as prose expounding and systemizing the Vedic rituals and their accompanying mythology. Their limited focus of justifying the priestly actions in the sacrifices restricted the themes of these first attempts at "imaginative" literature and the demise of the caste system. Nevertheless, the Brahmanas do give us information about the social customs of this period and serve as a transition from the Vedas to the Aranyakas and the mystical Upanishads.

Brahmin: priest. Also, the priestly caste.

Buddhi: intuitive intelligence.

Chakora: a type of bird: a Greek Partridge.

Chakra: "wheel"; the "wheel of a wagon". According to the wisdom of Yoga, a Chakra is an energy center within and around the body which clairvoyants perceive as spinning like a wheel. The Seven Major Chakras run from the base of the spine to the crown of the head and occur wherever Pingala and Ida Nadis intersect with the Sushumna Nadi. According to Yoga philosophy, the life-force or Prana of the body activates these centers. If any of the Chakras are over- or under-energized, there is disharmony or disease within the body. One can then be said to be "out of balance". One of the principal aims of Hatha, Kundalini and Tantra Yogas is to keep these Chakras "well-tuned" and in balance so that Divine energy can manifest through them. Each major Chakra represents a state of consciousness.

Chalana: to churn.

Chandra: the moon.

Chandra-Surya-Kumbhaka Pranayama: "Moon-Sun-Holding Breathing Exercise." The main breathing exercise, a form of Alternate Nostril-Breathing with holding.

Chatur: four.

Chin Mudra: "Consciousness Seal." A hand gesture in meditation which is formed by bringing the tips of the index finger and the thumb together, while the remaining fingers are kept straight. A synonym of Jnana Mudra (Seal of Knowledge).

Conch: a large seashell which, when cleaned and properly blown into, acts as a primitive, single-toned wind instrument and is used in both Vedic rites and in the context of those who practice Yoga to announce auspicious occasions. The sound that emanates from the conch is the sound of the sacred syllable Om.

Danda: staff, stick.

Devanagari: The script classically used for writing Sanskrit.

Dhanu: bow.

Dharana: the act of holding or "firmness," meaning "to hold one thought firmly in the mind." Dharana is the sixth limb of Patajanli's Astanga Yoga system and is understood as "concentration" in this context.

Dharma: "Bearer"; a term signifying "law", "virtue", "righteousness" and "duty". Bearer and upholder of the laws, both Divine and worldly; duty to participate in the Divine plan for humankind's higher evolution.

Dhauti: to wash. One of the six cleansing duties (Shat Kriyas) outlined in both The Hatha Yoga Pradipika and The Gheranda Samhita. Swallowing and retracting of a milk or water-soaked length of cloth or gauze.

Dhyana: meditation, thought or reflection. The seventh limb of Patanjali's Astanga Yoga system. Whereas Dharana (concentration) is simply holding one thought in mind, Dhyana allows the mind to expand or reflect on that one thought. Dhyana is concentration without interruption.

Drishthi: gazing point; the unmoving point upon which the Yogi fixes his or her attention. Some are external like a spot on the ceiling, while others are internal such as the space between the eyebrows or the very base of the spine.

Dukkha: affliction.

Dur: difficult.

Durga: represents the power of the Supreme Being that preserves moral order and righteousness in the world. The Sanskrit word "Durga" means "a fort" or "place of refuge" that is protected and difficult to reach. Durga, also called "Divine Mother", protects mankind from evil and misery by destroying evil forces such as selfishness, jealousy, prejudice, hatred, anger and ego. A tiger symbolizes unlimited power and Durga riding a tiger indicates that She possesses unlimited power and uses it to protect virtue and destroy evil.

Dwi: two.

Dwi-Hasta: two hands.

Dwi-Pada: two feet or legs.

Eka: one.

Ekagrata: one-pointedness.

Ganda: the cheek or side of the face, including the temple.

Ganesha: God representing the power of the Supreme Being that removes obstacles and brings success in human endeavors. Because of this, he is worshiped first before beginning any religious, spiritual or worldly activity. Lord Ganesha is the first son of Lord Shiva and the Divine Mother Parvati. He is usually depicted as having the head of an elephant and the body of a man. The large head of an elephant symbolizes wisdom, understanding and a discriminating intellect that one must possess to attain perfection in life. The large elephant ears signify that a perfect person is the one who possesses a great capacity to listen to others and assimilate ideas. The mouse often sitting at Lord Ganesha's feet indicates that a perfect person is one who has conquered his or her ego. It is also the vehicle of Ganesha signifying that one must control ego in order for wisdom to shine forth.

Garbha: infant.

Garuda: eagle.

Gheranda Samhita: "Gheranda's Compendium" was written during the 17th century C.E., and is still one of the three major surviving classical treatises on Hatha Yoga. Like many early writings on Yoga, the written text is little more than a set of instructor's lecture notes, covering only the highlights and leaving the rest to be filled in orally or by actual demonstration. The Gheranda Samhita consists of 351 verses divided into seven sections as follows: Shat Kriyas (6 categories of hygiene and purification techniques making for a total of 20 techniques), Asanas (32 physical postures described along with their benefits), Mudras

(20 physical Mudras and Bandhas; 5 Dharana-Mudras describing purely mentally focusing on the Chakras), Pratyahara (a short section on retraining the mind to ignore sensory input), Pranayama (8 breathing techniques with instruction regarding the use of Kumbhakas, Chakra focal-points and application of Mudras), Dhyana (5 meditation techniques), and Samadhi (the 6 variations of mental absorption).

Go: cow.

Gorakhnath (Gorak, Goraksha, GorakhNath or Gorakhnata): a disciple of Matsyendranath (Matsyendra) and an early exponent of Hatha Yoga. Goraksha is credited with founding Laya or Kundalini Yoga, as well as Hatha Yoga. Specifically, he founded an order called the "Kanphata Yogis," which is founded on the principles of Hatha Yoga and which survives to this day. Gorasksha and Matsyendra were both famous Yogis who lived sometime between the 9th and 12th centuries of the Common Era. Little is known about them historically, because soon after their deaths, their accomplishments quickly blended with myth, folklore and magical invention to the point of virtual deification. Gorakhnath is known to have authored innumerable works including The Goraksha Shataka, a conversation between himself and his teacher, Matsyendra. This text survives in translation, but not in the original Sanskrit. Hatha Yoga was lost except for brief passages included in The Hatha Yoga Pradipika of Svatmarama. This later work is now the oldest significant surviving manuscript on Hatha Yoga.

Goraksha: cowhead.

Granthi: psychic knot.

Granthi Mudra: lock performed by placing the palms together and interlacing the fingers.

Grishastha: "householder." The second Ashrama or stage of life in classical Indian thought. It encompasses the years of homemaking, earning a living and supporting a family.

Guna: "Strand." Energy that underlies and defines all phenomena on the material plane is always defined or under the sway of one of the three Gunas according to the Bhagavad-Gita. The three Gunas are: Rajas (fiery activity), Tamas (inertia) and Sattva (contentment, calm, equanimity, equipoise, purity). One of the great goals of Yoga is to become established in Sattva.

Guru: "He who is heavy or weighty." A spiritual teacher; the one who sheds light on the path's dark places.

Hala: plough.

Hamsa: "swan." Lord Shiva rides a white swan at the Crown Chakra when Kundalini Shakti and Shiva Shakti unite there. The swan is a symbol of the Divine Spirit or Liberated Self.

Hamsa Mantra (Hamsa Japa): the continuous chanting of Hamsa. If the word Hamsa is repeated rapidly, it becomes indistinguishable from Sohum being chanted rapidly. Taken together, they mean, "I am that swan or liberated spirit."

Hanuman: the giant, flying monkey who assists Lord Rama in his battle with the demon Ravana to rescue his kidnapped wife Sita in the Indian epic of The Ramayana. Hanuman embodies the qualities of a devotee to Lord Ram: knowledge, physical and mental strength, truthfulness, sincerity, selflessness, humility, loyalty, devotion and worship of the Supreme Lord. Hanuman is seen as the ultimate Karma Yogi and many followers of the modern Indian saint Neem Karoli Baba believe him to have been an incarnation of Hanuman.

Hanuman Chaleesa (Chalisa): a forty verse Bhajan or hymn in Hindi attributed to Tulsidas extolling the virtues of the monkey-god Hanuman.

Hasta: hand.

Hatha: the syllable "Ha" represents the sun and "Tha" represents the moon. Bringing together both the sun and moon is the path of Hatha Yoga. Ha and Yang both represent the masculine or solar polarities, while Tha and Yin represent the feminine or lunar polarities. The term Hatha Yoga refers to the integration of opposites into a more complete union or whole. The word Hatha can also mean "forceful," and this is probably the original sense in which it was applied to the new form of Yoga promoted by the likes of Matsyendra and Goraksha centuries ago.

Hatha Yoga: in India during the Middle Ages, Hatha Yoga and Tantra Yoga branched out separately from their common, ancient roots which extended back to the advanced, yet essentially prehistoric, Indus Valley Culture of 3000 B.C.E. Hatha Yoga represented an existential, ascetic approach which postulated that integration with the Divine could be more quickly or "forceful-ly" obtained by a person living a solitary, ascetic life of celibacy and seclusion. Most of the Yoga postures familiar to Western-ers are part of the Hatha Yoga tradition. Technically, the term means, "Self-integration through the union of opposites". Hatha Yoga aims to eliminate any false sense of duality between the practitioner and Universal spiritual reality or Brahman. The mindful performance of physical postures (Asanas), specific breathing modifications (Pranayama) and other techniques are thought to aid in the process of body, mind and spirit integration. Tantra Yoga developed in sharp contrast to the Yoga hermitage and wandering ascetics common to Hatha Yoga. Tantrikas (practitioners of Tantra) typically approached the integration of polarities either as householders (i.e.: couples living together and enjoying all of life's pleasures, joys and comforts (Right-Handed Tantra)) or in other, more exotic liasions (Left-Handed Tantra).

Hatha Yoga Pradipika: this 14th-century text written by the sage Svatmarama is the oldest significant surviving manuscript devoted specifically to the exposition of Hatha Yoga. Earlier texts all describe material that predates the foundation of Hatha Yoga which was not established as a separate form until sometime around 700-1000 C.E. One earlier text written by Gorakhnath himself and called simply Hatha Yoga was available in Svatmarama's day, and parts of it are reproduced in his Pradipika. The Hatha Yoga Pradipika consists of 390 verses divided into four sections: Asanas, Pranayama, Mudras and Samadhi.

Hindu Deities: Hindu deities represent different aspects of the Supreme Being in the form of gods and goddesses. Hindu worship of deities is monotheistic polytheism, as it is believed there is only one Supreme Being: the "God" of all religions. It is understood that the Supreme Being has three tasks: creation, preservation and dissolution for the purpose of recreation. These tasks are associated with the Hindu Trinity: Brahma, Vishnu and Shiva. Lord Brahma brings forth the creation and represents the creative principle of the Supreme Being. Lord

Vishnu maintains the universe and represents the eternal principle of preservation. Lord Shiva represents the principle of dissolution and recreation. Brahma, Vishnu and Shiva are not three independent deities, but represent three different aspects of the same truth.

Ida: "Channel of Cooling." One of three primary currents of life-force or Prana which circulate in the body. Representing the left side of the body, the negative current associated with the cooling energy of the internal moon travels along the left channel (Ida) criss-crossing the major Chakras along the spine. The Ida current corresponds with the parasympathetic nervous system. One seeks to draw the energy of the Ida and Pingala Nadis and redirect it up the Sushumna Nadi.

Ishta-Devata: the name and form of God with which one personally identifies with.

Ishvara: God; the term used for Him/Her by Patanjali in his Yoga-Sutras.

Ishvara Pranidhana: "Surrender to God". The fifth Niyama or observance of Patanjali's Astanga Yoga system.

Jala: water.

Jala Dhauti: a Kriya or cleansing duty which involves drinking a glass of warm lemon water first thing in the morning to help induce defecation and stimulate the liver to produce bile.

Jala Neti: Kriya wherein warm saline is generally poured into one nostril from a Neti Pot with the head at an angle and allowed to exit either through the other nostril or the mouth.

Jalandhara Bandha: "Cloud" or "Web-Lock"; it is used to prevent the premature upward movement of the Prana Vayu and to redirect it back down to the Manipura Chakra where it can be transmuted and sent up the central Sushumna Nadi.

Japa: "Repetition"; constant mental or verbal practice of recitation of a name of God or Mantra.

Japa Yoga (Mantra Yoga): one of the Nine Forms of Yoga, Union is achieved through repetition of a Mantra.

Jathara: abdomen, stomach.

Jivan-Mukta: one who has achieved immortality (Self-realization).

Jivan-Mukti: "Spiritual liberation". Jiva means "life" and Mukta means "liberation". Jivan-Mukti is liberation from the cycle of birth and death while still living.

Jnana Mudra: a hand gesture in which the tip of the index finger touches the tip of the thumb. The symbol or "seal" of knowledge; the sign of the initiate.

Jnana Yoga: one of the Nine Forms of Yoga by which the practitioner achieves Self-realization through the vehicle of the intellect. Study of sacred texts is a main feature of this path and the accumulated wisdom helps illumine Supreme Truth.

Jyotish: Yogic system of Astrology.

Kalpa: "Ageless" or "timeless". An immense period of time equal to one thousand ages or "Yugas". A Kalpa is designated as "one day of Brahma," and said to measure the duration of the world (being one thousand Yugas or 4,320 million human years).

Kapalabhati: "Skull-Shining Breath." A process of sharp, quick exhalations immediately followed by automatic, complimentary inhalations that clears the sinuses. Kapalabhati is both a Kriya and a Pranayam.

Kapota: dove or pigeon.

Kali Mudra: "Seal of Kali." The palms and index fingers of both hands pressed together with all the other fingers interlaced.

Karma: "Action." In the west, Karma is often misunderstood to mean what happens to us as a result of our actions. This is backwards. Phalam (fruit) is what happens to us as a result of our actions. Karma is our actions. It is what we do, not what we get back. Karma (action) is the law of cause and effect and Karma is the cause of resulting effects or Phalam. Karmas are of three kinds: actions of the body, actions of speech and actions of thought.

Karma Yoga: method of Yoga founded upon selfless-service. Through constant service to humanity, aspirants purify their hearts, eventually wiping clean the Karmic slate. Selfless-service is the vehicle that leads to Self-realization on this path of devotion.

Karna: ear.

Kevala Kumbhaka: spontaneous or intuitional breath retention independent of inhalation or exhalation.

Khechari Mudra: "Seal" or "Gesture of Moving into the Void". An intense form of tongue lock, this energy seal requires months of gradually cutting the frenulum linguae or lower tendon of the tongue so that the tongue can actually extend back and up into the root of the nasal cavity. Note: Khechari Mudra is NOT recommended for householders. Instead, the Nabho Mudra is recommended, as it only requires turning the tip of the tongue up and backwards as far as possible. The tongue's capacity to stretch gradually increases with regular practice. Khechari Mudra is sometimes used either with or instead of Jalandhara Bandha (chin lock) to reverse the upward-moving Prana Vayu and send it back downwards to be heated and re-energized at the Manipura Chakra. In some texts, the term Khechari Mudra refers to a combination of the tongue lock and the eye lock (Sambhavi Mudra).

Klesha: "Obstacle". According to Patanjali, they are five in number: Avidya (ignorance of your own Self), Asmita (egoism), Raga (attachment), Dvesha (aversion) and Abhinevesha (fear of death).

Kosha: "Sheath" or "Subtle Body". The True Self is thought to be hidden beneath five sheaths.

Krishna: the eighth incarnation of Lord Vishnu. Krishna's contributions throughout his life include the teachings of The Bhagavad-Gita to Arjuna. He was born around 3200 B.C.E. in Vrindavan into a family of cowherders. His childhood playmates were Gopas (cowherd boys) and Gopis (cowherd girls) who were greatly devoted to him. Of all the Gopis, Radha loved Krishna the most. The Gopis' love signifies the eternal bond between the individual soul and God. The dance of the Gopis and Krishna signifies the union of the human and Divine. Krishna is one of the most beloved and widely worshipped avatars of God in India today.

Kriya: "action", "intention", "undertaking", "activity" or "process". In Yoga, Kriya refers to any one of the six categories of hygiene and purification processes known collectively as the Shat-Kriyas or the "six cleansing-actions". Actually, there are about 20 different Kriyas because there are several specific techniques included under each of the six categories. Each is described in detail in The Gheranda Samhita.

Kriya Yoga: one of the Nine Forms of Yoga, this approach is Tapas, Svadhyaya and Ishvara Pranidhana.

Krouncha: heron.

Kukkuta: rooster, cock.

Kulpha: the ankle.

Kumbhaka: "like a pot" or "like a chalice." Kumbhaka is retention of the breath. The breath may be held after inhaling (Antara Kumbhaka), after exhaling (Bahya Kumbhaka) or automatically at any point in between (Kevala Kumbhaka). In Yogic breathing where the focus is placed on the sacred breath (Prana), we encourage the body to become a sacred "chalice" of this Divine "fluid".

Kundalini: the Divine "serpent energy" resting or sleeping at the Muladhara Chakra. This energy is stimulated by Yoga practices and can be raised to pierce the major Chakras along the Sushumna Nadi to the "Thousand-Petaled Lotus" at the crown of the head (Sahasrara Chakra). This is the goal of most physical Yoga paths.

Kundalini Yoga: one of the Nine Forms of Yoga; an intense form that places emphasis on powerful Pranayama techniques to heat up the body, which in turn is believed to awaken the sleeping Kundalini Shakti that resides at the base of the spine. Some say that Gorakhnath founded both Hatha and Kundalini Yoga. This is possible, since the two are so similar to one another, except in the details, which may well have developed over centuries from a common form.

Kunta: spear, lance.

Kurma: tortoise.

Lakshmana: symbolizes the ideal of sacrifice in the Indian epic of the Ramayana. Lakshamana leaves his young wife behind in the palace to accompany his brother Rama in exile. He sacrifices his personal life to serve his elder brother.

Lakshmi: the Hindu goddess of wealth and prosperity, both material and spiritual. The word "Lakshmi" means "goal," and represents the goal of all life, which includes worldly, as well as spiritual prosperity. Goddess Lakshmi is the Divine spouse of Lord Vishnu, and provides him with wealth for the maintenance and preservation of the creation.

Lalata: forehead. Also the name of a Chakra.

Laya Yoga: Laya means "absorption" or "dissolution" of the mind. A variant of Kundalini Yoga and one of the Nine Forms of Yoga, Laya Yoga awakens the latent power of Kundalini Shakti, causing it to rise from the Muladhara Chakra to the Ajna Chakra or beyond, thus dissolving the (conscious) mind and giving birth to the supra-conscious state of Samadhi or Turiya. Also, the "Yoga of Absorption" into the sound-current (Nadam), a.k.a. Nada Yoga.

Lingam (Lingham): The masculine principal and male symbol, the Lingam is a common symbol of Shiva. A Lingam is most often an oblong chunk of a meteorite in whose smooth face the Shaivite worshipper can see an image of Lord Shiva.

Lola: tremulous; swinging like a pendulum.

Loma: hair.

Madhya: middle (of the body).

Maha Mudra: the "Great Seal" or "Great Gesture." The Head-to-Knee Pose (alternate leg-stretch) performed with Bahya Kumbhaka, Bandha Triya and Yantra meditation.

Maha Samadhi: the "Great Samadhi" or "Great Absorption". Ideally, this would be a spiritual master's final conscious exit from his body as when Lord Jesus "yielded up his breath" on the cross or when Paramahansa Yoganada left this world in 1952. In practice, it means a revered figure has died.

The Mahabharata: The Mahabharata is one of the longest epic poems in history. It tells the story of a civil war in ancient India between the sons of Kuru (Kauravas) and the sons of Pandu (Pandavas) over a kingdom the Pandavas believe was stolen through the deception of the Kauravas. Every attempt by the Pandavas brothers to regain their kingdom without war had failed. The most famous part of The Mahabharata is The Bhagavad-Gita ("Song of God").

Makara: crocodile.

Mala: wreath.

Manas: the lower mind.

Mandala: a circular design symbolizing the cosmos.

Manduka: frog.

Manipura Chakra: "Wheel of the Jeweled City." This Chakra is the third major energy center, and is located at the height of the navel in the spine. Known as the "store-house of Prana," meditation on this Chakra will bestow all information needed on the physical body.

Manomaya Kosha: the third sheath; the mental body.

Mantra: "Instrument of thought"; a "prayer" or "song of praise". A mystical verse or magical formula used to invoke a deity or to acquire a Divine power. Commonly used to refer to any word, phrase or prayer used as an object of meditation containing a name of God. "Om Namah Shivaya" and "Om Namo Narayanaya" are two common examples.

Mantra Yoga (Japa Yoga): one of the Nine Forms of Yoga, Divine Union is achieved through complete absorption in a Mantra.

Marga (Margha): "path" or "way". In Yogic terminology, Marga is often used to indicate a particular spiritual path. For example, Bhakti Marga means "the path of devotion."

Matsya: a fish.

Mauna (Mouna): "Spiritual Silence."

Matsyendranath (Matsyendra, Matsyendra Nath, Matsendranatha): the teacher (Guru) of Goraknath (Goraksha) and an early exponent of Hatha Yoga. In mythological terms, Matsyendra was a fish who overheard Lord Shiva attempting to share the Divine secrets of Yoga with his wife Paravati, who was not interested. Matsyendra learned all he could, and then shared this sacred knowledge with mankind.

Mayura: a peacock.

Meru-Dhanda: the spinal column.

Mrita: dead; a corpse.

Mudra: "Seal" or "Gesture." In many Indian dance forms, thousands of such Mudras (specific gestures of the face, hands, arms and body) are recognized. In Yoga, Mudra is the name given to specific muscular contractions (Bandhas), body positions (Asanas) and points of concentration (Dharanas), that are used either to fix the location of or control the movement of Prana. The Gheranda Samhita lists 20 physical Mudras and 5 Dharana

Mudras. The latter specify the means of concentration (Dharana) on each of the first five Major Chakras (the five centers associated with the physical elements).

Mukha: face.

Mukta: free.

Mula: root.

Mula Bandha: "Root Lock." Performed by contracting the muscles of the anal sphincter, it is used to redirect the Apana Vayu upwards.

Muladhara Chakra: "Wheel of the Root Support". This Chakra is the first major energy center located near the coccyx at the coccygeal plexus (at the base of the spine). It opens to the rear.

Nabho Mudra: turn the underside of the tongue up, press it against the hard palate, extend the tip of the tongue back and towards the soft palate, and retain the breath in the lungs (Kumbhaka). This tongue lock technique should be practiced as a true Bandha by pressing the tongue firmly up and back. When performed in this manner, Nabho Mudra immediately suppresses spurious self-talk, internal dialog and mind chatter. It is used in place of Khechari Mudra, as it does not require cutting the frenulum linguae.

Nada: the inner sound, experienced (heard, realized) through the practice of Nada Yoga or Kundalini Yoga.

Nadi: "flowing water"; a "river" or "current"; any "tube" or "pipe", especially a tubular organ (a nerve, vein or artery in the physical body). In Yoga, Nadi often refers to channels in the subtle body through which Prana flows, as well as to the normal tubes and vessels of the physical body. The principal Nadi is Sushumna, the central nerve channel connecting the major Chakras, through which Kundalini Shakti is coaxed to rise. Sushumna is said to reside in the very center of the spinal cord. Wrapped around it are two secondary Nadis: Ida and Pingala (loosely associated with the parasympathetic and sympathetic nervous systems). For many Pranayama techniques, Ida and Pingala represent the left and right nostrils respectively. Ida is feminine: Yin, lunar and receptive. Pingala is masculine: Yang, solar and active. Recent studies have shown that left nostril lunar breathing called "Chandra Bheda" helps activate the right (more intuitive) cerebral hemisphere, while right nostril solar breathing called "Surya Bheda" helps activate the left (more logical or analytical) cerebral hemisphere. There are thousands of Nadis extending throughout the subtle body, just as there are thousands of nerves and vessels running throughout the physical body. The Shiva Samhita says there are 350,000 Nadis, of which it elaborates on only fourteen. Of these fourteen, only Ida, Pingala and Sushumna are considered vitally important to the practice of Yoga. The Hatha Yoga Pradipika and other sources claim that there are 72,000 Yoganadis. These numbers are symbolic and based on Indian systems of numerology. Their exact significance may have been understood differently by the ancient teachers. All agree on the importance of Ida, Pingala and Sushumna, with Sushumna being of primary importance.

Nadi-Shodhana "Channel-Cleansing." The practice of purifying the conduits through breath-control (Pranayama).

Nakra: crocodile.

Namaskara: worship; salutation; prostration.

Nama-Rupa: "name and form" being the standard linguistic, visual and tactile reference points for a living being or any other object residing on the material plane of existence. Distinguished from Sva-Bhava, a person's or thing's "own true being" or from Atman, a being's True Self, the term Nama-Rupa is used frequently in Buddhist literature and post-Buddhist Yoga literature to represent the esoteric nature of things as distinct from their true nature.

Nara: a man.

Nataraj: name of Shiva as the cosmic dancer.

Natya: dancing.

Nauli: a process in which the abdominal muscles and organs are made to move vertically and laterally in a surging motion.

Nava: boat.

Nir: without.

Nirbija-Samadhi: Samadhi without seed; one of the higher forms of absorption.

Nirguna-Samadhi: Samadhi without attributes; one of the higher forms of absorption.

Nirvichara-Samadhi: Samadhi without reflection; one of the higher forms of absorption.

Nirvikalpa-Samadhi: Samadhi without change or differences; one of the higher forms of absorption.

Nirvitarka-Samadhi: Samadhi without deliberation; one of the higher forms of absorption.

Niyama: moral observance. The second limb of Patanjali's Astanga Yoga system.

Ojas: "vitality." The subtle energy produced through practice, especially the discipline of sexual abstinence (Brahmacharya).

Om (Aum): the Pranava. The name of God as rendered in human speech.

Om Mani Padme Hum: "Jewel in the Lotus," signifying "Lingam in the Yoni." An ancient and sacred Tantric Mantra relating (among other things) to the Maithuna ritual, and often employed by Buddhists of various lineages today.

Pada: foot or leg.

Padangustha: big toe.

Padma: "lotus" or "lotus flower." Another name for the Chakras, since sometimes they are seen as spinning wheels, and at other times as lotus flowers.

Parampara: succession.

Parigha: bolt lock on a gate.

Parivrtta: revolving.

Parivartana: turning around; revolving.

Parivartana-Pada: with one leg turned around.

Parshva: the side; flank; lateral.

Parvata: mountain.

Paryanka: bed or couch.

Pasha: noose.

Paschima: West; the backside of the body.

Patanjali: the author of the Yoga-Sutras, Maharishi Patanjali lived sometime between 200 B.C.E. and 200 C.E. -- the exact date is unknown. Patanjali traveled throughout much of India, studying and analyzing what different practitioners and teachers were doing under the name of Yoga. Patanjali probably did not actually contribute new ideas or practices to Yoga -- rather he provided a valuable structural analysis and treatise on the Yoga of his day.

Phalam: fruit; the fruit of Karma. Used in esoteric texts to refer to the results, outcome or consequences of our actions (Karmas).

Pid: squeeze.

Pincha: chin; a feather.

Pinda: fetus; embryo; ball.

Pingala: "tawny current." One of the three primary channels through which the life-force (Prana) courses. It is associated with the sun, and responsible for the heating of the body. It corresponds on the physical level to the sympathetic nervous system.

Pitta: element of fire

Prajna: intelligence; wisdom.

Prakriti: "She who brings forth" is Nature manifest; all that exists in the material world. Prakriti stands in opposition to Purusha (pure consciousness). The goal of Yoga is the union of Prakriti with Purusha.

Prana: the root "Pra" means "to fill". The root "An" means "to breathe" or "to live". Prana is "the life that fills with the breath" or the "life principle in action". Prana commonly translates as air, breath, spirit, life, life-force, energy, subtle energy or the upward-moving energy currents within the body.

Pranama: a prayer.

Pranamaya Kosha: the second sheath; the Vital Life-Force Body.

Pranava: the Sanskrit name for the syllable Om.

Pranayama: "Breath Control." Any of hundreds of therapeutic breathing patterns used in any of the forms of Yoga or the Martial Arts. The fourth limb of Patanjali's Astanga Yoga system.

Prapada: the tip of the feet.

Prasarita: spread out; stretched out.

Pratyahara: "Sensory Withdrawal." Turning the senses inward, so as to detect the subtle currents and energy centers within the body. The fifth limb of Patanjali's Astanga Yoga system.

Puraka Kumbhaka: breath retention after inhaling; same as Antara Kumbhaka. Also known as "internal breath retention."

Purusha: pure consciousness, as opposed to Prakriti which is nature manifest. Prakriti is the field of play on which Purusha may come to know itself. The goal of Yoga is to unite Purusha, pure consciousness, with Prakriti, the material world. Also, Atman or the soul.

Purva: East; the front of the body.

Purvottana: an intense stretch of the front side of the body.

Raja Kapota: King Pigeon.

Rajas: activity; one of the three Gunas (qualities of nature).

Rajasic: always busy, active in outward activities.

Raja Yoga: "Royal Union." Royal Yoga is one of the Nine Forms of Yoga, and the path to enlightenment through the study of the mind and the practice of meditation as outlined in Patanjali's Yoga-Sutras. Raja Yoga distinguishes itself from Hatha Yoga as emphasizing the final three branches of Astanga

Yoga in practice. Union with the Supreme Spirit by becoming ruler of one's own mind. Also another name for Patanjali's Eight-Fold Path of Yoga.

Rama: the seventh incarnation of Lord Vishnu, Rama is usually shown with his faithful wife Sita, brother Lakshmana and his beloved devotee, Hanuman. In The Ramayana, Rama is depicted as the perfect son, devoted brother, true husband, loyal friend and ideal king. His bow and arrow convey that he is always ready to destroy evil and protect righteousness. He is himself an embodiment of Dharma.

The Ramayana: The Ramayana is the story of Rama and of his consort, Sita. Dasharatha, King of Ayodhya, has three wives and four sons. Rama is the eldest and his mother is Kaushalya. Bharata is the son of Dasharatha's second and favorite wife, Queen Kaikeyi. King Dasharatha decides it is time to give his thrones to his eldest son Rama and retire to the forest to seek Moksha (liberation). However, Rama's stepmother, the king's second wife, is not pleased. She wants her son, Bharata, to rule. Because of an oath Dasharatha had made to her years before, she gets the king to agree to banish Rama for fourteen years and to crown Bharata king. Rama, always obedient, is as content to go into banishment in the forest as to be crowned king. Sita and Rama's brother, Lakshmana, also decide to accompany Rama to the forest. Years pass and Rama, Sita, and Lakshmana are happy in the forest. One day, a Rakshasa (demon) princess tries to seduce Rama and Lakshmana wounds her and drives her away. She returns to her brother Ravana, the ten-headed ruler of Lanka, and tells him about lovely Sita. Ravana devises a plan and abducts the innocent Sita. Rama is broken-hearted and promises to find Sita and avenge her abduction. A band of giant monkeys offer to help find Sita, among them the most heroic of all monkeys, Hanuman. Ravana has carried Sita to his palace in Lanka and attempts to get her to agree to marry him. Hanuman, the general of the monkey band, finds Sita there, comforting her and tells her Rama will soon come and save her. Ravana's men capture Hanuman, but he escapes to fly to Rama to tell him where Sita is. Rama, Lakshmana and the monkey army cross over to Lanka and a battle ensues. Rama kills Ravana and frees Sita, but Rama cannot accept Sita back into his heart, fearing her impurity. Sita cannot believe what she is hearing and enters a fire to end her life. The god of fire dares not burn a pure soul, and so Agni takes human form and declares to Rama that Sita has been faithful. Upon her return home, the townspeople of Ayodhya cannot accept Sita's purity and Rama, bowing to public opinion, banishes pregnant Sita to the forest. Sita is broken-hearted and gives birth to twin sons, Lawa and Kusya. Upon seeing his sons, Rama begs Sita's forgiveness, but her heart is broken. She asks the earth to open up and take her, and it does.

Rechaka Kumbhaka: breath-retention after exhaling; same as Bahya Kumbhaka. Also called "external breath-retention."

Rig Veda: the hymns of the Rig Veda are considered the oldest and most important. Essentially, the Rig Veda praises a Supreme Power, and is the fountainhead of Hinduism. Its hymns offer thanks for victories and wealth, as well as prayers for further worldly benefits, such as wealth, health, long-life, protection and victory. Many of the hymns refer to the intoxicating juice Soma, which is credited with making one feel immortal, possibly because of its psychedelic properties.

Rishi: sage

Sa: with.

Sabija-Samadhi: Samadhi with seed; one of the lower forms of absorption.

Sadhana: regular spiritual practice.

Saguna-Samadhi: Samadhi with attributes; one of the lower forms of absorption.

Sahasrara Chakra: "Wheel of a Thousand Petals". The Crown Chakra is the seventh major energy center, located just behind the top of the head (where the soft spot is on a baby). It opens slightly to the rear.

Salamba: with support.

Sama: same, equal, even; upright.

Sama Veda: the Sama Veda contains the melodies or music for the hymns of the Rig Veda. This is considered to be the original Indian music. The Sama Veda helped to train musicians and functioned as a hymnal for religious rites.

Samadhi: "putting together", "joining" or "combining with" – hence, a state of Oneness. In Yoga, specifically, Samadhi may mean any of the following: absorbed in meditation, a state of profound meditation or devotion, intense application of or fixing the mind on something, attention; intense absorption or a kind of trance, concentration of thoughts, profound or abstract meditation, intense contemplation of any particular object so as to identify the meditator with the object meditated upon. In other words, in Samadhi, the practitioner becomes perceptually and experientially one with the environment. This state of Atman or Turiya (fourth Samadhi), may refer to any of the highest levels of consciousness, in or out of trance. These states may be achieved by Yoga practice or other means. It is the eighth and final limb of Patanjali's Astanga system of Yoga. Most systems of Hatha Yoga view Samadhi as the state of ultimate achievement. In Buddhism, Samadhi is the fourth and final state of Dhyana or intense, abstract meditation. There are many levels of Samadhi which are given different names.

Sambhavi Mudra: "Related to Shiva". There are several different techniques that go by this name and English spellings are inconsistent. What is referred to in this text is the "seal" or" gesture of the eyes" in which one turns the eyes upwards and inwards toward the "third-eye" or "Eye of Shiva" located at the space between the eyebrows (Ajna Chakra). Turning the eyes up and left allows the brain to access remembered visual images. Turning them up and right allows it to construct new visual images. This technique has the right eye accessing remembered images, while the left eye is accessing creative images. At the cognitive level, this produces a third way for the brain to see; creating almost literally a "third eye". It also strengthens the eye muscles. This dual-modality visual accessing technique also has the effect of limiting one's ability to engage in internal dialogue. Khechari or Nabho Mudras also help to suppress internal self-talk by dampening the micro-motor movements of the tongue that are concomitant with internal self-talk and sub-vocalizations, whether conscious or unconscious. These two techniques, the Eye Lock and the Tongue Lock, are therefore often practiced together, and are excellent techniques to use while doing Yantra and Mantra meditations because together they help to control both the visual and the auditory processing modes of the brain.

Samavritti (Samavritti Kumbhaka, Samavritti Pranayama):
"Equal Movements"; the "Equal Breathing Technique". This
measured breathing technique may be practiced using 2, 3 or 4
equal parts to the breath, i.e.: inhale-exhale, inhale-hold-exhale
or inhale-hold-exhale-hold.

Samhita: any methodically arranged collection of texts and verses.
Also the name of various works: Shiva Samhita, Gheranda
Samhita, etc.

Samsara: "confluence." The finite world of change, as opposed
to the ultimate reality. The cycle of birth, life/suffering and
death.

Samskara: Subliminal, habitual impression upon the mind, like
a groove in consciousness, that continues our Karmic cycle and
keeps us bound to the cycle of re-birth. Samskaras are the content
of our "baskets of Karma".

Sanchalana: shaking.

Sannyasa (Sannyasin): a renunciate: "he who has cast off." The
fourth Ashrama or stage of life in classical Indian thought when
one leaves the security of the hermitage and lives as a wandering
ascetic, owning nothing, save the clothes one is wearing, a staff
and a small wooden bowl for collecting alms or food.

Sanskrit: Sanskrit is an Indo-European classical language of Indian sub-continent; liturgical language of Hinduism, Buddhism,
Sikhism, Jainism and one of the 23 official languages of India.
Its position in the cultures of South and Southeast Asia is akin
to that of Latin and Greek in Europe, and it has evolved into,

as well as influenced, many modern day languages of the world. It appears in pre-Classical form as Vedic Sanskrit with the language of the Rigveda being the oldest and most archaic stage preserved. Dating back to as early as 1500 B.C.E., Vedic Sanskrit is the earliest known Indo-Aryan language and one of the earliest attested members of the Indo-European language family" Indo-European language family. The corpus of Sanskrit literature encompasses a rich tradition of poetry and drama, as well as scientific, technical, philosophical and religious texts. Today, Sanskrit continues to be widely used in Hindu religious rituals through the medium of hymns and Mantras. Spoken Sanskrit is still in use in a few traditional institutions in India, and there have been some attempts to foment a revival.

Santosha: "Contentment." The second Niyama or observance of Patanjali's Astanga Yoga system.

Saraswati: the Hindu goddess of learning, knowledge and wisdom needed for creation. Saraswati means the "essence of the self". She is the Divine consort of Lord Brahma, the creator of the universe. Saraswati symbolizes the creative power of Brahma.

Satsanga: "company of truth." The practice of frequenting the good company of saints, Sages, and their disciples.

Sarva: all; whole.

Sarvanga: the whole body.

Sattva: a state of balance; peace; one of the three Gunas (qualities of nature).

Satya: "non-lying." The second Yama or restraint of Patanjali's Astanga Yoga system.

Saucha: "Purity." The first Niyama or observance of Patanjali's Astanga Yoga system.

Savichara-Samadhi: Samadhi with reflection; one of the lower forms of absorption.

Savikalpa-Samadhi: Samadhi with change; one of the lower forms of absorption.

Savitarka-Samadhi: Samadhi with deliberation; one of the lower forms of absorption.

Setu: bridge.

Shalabha: locust.

Shaivism: the worship of Shiva as the Supreme Lord: one of the major sectarian branches of Hinduism.

Shakti: "power", "ability", "strength" or "energy". The Yin or feminine aspect of Divine creative expression, which in Yoga is considered to reside at the base of the spine in the Muladhara Chakra. Sometimes used as a synonym for Kundalini. Also, the female person in a Tantric relationship.

Shanti: peace; the deep peace of Yoga.

Shat: six.

Shat Kriyas (Shat Karmas): the six fundamental cleansing duties or actions.

Shava: corpse.

Shirsha: head.

Shiva (Siva): "auspicious", "favorable", "benign" or "benevolent". The Yang or masculine aspect of the Divine, creative expression which in Yoga is considered to reside at the crown of the head in Sahasrara Chakra. Shiva is distinguished from Shakti, the Yin or feminine aspect of the creative force which resides (as Kundalini) at the base of the spine in Muladhara Chakra. As a member of the Hindu trinity, Shiva is the Destroyer (of ignorance). He represents the aspect of the Supreme Being (Brahman of the Upanishads) that continuously dissolves to recreate in the cyclic process of creation, preservation, dissolution and recreation of the universe. Also the male person in a Tantric relationship. Shiva is the patron deity of Yoga - its author and protector. All of Yoga Vidya (the knowledge or science of spiritual integration with the Divine) emanates from Lord Shiva.

Shiva Samhita: "Shiva's Compendium" was written during the 18th century by an unknown author who writes as though Shiva himself were speaking. The work alludes frequently to the Tantras and there is a distinct Buddhist influence that runs throughout the text. This is one of three major, surviving classical treatises on Hatha Yoga. Like many early writings on Yoga, the text resembles an instructor's set of notes. It covers the highlights, but leaves the details to be filled in orally. The Shiva Samhita consists of five sections divided as follows: Non-dualism (In stating that consciousness alone exists, the first section has suggestions of both

Advaita-Edenta -- the Hindu school of non-dualism introduced in the Mandukay Upanishad and popularized by Shankara, and Vijnanavada -- a Buddhist philosophy which maintains that ultimately, consciousness alone exists), Subtle body (The system of Nadis is described, the most important in some detail, and the idea of Chakras is briefly introduced. The role of Karma is also explained.), Pranayama (The relationship between student and teacher is discussed, the requirements for success in Yoga are explained, Pranayama is introduced, but not well explained, and the Siddhis are mentioned.), Mudras (Yoni Mudra is introduced to arouse Kundalini, then ten other Mudras are described to fully awaken her, but the instructions here are not as precise as those given in the Gheranda Samhita or the Hatha Yoga Pradipika.), and the Practice of Yoga. (Three main obstacles to the practice of Yoga are cited, four types of Yoga are mentioned and the seven Major Chakras are described in great detail. It is in this final section that the text really shines, although it is not without several technical errors, at least in the 1914 English translation.)

Simha: lion.

Sita: she represents the ideal female; daughter, wife and mother. The wife of Rama in the Indian epic the Ramayana, she is all that is great and noble in womanhood. Sita is revered as an incarnation of the Hindu goddess Lakshmi, the consort of Lord Vishnu.

Sohum: "I am that." If Sohum is chanted rapidly, it becomes indistinguishable from Hamsa being chanted rapidly. Taken together, they mean "I am that swan" or "liberated spirit". One of the greatest of all Mantras, it is already a part of each inhaled and exhaled breath. We say this Mantra, subconsciously, about 12,000 times each day.

Sthiti: stability.

Sukha: easy, comfortable.

Sunyata: "to strive after the void," without which nothing would have any value or function. A cup that is not void cannot hold liquid. A room that is not void cannot house people. A person who is not "void" or "pure" cannot achieve the Divine State (Atman).

Supta: sleeping.

Surya: the sun.

Sushumna Nadi: the central nerve or channel of the subtle body, it rises up from the Root Chakra (Muladhara) to the Crown Chakra (Sahasrara). Sushumna Nadi connects all seven of the major Chakras. This is the only path for Shakti to take if she is to reach the gate of Sahasrara and awaken us to awareness of Shiva (Atman). Synonymous with Brahma Nadi.

Sutra: "thread." A work consisting of aphoristic statements, such as Patanjali's Yoga-Sutras.

Sutra Neti: Kriya wherein a string is threaded into a nostril, caught at the back of the mouth in the throat, and then used to clean the area inside where contact is made by manipulating the thread like dental floss.

Sva-Bhava (Svabhava or Swabava): "own-being." The true nature of anything, as distinguished from its appearance (Nama-Rupa).

Svadishthana Chakra: "One's Own Abode" or "Home of the Self". The second major Chakra, located in the region of the regenerative organs. This is the creative and generative center of the subtle body.

Svadhyaya: "self-study" is the fourth Niyama or observance of Patanjali's Astanga Yoga system. Self-study not only applies to reading and studying sacred texts, but also suggests that study of one's own self will lead to liberation.

Svana: a dog.

Svatmarama Yogendra (Atmarama): This 14th Lord of Yoga (Yogendra) is the author of the Hatha Yoga Pradipika, the oldest and most well-known of the surviving early manuscripts on Hatha Yoga. An earlier work (now lost) called simply Hatha Yoga written by Goraksha, was apparently available to Svatmarama, since scholars maintain that parts of it are incorporated into the Pradipika. His name may either indicate that he was of an order of Swamis (Swami Rama) in the Shiva Yoga tradition, or it may be a contracted form of Sva-Atma-Rama (own-spirit-god), suggesting that he had achieved the common goal of both Yoga (Nirguna-Samadhi) and Vedanta (Turiya), and that he therefore shared the "same spirit with God". Both of these schools are represented in his writings, along with the Shiva Yoga tradition of his time.

Tada: mountain.

Tamas: inertia; dullness; one of the three Gunas (fundamental qualities of nature).

Tan: to stretch or lengthen.

Tantra: "loom", "framework", "structure" or "essential part". "Loom" is used to suggest the two cosmic principles (male-female; Ying-Yang; Ha-Tha) that make up the warp and woof of the woven fabric of life in the universe. The term "Tantra" refers to a post-Upanishadic class of literature dating from 700-1000 C.E. The Tantra texts deal mainly with folk magic and heterodox religious practices, especially those used to attract Divine or magical powers. These medieval Tantras form the basis of modern Tantric beliefs and practices. Modern Tantra (c. 1000 C.E. to present) is often divided into two paths: The "Left-Handed Path" (Vama Margha) is much like the darker side of Voodoo. It uses the power of magic for personal aggrandizement and to frighten or control ignorant and superstitious people. This aspect of Tantra is greatly feared in many parts of rural India, even to this day. The "Right-Handed Path" (Dakshina Margha) is a system of spiritual beliefs and practices designed to attract spiritual or magical powers by tapping into Divine forces or energy currents that permeate throughout the universe. Tantrikas (practitioners of Tantra) use these cosmic forces (collectively called "Shakti" or "Kundalini") to activate the various Chakras (or subtle glands) within the human body. Here the practices of Tantra and traditional Yoga begin to overlap.

Tapas: "heat" or "austerity" is the third Niyama or observance of Patanjali's Astanga Yoga system. It is the deliberate self-discipline effort involved in the personal purification process. It relates to the internal fires of the body, meaning sacred heat created through the practice.

Tittibha: firefly.

Tolana: weighing.

Trataka: "to Gaze." Name for both a Kriya (cleansing-action) and Dharana (concentration) technique.

Trikona: a triangle.

Trikuti: the Third Eye Point; the seat of the mind.

Ubhaya: both.

Uddiyana Bandha: the "Flying-up Lock" is performed only during external breath retention. The upper abdominal muscles raise the diaphragm up against the heart and lungs to create an intense vacuum in the thorax.

The Upanishads: The term "Upanishad" literally means "those who sit near", and implies listening closely to the secret doctrines of a spiritual teacher. The primary message of the over 200 texts of The Upanishads is that the caste system does not matter, and that one can connect with God simply through awareness and meditation. The Upanishads are the final part of the Vedas and the basis for the philosophy of Vedanta or the end of the Vedic age. Yoga really came into its own with The Upanishads which are Gnostic texts expounding the hidden teachings about the ultimate unity of all things.

Upavistha: seated.

Urdhva: raised, elevated.

Urdhva-retus: upward-facing.

Ushtra: camel.

Utkata: powerful.

Uttana: an intense stretch.

Utthita: raised up; extended, stretched.

Vahnisara: "cascading-fire"; a synonym for the Kriya: Agnisara Dhauti; performing Uddiyana Bandha with the lungs empty repeatedly, either fast or slow, to stoke the gastric fire or Agni, located in the navel region.

Vakra: crooked.

Vama: the left side.

Vata: air element.

Vatayana: a horse.

Vayu: wind or vital air.

Vedanta: philosophy of the reality of nature.

The Vedas: Veda literally means "knowledge." The Vedas are considered the most sacred scriptures of Hinduism. Composed by sages or seers who lived in India several thousand years ago, the Vedas were among the first works to articulate the interconnection between all things in the known and unknown universe. They taught about the Laws of Karma and Reincarnation. It is clear that Vedic Yoga was intimately connected with the ritual life of ancient Indians. This life revolved around the idea of sacrifice as a means of joining the material world with the invisible world of spirit. In order to perform the exacting rituals successfully, the sacrificers had to be able to focus their mind for prolonged periods of time. Such "inner focusing" for the sake of transcending the limitations of the ordinary mind is the root of Yoga. When successful, the Vedic Yogi was graced with a vision or experience of transcendental reality. A great master of Vedic Yoga was called a "Rishi" which is Sanskrit for "seer". The Vedic seers were able to see the very fabric of existence and their hymns speak of their marvelous intuitions. The most holy hymns and Mantras are to be found in four Vedas: Rig, Sama, Yajur and Atharva. It is difficult to accurately date the Vedas because they passed down orally for about a thousand years before they were written.

Vedic Sanskrit: Sanskrit, as defined by Panini, had evolved out of the earlier "Vedic" form. Scholars often distinguish Vedic Sanskrit and Classical or Paninian Sanskrit as separate dialects. Classical Sanskrit is considered to have descended from Vedic Sanskrit. Though the two dialects are quite similar, they differ in a number of essential points of phonology, vocabulary, grammar, and syntax that make the understanding of Vedic Sanskrit difficult. Vedic Sanskrit is the language of the Vedas: a large collection of hymns, incantations (Samhitas), theological discussions and religio-philosophical discussions (Brahmanas, Upanishads), which are the earliest religious texts of the original Indian religion; i.e.: the precursor of the Hindu religion. Modern linguists consider the metrical hymns of The Rig Veda Samhita to be the earliest, composed by many authors over centuries of oral tradition. The end of the Vedic period is marked by the composition of The Upanishads which form the concluding part of the Vedic corpus in the traditional compilations. The current hypothesis holds that the Vedic form of Sanskrit survived until the middle of the first millennium B.C.E. It is around this time that Sanskrit began the transition from a first language to a second language of religion and learning, marking the beginning of the Classical period.

Vidya: "knowledge", "wisdom" or "science". A term such as Yoga Vidya may be translated (according to the context) as either "knowledge of Yoga", "Yogic wisdom" or "the science of Yoga".

Vijnanamaya Kosha: the fourth sheath, the intelligence body.

Vinyasa: going progressively; postures (Asanas) linked in a flow by the breath.

Vairagya: non-attachment.

Viparita: inverted; reversed.

Viparita Karani Mudra: "Legs in the Air Seal." Another name for Sirshasana or Sarvangasana when combined with other techniques.

Vira: a hero.

Vrksha: a tree.

Vrschika: a scorpion.

Vrt: to turn or revolve.

Vishnu: Vishnu is the aspect of Supreme Reality that preserves and sustains the universe. When Brahma finished creating the world, he found it lifeless. He prayed for help and the god Vishnu entered into the Earth (Vish means "to enter") and filled it with living beings. He is seen as possessing a human body with four arms. Lord Vishnu carries a conch in the upper left hand indicates that the Lord communicates with His devotees with love and understanding. When blowing the conch, his devotees are reminded to live in this world with kindness and compassion towards all living beings. A Chakra in the upper right hand conveys the idea that the Lord uses this weapon to protect his devotees from evil.

Vishnu Mudra: "Seal of Vishnu". Formed with the hand by folding the index and middle fingers to the palm, often assumed by the right hand and used to close the nostrils during Pranayama.

Vishuddha Chakra: "Wheel of Great Purity". The fifth major energy Center or Chakra, located at the base of the throat in the spine.

Yajur Veda: the Yajur Veda consists of hymns dealing with the knowledge of how to properly execute religious rites and ceremonies. It explains in detail how to construct the altars for new and full-moon celebrations.

Yama: "restrain"; "hold-back"; "to control" or "regulate." A moral injunction or self-restraint. The first of the eight limbs of Patanjali's Astanga Yoga system. Yama can also be a "road" or "path" that keeps one from wandering or getting lost. Yama also refers to the planet Saturn whose orbit is the slowest (or most restrained) of all the planets that can be seen by the naked eye.

Yantra: Any instrument used for "holding", "restraining" or "fastening". In Yoga, a Yantra is a visual symbol used to hold or restrain the mind from wandering during meditation. Each Chakra has its own Yantra (a simple geometric design), to which more and more can be added in terms of color, surrounding images of each lotus flower, resident deities (male and female), plus their vehicular animals, followed by sounds as perceived in the inner ear and on and on. In Hatha and Tantra Yogas, the Yantra is studied over time in progressive levels of detail. As each level of detail is committed to memory, it is taken into the meditation. The meditation is typically done during breath retention in either the Swan Breath or the Fire Breath.

Yantra Yoga: one of the Nine Forms of Yoga. Divine Union is achieved through focus on forms.

Yoga: "Integration" or "Union." From the root word "Yuj" meaning a yoke that unites animals together to combine their strength and control their direction. In Hatha and Tantra Yogas, we use Pranayama, Kumbhaka, Mudra and Bandha to combine the Vayus (internal energies or Pranas) and to direct this combined energy up through the central channel (Sushumna Nadi) to create a Divine Union or Yoga. This is why the breathing exercises are so important. The purpose is to coax Kundalini Shakti up to join with Shiva so we may, in that Divine Union, discover our essential nature.

Yoga Mudra: a posture; a seal.

Yoganadis: full name for the psychic channels.

Yoga Nidra: "Yogic Sleep," where the body is at rest, but the mind remains fully conscious. A Tantric technique.

Yogasanas: another term for Asana.

Yoga-Sutras: the writings of Patanjali which set down most of what he had studied throughout India under the name of "Yoga". An excellent treatise on the subject, and an early example of both structural and functional analysis.

Yogi (Yogin) or Yogini: one who practices and follows the path of Yoga. "Yogi" can be male or female, while "Yogini" is feminine.

Yoni: "source"; "vagina" or "womb". The feminine principle and female symbol.

Yoni Mudra: "The Seal of the Yoni" or "Gesture at the Source". A contraction either of the vaginal muscles or of the testicular muscles. In individual practice, this Mudra is used to redirect energy, both subtle and physical. In Tantric couples practice, it is used to heighten and prolong pleasure. Yoni Mudra may also be the closing off of the sensory organs on the face to practice Pratyahara.

108: the sacred number upon which the entire universe rests in Vedic thought. The number of Upanishads.

Om Shanti, Shanti, Shantih.